'The central message is that we are going to hell in a handcart, as free markets rip up established communities. The idea of a world of liberal democratic and prosperous states on the American model is, he argues, a fantasy . . . Gray is right.' Andrew Marr, *Independent*

'Gray's message is that the hell-for-leather pursuit of capitalism US-style, which is to say of the highly deregulated variety, is based on a number of false premises . . . the result, in Gray's none too comforting analysis, will not be the Utopia of a single, super-efficient, wealth-generating global market we were promised, but its opposite: a sort of permanent anarchy . . . It is sharply written, draws on a wealth of practical and theoretical knowledge, and deserves to provoke more thinking than we have yet seen on a subject which could scarcely be more important.' *Evening Standard*

'Essentially this is a pessimistic book . . . Global capitalism seems to work in much the same way as natural selection; it destroys those who fail to adapt, and rewards, often to an absurd degree, those who adapt successfully.' William Rees-Mogg, *Spectator*

'[Gray] concludes that the effect of unrestricted international free enterprise will be socially and culturally destructive . . . Gray's analysis – combining what he thinks is essential for future stability with an explanation of why it cannot be provided – is more apocalyptic than Utopian.' *Guardian*

'[*False Dawn*] introduces a sense of economic and historical perspective to these dissident-free days.' *Esquire*

D0031960

FALSE DAWN

John Gray is Professor of European Thought at the London School of Economics. He is a regular contributor to the *Guardian* and the *Times Literary Supplement*, and his books include *Isaiah Berlin, Enlightenment's Wake* and *Voltaire and Enlightenment*.

Also by John Gray

Enlightenment's Wake: Politics and Culture at the Close of the Modern Age

Isaiah Berlin

Endgames: Questions in Late Modern Political Thought

Voltaire and Enlightenment

FALSE DAWN

The Delusions of
Global Capitalism

John Gray

Granta Books
London

Granta Publications, 2/3 Hanover Yard, London N1 8BE

First published in Great Britain by Granta Books 1998
This edition published by Granta Books 1999

A CIP catalogue record for this book is available from the British Library.

3 5 7 9 10 8 6 4 2

Typeset in Times New Roman by M Rules
Printed and bound in Great Britain
by Mackays of Chatham PLC

Contents

Acknowledgements & Author's note   viii

1 From the Great Transformation to the global free
    market   1
2 Engineering free markets   22
3 What globalization is not   55
4 How global free markets favour the worst kinds of
    capitalism: a new Gresham's Law?   78
5 The United States and the Utopia of global capitalism   100
6 Anarcho-capitalism in post-communist Russia   133
7 Occidental twilight and the rise of Asia's capitalisms   166
8 The ends of *laissez-faire*   194

Postscript   209
Notes   236
Index   257

Acknowledgements

There are a great many people without whom I could not have written this book. Without the encouragment given me by Neil Belton I would not have begun, still less finished it. His unflagging support and incisive criticisms have been decisive at every stage. I could not have asked more from an editor.

Several people were kind enough to comment on all or part of the book. David Barron, Nick Butler, Colin Clarke, Tony Giddens, Will Hutton, James Sherr, Geoff Smith and George Walden all gave me helpful comments, and their conversation has stirred my thoughts on many of the themes of the book. Jane Robertson has made many invaluable suggestions at the copy-editing stage.

Since I have not accepted all of the suggestions made by any of the people who have read the book, and none of them would accept everything that I argue, all the usual disclaimers apply.

Author's note

The original text of *False Dawn* is reprinted here unaltered. A new postscript has been added to update the argument. Neil Belton's comments were, as always, invaluable. Conversations with George Soros stimulated and clarified my thoughts. The arguments and opinions I express are mine alone.

John Gray, August 1998

1   From the Great Transformation to the global free market

The collapse of the global marketplace would be a traumatic event with unimaginable consequences. Yet I find it easier to imagine than the continuation of the present regime.

GEORGE SOROS[1]

The origins of the catastrophe lay in the Utopian endeavour of economic liberalism to set up a self-regulating market system.

KARL POLANYI[2]

Mid-nineteenth century England was the subject of a far-reaching experiment in social engineering. Its objective was to free economic life from social and political control and it did so by constructing a new institution, the free market, and by breaking up the more socially rooted markets that had existed in England for centuries. The free market created a new type of economy in which prices of all goods, including labour, changed without regard to their effects on society. In the past, economic life had been constrained by the need to maintain social cohesion. It was conducted in social markets – markets that were embedded in society and subject to many kinds of regulation and restraint. The goal of the experiment that was attempted in mid-Victorian England was to demolish these social markets, and replace them by deregulated markets that operated independently of social needs. The rupture in England's economic life produced by the creation of the free market has been called the Great Transformation.[3]

The achievement of a similar transformation is the overriding objective today of transnational organizations such as the World Trade Organisation, the International Monetary Fund and the

Organisation for Economic Cooperation and Development. In advancing this revolutionary project they are following the lead of the world's last great Enlightenment regime, the United States. The thinkers of the Enlightenment, such as Thomas Jefferson, Tom Paine, John Stuart Mill and Karl Marx never doubted that the future for every nation in the world was to accept some version of western institutions and values. A diversity of cultures was not a permanent condition of human life. It was a stage on the way to a universal civilization. All such thinkers advocated the creation of a single worldwide civilization, in which the varied traditions and cultures of the past were superseded by a new, universal community founded on reason.[4]

The United States today is the last great power to base its policies on this enlightenment thesis. According to the 'Washington consensus', 'democratic capitalism' will soon be accepted throughout the world. A global free market will become a reality. The manifold economic cultures and systems that the world has always contained will be redundant. They will be merged into a single universal free market.

Transnational organizations animated by this philosophy have sought to impose free markets onto the economic life of societies throughout the world. They have implemented programmes of policies whose ultimate objective is to incorporate the world's diverse economies into a single global free market. This is a Utopia that can never be realized; its pursuit has already produced social dislocation and economic and political instability on a large scale.

In the United States free markets have contributed to social breakdown on a scale unknown in any other developed country. Families are weaker in America than in any other country. At the same time, social order has been propped up by a policy of mass incarceration. No other advanced industrial country, aside from post-communist Russia, uses imprisonment as a means of social control on the scale of the United States. Free markets, the desolation of families and communities and the use of the sanctions of criminal law as a last recourse against social collapse go in tandem.

Free markets have also weakened or destroyed other institutions on which social cohesion depends in the US. They have generated a long economic boom from which the majority of Americans has hardly benefited. Levels of inequality in the United States resemble those of Latin American countries more than those of any European society. Yet such direct consequences of the free market have not

weakened support for it. It remains the sacred cow of American politics and has become identified with America's claim to be a model for
a universal civilization. The Enlightenment project and the free market
have become fatefully intertwined.

A single global market is the Enlightenment's project of a universal
civilization in what is likely to be its final form. It is not the only variant of that project to have been attempted in a century that is littered
with false Utopias. The former Soviet Union embodied a rival
Enlightenment Utopia, that of a universal civilization in which markets were replaced by central planning. The human costs of that
defunct Utopia were incalculable. Millions of lives were lost through
totalitarian terror, ubiquitous corruption and apocalyptic environmental degradation. An immeasurable price in human suffering was
exacted by the Soviet project – yet it failed to deliver the modernization it promised for Russia. At the close of the Soviet era Russia was
in some ways further from modernity than it had been in late Tsarist
times.

The Utopia of the global free market has not incurred a human cost
in the way that communism did. Yet over time it may come to rival it
in the suffering that it inflicts. Already it has resulted in over a hundred
million peasants becoming migrant labourers in China, the exclusion
from work and participation in society of tens of millions in the
advanced societies, a condition of near-anarchy and rule by organized
crime in parts of the post-communist world, and further devastation
of the environment.

Even though a global free market cannot be reconciled with any
kind of planned economy, what these Utopias have in common is
more fundamental than their differences. In their cult of reason and
efficiency, their ignorance of history and their contempt for the ways
of life they consign to poverty or extinction, they embody the same
rationalist hubris and cultural imperialism that have marked the central traditions of Enlightenment thinking throughout its history.

A global free market presupposes that economic modernization
means the same thing everywhere. It interprets the globalization of the
economy – the spread of industrial production into interconnected
market economies throughout the world – as the inexorable advance of
a singular type of western capitalism: the American free market.

The real history of our time is nearer the opposite. Economic modernization does not replicate the American free market system

throughout the world. It works against the free market. It spawns indigenous types of capitalism that owe little to any western model.

The market economies of east Asia diverge deeply from one another, with those of China and Japan exemplifying different varieties of capitalism. Equally, Russian capitalism differs fundamentally from capitalism in China. All that these new species of capitalism have in common is that they are not converging on any western model.

The emergence of a truly global economy does not imply the extension of western values and institutions to the rest of humankind. It means the end of the epoch of western global supremacy. The original modern economies in England, western Europe and north America are not models for the new types of capitalism created by global markets. Most countries which try to refashion their economies on the model of Anglo-Saxon free markets will not achieve a sustainable modernity.

Today's Utopia of a single global market assumes that the economic life of every nation can be refashioned in the image of the American free market. Yet in the United States the free market has ruptured the liberal capitalist civilization, founded on Roosevelt's New Deal, on which its post-war prosperity rested. The United States is only the limiting case of a general truth. Wherever deregulated markets are promoted in late modern societies they engender new varieties of capitalism.

In China they have spawned a new variant of the capitalism practised by the Chinese diaspora throughout the world. In Russia the collapse of Soviet institutions has not produced free markets but instead a novel variety of post-communist anarcho-capitalism.

Nor is the growth of a world economy promoting the universal spread of western liberal democracy. In Russia it has produced a hybrid type of democratic government in which strong presidential power is central. In Singapore and Malaysia economic modernization and the growth have been achieved without loss of social cohesion by governments that reject the universal authority of liberal democracy. With luck, a similar government may emerge in China when it becomes fully post-communist.

A world economy does not make a single regime – 'democratic capitalism' – universal. It propagates new types of regimes as it spawns new kinds of capitalism. The global economy that is presently under construction will not assure the free market's future. It will trigger a new competition between remaining social market economies and free markets in which social markets must reform themselves profoundly or be destroyed. Yet, paradoxically, free market economies will not be the winners in this contest. For they too are being transformed out of all recognition by global competition.

The free market governments of the 1980s and 1990s failed to achieve many of their objectives. In Britain, levels of taxation and state spending were as high, or higher, after eighteen years of Thatcherite rule than they were when Labour fell from power in 1979.

Free market governments model their policies on the era of *laissez-faire* – the mid-nineteenth century period in which government claimed that it did not intervene in economic life. In reality a *laissez-faire* economy – that is to say, an economy in which markets are deregulated and put beyond the possibility of political or social control – cannot be reinvented. Even in its heyday it was a misnomer. It was created by state coercion, and depended at every point in its workings on the power of government. By the First World War the free market had ceased to exist in its most extreme form because it did not meet human needs – including the need for personal freedom.

Yet, without diminishing the size of the state or reinstating the social institutions that supported the free market in its Victorian heyday, free market policies have encouraged new inequalities in income, wealth, access to work and quality of life that rival those found in the vastly poorer world of the mid-nineteenth century.

In nineteenth-century England the damage done by the free market to other social institutions and to human well-being triggered political counter-movements that changed it radically. A spate of legislation, provoked by different aspects of the free market in action, re-regulated it so that its impact on other social institutions and on human needs was tempered. Mid-Victorian *laissez-faire* showed that social stability and the free market cannot be compatible for long.

England had a market economy before and after the brief mid-Victorian experiment in *laissez-faire*. In each case markets were regulated so that their workings were less inimical to social stability. Only during these eras of *laissez-faire* – in mid-nineteenth century England and, in some parts of the world, the 1980s and 1990s of this century – has the free market been the dominant social institution.

The managed market economies of the post-war era did not emerge through a series of incremental reforms. They came about as a consequence of great social, political and military conflicts. In Britain the Keynesian and Beveridge settlement was made possible by the imperatives of a war of national survival that tore up pre-war social structures by the roots.

In nineteenth-century England, the free market ran aground on enduring human needs for economic security. In the twentieth century, the liberal international economic order perished violently in the wars and dictatorships of the 1930s. That cataclysm was the precondition of post-war prosperity and political stability. In the 1930s the free market proved to be an inherently unstable institution. Built by design and artifice, it fell apart in confusion and chaos. The history of the global free market in our time is unlikely to be much different.

There is no prospect of Britain returning to Keynesian economic management, of the United States reviving a Rooseveltian New Deal, or of any continental countries (aside perhaps from Norway and Denmark) renewing the levels of social provision associated with European Social and Christian Democracy.

The continental social market that spawned German post-war prosperity will be among the most notable casualties of global free markets. It will suffer this fate along with American liberal capitalism, which assured prosperity in the United States and throughout the world for a generation after the Second World War.

Some national governments may be able to use the freedom of manoeuvre they still retain to devise policies which in some degree reconcile the imperatives of global markets with the needs of social cohesion, but the narrow margin of reform that is still open to some sovereign states will not allow any of them a return to the past.

The transnational organizations that oversee the world economy today are vehicles of a post-Keynesian orthodoxy. At the level of sovereign states, they claim that the management of national economies by the control of demand is neither feasible nor desirable. All that is needed for free markets to coordinate economic activity is a framework providing monetary and fiscal stability. The Keynesian policies of the post-war era are rejected as unnecessary or harmful. At the global level, according to these transnational organizations, free markets are equally self-stabilizing. They need no overall governance to prevent economic and social dislocation.

Economic globalization – the worldwide spread of industrial production and new technologies that is promoted by unrestricted mobility of capital and unfettered freedom of trade – actually threatens the stability of the single global market that is being constructed by American-led transnational organizations.

The central paradox of our time can be stated thus: economic globalization does not strengthen the current regime of global *laissez-faire*. It works to undermine it. There is nothing in today's global market that buffers it against the social strains arising from highly uneven economic development within and between the world's diverse societies. The swift waxing and waning of industries and livelihoods, the sudden shifts of production and capital, the casino of currency speculation – these conditions trigger political counter-movements that challenge the very ground rules of the global free market.

Today's worldwide free market lacks the political checks and balances which allowed its mid-Victorian precursor in England to wither away. It can be made more humanly tolerable for the citizens of states which pursue innovative and resourceful policies, but such reforms at the margin will not render the global free market much less unstable. Today's regime of global *laissez-faire* will be briefer than even the *belle époque* of 1870 to 1914, which ended in the trenches of the Great War.

Engineering the free market in early Victorian England

The free market that developed in Britain in the mid-nineteenth century did not occur by chance. Nor, contrary to the mythic history propagated by the New Right, did it emerge from a long process of unplanned evolution. It was an artefact of power and statecraft. In Japan, Russia, Germany, and in the United States throughout decades of American protectionism, state intervention has been a key factor in economic development.

Laissez-faire is not a necessary condition of successful industrialization or of sustained economic growth. The political institutions that have gone with steady economic growth and rapid industrialization throughout most of the world have been those of a developmental capitalist state. The English case, in which *laissez-faire*, free trade and industrialization coincided, is *sui generis*.

Indeed, even in nineteenth-century England, state intervention on a most ambitious scale was an indispensable prerequisite of a *laissez-*

faire economy. A precondition of the nineteenth-century British free market was the use of state power to transform common land into private property. This was engineered through the Enclosures that occurred from the Civil War up to early Victorian times. These appropriations tilted the balance of ownership in England's agrarian market economy away from cottagers and yeoman farmers towards the great landowners of the late eighteenth and early nineteenth centuries. Ideologues such as Hayek, who developed grand theories wherein market economies emerge by a slow evolution in which the state plays little role, not only generalized wildly from a single case, they misrepresented that case.

As Barrington Moore summarizes the history of the Enclosure movement: ' . . . it was Parliament that ultimately controlled the process of enclosure. Formally the procedures by which a landlord put through an enclosure by Act of Parliament were public and democratic. Actually the big property owners dominated the proceedings from start to finish.' He comments: 'The span of time when these changes were most rapidly and thoroughly taking place is not absolutely clear. It seems most likely, however, that the enclosure movements had gathered greatest speed during the Napoleonic wars, to die out after 1832, by which time it had helped to change the English countryside beyond recognition.'[5]

It is hyperbolic to suggest, as Barrington Moore does, that the Enclosures transformed England from a peasant society to a market economy. A market economy pre-dated the enclosure movement by centuries. Yet the Enclosures helped form the nineteenth-century agrarian capitalist economy of large landed estates. The mid-Victorian free market was an artefact of state coercion, exercised over several generations, in which property rights were created and destroyed by Parliament.

The British state in which the free market was thereby engineered – unlike most of those in which it is being presently being constructed - was pre-democratic. The franchise was small and the overwhelming majority of the population was excluded from political participation. It is doubtful if the free market would ever have been engineered if working democratic institutions were in place. It is a matter of historical record that the free market began to wither away with the entry of the broad population into political life. As the more clear-sighted ideologues of the New Right have always recognized, the unfettered market is incompatible with democratic government.

The late-twentieth-century free market experiment is an attempt to legitimate through democratic institutions severe limits on the scope and content of democratic control over economic life. The pre-democratic preconditions of the mid-Victorian free market tell us a good deal about its prospects of political legitimacy today.

Among the measures which created the free market none was more important than the Repeal of the Corn laws, which established agricultural free trade. The Corn Law of 1815, which followed on protectionist legislation going back in various forms to the seventeenth century, was repealed in 1846 in a dramatic victory for the advocates of free trade.

Repeal of the Corn Laws represented a defeat for the landed interest and a triumph for *laissez-faire* thinking. The proposition that a market economy must always be subject to ultimate political oversight and control with the aim of safeguarding social cohesion had been until then an article of political commonsense – certainly among Tories. Free trade was little more than a radical theory. In England thereafter this was reversed. Free trade became the common property of the political classes of all parties, and protectionism a wild heresy, until the disasters of the 1930s.

Not much less significant in the formation of the free market was Poor Law Reform. The Poor Law Act of 1834 was a decisive piece of legislation. It set the level of subsistence lower than the lowest wage set by the market. It stigmatized the recipient by attaching the harshest and most demeaning conditions to relief. It weakened the institution of the family. It established a *laissez-faire* regime in which individuals were solely responsible for their own welfare, rather than sharing that responsibility with their communities.

Eric Hobsbawm captures the background, character and effects of the welfare reforms of the 1830s when he writes:

The traditional view, which still survived in a distorted way in all classes of rural society and in the internal relations of working-class groups, was that a man had a right to earn a living, and, if unable to do so, a right to be kept alive by the community. The view of middle-class liberal economists was that men should take such jobs as the market offered, wherever and at whatever rate it offered, and the rational man would, by individual or voluntary collective saving and insurance make provision for accident, illness and old age. The residuum of paupers could not, admittedly, be left actually to starve, but they ought not to be given more than the absolute minimum – provided it was less than the lowest wage offered in the market, and in the most discouraging conditions. The Poor Law was not so much intended to help the unfortunate as to stigmatize the self-confessed failures of society . . . There have been few more inhuman statutes than the Poor Law Act of 1834, which made all relief 'less eligible' than the lowest wage outside, confined it to the jail-like work-house, forcibly separating husbands, wives and children in order to punish the poor for their destitution.[6]

This system applied to at least 10 per cent of the English population in the mid-Victorian period. It remained in force until the outbreak of the First World War.

The central thrust of the Poor Law reforms was to transfer responsibility for protection against insecurity and misfortune from communities to individuals and to compel people to accept work at whatever rate the market set. The same principle has informed many of the welfare reforms that have underpinned the re-engineering of the free market in the late twentieth century.

In the era of the New Right, as in early mid-Victorian England, the unintended consequences of earlier welfare institutions were sufficiently serious to make welfare reforms politically unavoidable and indeed desirable. The nineteenth-century system of supplementing wages from local rates created a large system of outdoor poor relief which was not indefinitely sustainable. By the 1980s some of the institutions of the Beveridge welfare state no longer corresponded to late modern patterns of family and working life. They were in danger of institutionalizing poverty rather than ending it. New Right policy-makers seized on these dangers to reshape welfare provisions to match the imperatives of deregulated markets.

No less important than Poor Law reform in the mid-nineteenth century was legislation designed to remove obstacles to the determination of wages by the market. David Ricardo stated the orthodox view of the classical economists when he wrote, 'Wages should be left to fair and free competition of the market, and should never be controlled by the interference of the legislature.'[7]

It was by appeal to such canonical statements of *laissez-faire* that the Statute of Apprentices (enacted after the Black Death in the four-teenth century) was repealed and all other controls on wages ended in the period leading up to the 1830s. Even the Factory Acts of 1833, 1844 and 1847 avoided any head-on collision with *laissez-faire* ortho-doxies. 'The principle that there should be no interference in the freedom of contract between master and man was honoured to the extent that no direct legislative interference was made in the relation-ship between employers and adult males . . . it was still possible to argue for a further half-century, though with diminishing plausibility, that the principle of non-interference remained inviolate.'[8]

The removal of agricultural protection and the establishment of free trade, the reform of the poor laws with the aim of constraining the poor to take work, and the removal of any remaining controls on wages were the three decisive steps in the construction of the free market in mid-nineteenth-century Britain. These key measures cre-ated out of the market economy of the 1830s the unregulated free market of mid-Victorian times that is the model for all subsequent neo-liberal policies.

The reform of welfare institutions to compel the poor to take what-ever work was available, the scrapping of wage councils and other controls on incomes, and the opening up of the national economy to unregulated global free trade, have been central and fundamental neo-liberal policies during the 1980s and 1990s throughout the world. In every case the core of the free market that has been constructed is a deregulated labour market. In Britain, the United States and New Zealand, as well as countries such as Mexico which have had struc-tural adjustment imposed on them by transnational financial institutions, the outcome has been an approximation to a free market in which labour is traded freely as a commodity just like any other.

In many ways the establishment of the free market in nineteenth-century England was an historical singularity. It was generated, for a while with some success, in peculiarly fortunate historical circum-stances. In the rest of Europe, nothing like the English free-market experiment was tried. The nineteenth-century English project, like its modern equivalent, could not have advanced as far as it did if it had not gone with the flow of large economic and technological changes.

The statecraft which constructed the free market in England turned to its purposes the effects of a centuries-long development. In the course of this historical movement, market forces had come to be a dominant force in social life. Market exchange there had always been, and in England a market economy had existed for several hundred years; but it was at this juncture in history that the truly free market came into being, thereby creating a market society.

Karl Polanyi notes that, 'Ultimately . . . the control of the economic system by the market is of overwhelming consequence to the whole organization of society; it means no less than the running of society as an adjunct to the market. Instead of economy being embedded in social relations, social relations are embedded in the economic system.'[9] Here Polanyi makes a distinction between societies in which economic activities, including all the phenomena we group together under the category of market exchange, are inseparable from other areas of social activity, and societies in which markets form a separate realm, distinct and independent from all others.

In pre-modern traditional societies, prices often have the status of conventions, many goods cannot be bought or sold, exchange is tied up with locality and kinship, and 'the market' has not yet emerged as a distinct social and cultural institution. In such societies, there is no such thing as 'the market'.

In market societies, by contrast, not only is economic activity distinct from the rest of social life, but it conditions, and sometimes dominates, the whole of society. In several countries in northwest Europe in the early modern period, markets developed and freed themselves in varying degrees from the remnants of the social controls of medieval life. Yet in no country apart from England did the social institution of the free market come into existence. The countries of continental Europe were market economies but not market societies. They have remained so to this day.

Where market societies have emerged, Polanyi observes, it has not been as a result of chance or evolution but through the artifice of recurrent and systematic political intervention.

The step which makes isolated markets into a market economy, regulated markets into a self-regulating market, is indeed crucial. The nineteenth century . . . naively imagined that such a development was the natural outcome of the spreading of markets. It was not realized that the gearing of markets into a self-regulating system was not the result of any inherent tendency of markets . . . but rather the effect of highly artificial stimulants administered to the body social in order to meet a situation which was created by the no less artificial phenomenon of the machine.[10]

Here we must modify Polanyi's Marxian interpretation. We need to take the full account of the exceptional character of social conditions in England in the early nineteenth century. Unlike any country in continental Europe, England had long possessed a highly individualist legal culture of property ownership. Land had long been traded as a commodity, labour had long been mobile, the immobility of village life common in many continental European countries was rare or unknown, and family life was closer to modern nuclear families than to pre-modern extended families. England was not, as other European countries still were in the nineteenth century, a peasant society.

In this regard, Alan Macfarlane may be right to maintain that 'one of the major theories of economic anthropology is incorrect, namely the idea that we witness in England between the sixteenth and nineteenth centuries the "Great Transformation" from a non-market, peasant society where economics is "embedded" in social relations to a modern market, capitalist system where economy and society have been split apart? This view,' Macfarlane continues 'is most clearly expressed in the work of Karl Polanyi . . . when Adam Smith founded classical economics on the premise of the rational "economic" man, believing he was describing a universal and long-evident type, he was eluded. According to Polanyi, such a man had only just emerged, stripped of his ritual, political and social needs . . . [But] it was Smith who was right and Polanyi who was wrong, at least in relation to England. "Homo economicus" and the market society had been present in England for centuries before Smith wrote.' Macfarlane concludes, however, that 'Polanyi's insight that Smith was writing within a particular social environment is correct when we realize that in many respects England had probably long been different from almost every other agrarian civilization we know.'[11]

The free market was – and remains – an Anglo-Saxon singularity. It was constructed in a context not found in any other European society: it existed in full-blown form for only about a generation. It could never have been created at all if ownership and economic life had not long been thoroughly individualist in nineteenth-century England. It was an experiment in social engineering undertaken in exceptionally propitious circumstances.

Revising Polanyi's account of the Great Transformation to take account of these considerations does not restrict its application to our current circumstances. It enhances its relevance. It illuminates even more clearly the hubris of seeking to transplant worldwide a social institution that has figured only briefly in the history of one strand of capitalism – once in the nineteenth century, in the English paradigm case, and again in the 1980s of this century, in Britain, the United States, Australia and New Zealand, as a consequence of neo-liberal policies.

Taking a longer historical perspective, it is hardly surprising that these Anglo-Saxon countries are the only ones in which the free market has existed for even a short period. For, as Macfarlane notes, 'the only areas that had never had peasantries at all were those colonized by England: Australia, New Zealand, Canada and North America'.[12] These Anglo-Saxon countries were societies in which a culture and economy of agrarian individualism preceded industrialization. They incubated an economic culture in which the free market could for a short time be established, but which nonetheless presupposed exceptional legal, social and economic conditions, along with the ruthless use of the powers of a strong state. Even in these favourable environments, the free market proved so humanly costly and so disruptive of the life of society that it could not be rendered stable. It is the disappearance of the nineteenth-century free market, not its emergence, that occurred as a result of a slow historical evolution. In that evolution the unplanned workings of democratic political institutions were decisive.

The free market that existed in England from the 1840s to the 1870s could not be reproduced. In the strictly economic terms of rising productivity and national wealth, the mid-Victorian period was one of boom. But it was a boom whose social costs were politically insupportable.[13]

As the democratic franchise was extended, so was state intervention in the economy. From the 1870s to the First World War, a spate of reforms was implemented, limiting market freedoms for the sake of social cohesion (and sometimes economic efficiency). By 1870 the 'patently interventionist' Education Act was passed.[14] These reforms did not represent the execution of any comprehensive design. But by the close of the century they had put an end to the brief episode of *laissez-faire* in England. With the outbreak of the First World War the foundations of the welfare state had been laid in Britain.

Free trade survived until the impact on Britain of the Great Depression, persisting as a dogma long after its utility as an ideology had been exhausted. It was abandoned only when the loss of Britain's comparative advantage in international trade became intolerable. As Corelli Barnett has put it, 'It was only the coming of another great emergency, the world slump, which finally broke the taboo of liberal economic doctrine in Britain. Free Trade itself was abandoned in 1931. It was nearly a hundred years since it had opened the way to British dependence on overseas markets and supplies for its very existence . . . '[15] In the mid-nineteenth century free trade was adopted by Britain for several reasons, including the comparative advantage Britain still possessed in world markets as the first industrialized country. The power of *laissez-faire* ideas in Britain reflected that advantage.

Laissez-faire thinking was supplanted by the 'New Liberal' thinkers such as Hobhouse, Hobson, Bosanquet, Green and Keynes who were ready to harness the powers of the state to moderate the effects of market forces, to relieve poverty and promote social welfare. In the first decade of this century the New Liberals found in Lloyd George their first and greatest political architect.

The slow growth of welfare legislation in the last quarter of the nineteenth century was succeeded by a swift advance towards a welfare state. Both the philosophy and the policies that had created the free market were discarded. The economic insecurities of the free market interacted with the imperatives of party competition in an emerging democracy. The result was to kill off the political influence of *laissez-faire*.

Yet the classical liberal illusion of the free market as a self-regulating system still lingered through the interwar years. It inspired the deflationary expenditure cuts which deepened the Great Slump. Even the growth of fascist movements which fed on Europe's post-war economic dislocations was not sufficient to shake the faith in self-correcting markets. It took the catastrophe of the Second World War to jolt economic orthodoxy into accepting Keynesian ideas.

The managed economies of the post-war period did not arise from an intellectual conversion from *laissez-faire*, however. They grew out of a horror of the economic collapses and dictatorships that had led to the Second World War and from the resolute refusal of voters in Britain to return to the social order of the interwar years.

The idea of a self-stabilizing international economic order perished in the totalitarian dictatorships, forced migrations, Allied saturation bombing and the measureless horror of the Nazi genocide. In Britain, the idea was killed by the experience of a war economy, far more efficient than that of Nazi Germany, in which joblessness was unknown and nutritional and health standards higher for the majority than they had been in peacetime.

Laissez-faire made an anachronistic and ephemeral return to political life during the 1980s and 1990s. The declining productivity and social and industrial conflicts of British corporatism were the catalysts for the intervention of the International Monetary Fund in the management of the British economy in 1976. That intervention began the swift unravelling of Britain's post-war Keynesian economic consensus which culminated with Margaret Thatcher's rise to power in 1979.

Mrs Thatcher's government captured the spirit of the age and responded to some of Britain's needs. In their earlier years the Tories completed, as Labour could not, the dismantling of British corporatism that was a precondition of economic modernization; but this necessary response to a particular national dilemma degenerated into a universal ideology. Thatcher became an icon of the global free market, and her policies were emulated throughout the world.

The fate of the regime of deregulation and marketization which was installed in many countries in the 1980s is likely to be similar to that of the nineteenth-century English free market. But it will be harder now than it was then to moderate the social costs of free markets. The leverage of national governments over their economies is much weaker. If social markets are to survive or be rebuilt they will need to be embodied in new and more flexible institutions.

Large and widening economic inequalities threaten the political stability of the free market at both national and global levels. It is not easy to see how the American-led concert of the great powers on which today's global market relies can withstand a prolonged setback in the world economy. The policies of crisis management that have averted catastrophe in the recent past will not now be adequate.

A breakdown of the present global economic regime could well result from current policies. Those who imagine that great errors of policy are not repeated in history have not learnt its chief lesson – that nothing is ever learnt for long. We are at present in the midst of an experiment in utopian social engineering whose outcome we *can* know in advance.

The false dawn of the global free market

The *laissez-faire* policies which produced the Great Transformation in nineteenth-century England were based on the theory that market freedoms are natural and political restraints on markets are artificial. The truth is that free markets are creatures of state power, and persist only so long as the state is able to prevent human needs for security and the control of economic risk from finding political expression.

In the absence of a strong state dedicated to a liberal economic programme, markets will inevitably be encumbered by a myriad of constraints and regulations. These will arise spontaneously, in response to specific social problems, not as elements in any grand design. The parliamentarians who passed Factory Acts in the 1860s and 1870s were not reconstructing society or the economy according to a plan. They were responding to problems of working life – danger, squalor, inefficiencies – as they became aware of them. *Laissez-faire* withered away as the unintended consequence of a multitude of such uncoordinated responses.

Encumbered markets are the norm in every society, whereas free markets are a product of artifice, design and political coercion. *Laissez-faire* must be centrally planned; regulated markets just happen. The free market is not, as New Right thinkers have imagined or claimed, a gift of social evolution. It is an end-product of social engineering and unyielding political will. It was feasible in nineteenth-century England only because, and for so long as, functioning democratic institutions were lacking.

The implications of these truths for the project of constructing a worldwide free market in an age of democratic government are profound. They are that the rules of the game of the market must be insulated from democratic deliberation and political amendment. Democracy and the free market are rivals, not allies.

The natural counterpart of a free market economy is a politics of insecurity. If 'capitalism' means 'the free market', then no view is more deluded than the belief that the future lies with 'democratic capitalism'. In the normal course of democratic political life the free market is always short-lived. Its social costs are such that it cannot for long be legitimated in any democracy. This truth is demonstrated by the history of the free market in Britain, and it is well understood by more far-sighted neo-liberal thinkers who plan to make the free market global.

Those who seek to design a free market on a worldwide scale have always insisted that the legal framework which defines and entrenches it must be placed beyond the reach of any democratic legislature. Sovereign states may sign up to membership of the World Trade Organisation; but it is that organization, not the legislature of any sovereign state, which determines what is to count as free trade, and what a restraint of it. The rules of the game of the market must be elevated beyond any possibility of revision through democratic choice.

The role of a transnational organization such as the WTO is to project free markets into the economic life of every society. It does so by trying to compel adherence to the rules which release free markets from the encumbered or embedded markets that exist in every society. Transnational organizations can get away with this only insofar as they are immune from the pressures of democratic political life.

Polanyi's description of the legislation that was required to create a market economy in the nineteenth century applies with equal force to the project of the global free market today, as has been advanced through the World Trade Organisation and similar bodies.

> Nothing must be allowed to inhibit the formation of markets, nor must incomes be permitted to form other than through sales. Neither must there be any interference with the adjustment of prices to changed market conditions – whether the prices are those of goods, labour, land, or money. Hence there must not only be markets for all elements of industry, but no measure or policy must be countenanced that would influence the action of these markets. Neither price, nor supply, nor demand must be fixed or regulated; only such policies and measures are in order which help to ensure the self-regulation of the market by creating conditions which make the market the only organizing power in the economic sphere.[16]

To be sure, this is an unrealizable fantasy; its pursuit by transnational bodies has produced economic dislocation, social chaos and political instability in hugely different countries throughout the world.

In the conditions in which it has been attempted in the late twentieth century, reinventing the free market has involved ambitious social engineering on a massive scale. No reformist programme today has a chance of success unless it understands that many of the changes produced, accelerated or reinforced by New Right policies are irreversible. Equally, no political reaction against the consequences of free-market policies will be effective that does not grasp the technological and economic transformations that such policies were able to harness.

Reinventing the free market has effected profound ruptures in the countries in which it has been attempted. The social and political settlements which it has destroyed – the Beveridge settlement in Britain and the Roosevelt New Deal in the United States – cannot now be recreated. The social market economies of continental Europe cannot be renewed as recognizable variants of post-war social or Christian democracy. Those who imagine that there can be a return to the 'normal politics' of post-war economic management are deluding themselves and others.

Even so, the free market has not succeeded in establishing the hegemonic power that was envisaged for it. In all democratic states the political supremacy of the free market is incomplete, precarious and soon undermined. It cannot easily survive periods of protracted economic setback. In Britain the unintended consequences of neo-liberal policies themselves weakened the New Right's hold on political power. The delicate coalition of electoral and economic constituencies that the New Right mobilized in support of its policies was soon scattered.

It was dissolved partly by the effects of New Right policies and partly by the forces that are loose in the world economy at large. New Right policies offered those who voted for them a chance of upward social mobility. Over time they undid the social structures in which such aspirations were framed. Moreover, they imposed heavy costs and risks on some aspirants to property-ownership. Those who have been immobilized by negative equity in their homes can hardly be expected to be enthusiastic about the regime of deregulation that landed them in their difficulties. The economic insecurities which New Right policies exacerbate were bound to weaken the initial coalitions that supported and benefited from these policies. Labour's landslide victory in May 1997 resulted partly from these self-undermining effects of the Tories' New Right policies.

However, the dislocations of social and economic life today are not caused solely by free markets. Ultimately they arise from the banalization of technology. Technological innovations made in advanced western countries are soon copied everywhere. Even without free-market policies the managed economies of the post-war period could not have survived – technological advance would have made them unsustainable.

New technologies make full employment policies of the traditional sort unworkable. The effect of information technologies is to throw the social division of labour into a flux. Many occupations are disappearing and all jobs are less secure. The division of labour in society is now less stable than it has been since the Industrial Revolution. What global markets do is to transmit this instability to every economy in the world, and in doing so they make a new politics of economic insecurity universal.

The free market cannot last in an age in which economic security for the majority of people is being reduced by the world economy. The regime of *laissez-faire* is bound to trigger counter-movements which reject its constriants. Such movements – whether populist and xenophobic, fundamentalist or neo-communist – can achieve few of their goals; but they can still rattle to pieces the brittle structures that support global *laissez-faire*. Must we accept that the world's economic life cannot be organized as a universal free market and that better forms of governance by global regulation are unachievable? Is a late modern anarchy our historical fate?

A reform of the world economy is needed that accepts a diversity of cultures, regimes and market economies as a permanent reality. A global free market belongs to a world in which western hegemony seemed assured. Like all other variants of the Enlightenment Utopia of a universal civilization it presupposes western supremacy. It does not square with a pluralist world in which there is no power that can hope to exercise the hegemony that Britain, the United States and other western states possessed in the past. It does not meet the needs of a time in which western institutions and values are no longer universally authoritative. It does not allow the world's manifold cultures to achieve modernizations that are adapted to their histories, circumstances and distinctive needs.

A global free market works to set sovereign states against one another in geo-political struggles for dwindling natural resources. The effect of a *laissez-faire* philosophy which condemns state intervention in the economy is to impel states to become rivals for control of resources that no institution has any responsibility for conserving.

Nor, evidently, does a world economy that is organized as a global free market meet the universal human need for security. The *raison d'être* of governments everywhere is their ability to protect citizens from insecurity. A regime of global *laissez-faire* that prevents governments from discharging this protective role is creating the conditions for still greater political, and economic, instability.

In advanced economies that are competently and resourcefully governed, ways may be found in which the risks imposed on citizens by world markets can be mitigated. In poorer countries, global *laissez-faire* produces fundamentalist regimes and works as a catalyst for the disintegration of the modern state. At the global level, as at that of the nation-state, the free market does not promote stability or democracy. Global democratic capitalism is as unrealizable a condition as worldwide communism.

2　Engineering free markets

The road to the free market was opened and kept open by an
enormous increase in continuous, centrally organized and
controlled interventionism.

KARL POLANYI[1]

On the morning of 20 December 1994, one of the world's most ambitious free-market experiments aborted. Just three weeks after his
inauguration President Ernesto Zedillo of Mexico announced a devaluation of the country's currency. American investors who had placed
their savings in funds managed by firms such as Fidelity, Scudder,
Goldman Sachs and Salomon Brothers lost over $30 billion. On the
Mexican stock market, there was an estimated loss of $70 million in
the stock market worth of Mexican corporations. In addition, Mexico
suffered a loss of somewhere between a quarter of a million and one
million jobs by the end of 1995, capital flight on an unknown scale, a
leap in annual inflation to over 50 per cent, a rise in the cost of mortgages and loans far in excess of the inflation rate and, as a
consequence, a rash of business and bank failures, with the threat of
bankruptcy overshadowing some state governments.[2]

What collapsed that day was more than a currency: it was an entire
model of economic development. Prior to the devaluation, the
Mexican experiment was held up as something to be emulated by
developing countries throughout the world. Animated by the
Washington consensus – the dogma that minimum government and

free markets are achievable and desirable throughout the world – transnational organizations had attempted to implant in Mexico a variant of the American free market. A similar project was attempted in Thatcherite Britain and in Labour-governed New Zealand in the 1980s. In each case, despite major differences between these countries, the results were similar. The experiments were at best only very partial successes, but they wrought irreversible change on the societies.

A global single market is very much a late-twentieth-century *political* project. It is good to remind ourselves of this, and to make an important distinction. This political project is far more transient than the globalization of economic and cultural life that began in Europe in the early modern period from the fifteenth century onwards, and is set to advance for centuries. For humankind at the close of the modern period globalization is an historical fate. Its basic mechanism is the swift and inexorable spawning of new technologies throughout the world. That technology-driven modernization of the world's economic life will go ahead regardless of the fate of a worldwide free market. Growing economic interconnectedness does not depend on the orthodoxies of the IMF. Only an ecological catastrophe can halt or retard it.

Yet the consequences of this spread of modern means of production and communication throughout the world are practically the reverse of those that are confidently expected by the Washington consensus. It means a metamorphosis of the American free market rather than its universal replication. It is more likely to engender a new international anarchy rather than recapture the supposed harmonies of the nineteenth-century system; and it permits the appearance of new types of capitalism, most of which differ sharply from the free market. The most successful economies in the coming century will not be those that have tried to graft American free markets onto the stem of their native cultures; they will be economies whose modernization is indigenous.

Among recent experiments in engineering the free market in late-twentieth-century conditions, those in Britain, New Zealand and Mexico are particularly notable. Each of them exemplifies, in the context of a particular national political culture, the ironies and paradoxes of the free market in the late modern world.

In each, the initial impetus of the experiment was the fact that corporatist economic structures had become unsustainable; at the same time neo-liberal ideology came to be a powerful influence in its own right. In each case, economic globalization was the catalyst that triggered the neo-liberal experiment; but the politics of insecurity fuelled by an expanding world economy scattered the initial coalition of interests that propelled the experiment into power and weakened or destroyed the political vehicle that implemented it.

As a result, the free market has used the power of the state to achieve its ends but has weakened the institutions of the state in vital respects. In every case free market policies lost political legitimacy while at the same time altering the economy and society in ways that democratic choice cannot reverse.

The Thatcherite experiment

Margaret Thatcher's attempt to resurrect the free market in late-twentieth-century Britain is instructive not only for its strategies and successes, but for the manner and causes of its downfall. In one respect Thatcherite policy was an attempt to impose a much needed modernization on the British economy; in another, it tried to reshape British institutions along the lines of an irrecoverable past. These two aspects of Thatcherite policy are intimately, even inseparably, linked.

The electoral coalition which Thatcher mobilized behind her key policies – reducing trade union power, removing council houses from municipal ownership and lowering direct taxes – enabled her to win three successive elections. Her demolition of Britain's post-war consensus triggered a far-reaching transformation in the Labour Party that resulted in its return to power after a landslide victory in May 1997.

Thatcherism did not begin as a political project in which ideology was central. The Labour government of James Callaghan had already begun dismantling British corporatism when, in response to the imperatives imposed upon it by the International Monetary Fund in the autumn of 1976, it announced that the pursuit of full employment through Keynesian policies of economic management was no longer feasible. But it could not do more than inaugurate that break with Britain's post-war settlement. It could not reform British industrial relations.

Thatcherism began as a local response to a British problem. In its initial policy agenda nothing was more important than trade union reform. Margaret Thatcher understood that British corporatism – the triangular coordination of economic policy by government, employers and trade unions – had become an engine of industrial conflict and strife over the distribution of the national income rather than an instrument of wealth creation or a guarantor of social cohesion. For much of the 1980s 'Thatcherism' was a gloss on this perception.

The early years of the Thatcher era were not informed by any coherent political doctrine. Indeed, the very idea of Thatcherism may well have been invented by the Left. A handful of perceptive Marxists, notably Martin Jacques, editor of the pioneering journal *Marxism Today*, were among those who first grasped that Thatcher's governments marked an irreversible break with post-war British social democracy.

Yet, by the time Thatcher was toppled, a callow New Right ideology had become pervasive in her government's thinking, evident in such fateful policies as the poll tax. A circle of folly and hubris had closed around Thatcher and her advisers. Within that circle she was sheltered from public and business alarm that her policies – not only on the poll tax but, more significantly, on Britain's relations with the European Union – were driven by ideology rather than practical necessity.

The government of John Major which followed in 1990 did not temper her policies; they were simply applied more mechanically. Britain's railway network was broken up into four score privatized companies, a move that was popular with no one apart from a few *rentiers* of railway rolling stock. It merely compounded the electoral difficulties of Major's last government. The project of re-engineering the free market was not, then, set back when Thatcher was toppled from power; it was merely given a long second wind. Britain was thus subjected to free-market policies for nearly two decades.

And what of the touchstones of New Right obloquy? The size of the British state did not shrink. It pre-empted as much of the nation's economic resources as it had in the 1970s – far more than had the Labour government of 1945. Levels of tax for most families were higher at the end of the Thatcherite period than they had been at its start. In some areas, such as the reduction of union power, Thatcherite policy – helped by major changes in the real economy – achieved its objectives; but its overall result was to set in place the conditions for its political defeat.

Thatcherite policies eroded the class culture on which the almost unbroken dominance of the Conservative Party on British political life for over a century depended. A set of policies which put into the melting pot a whole range of industries, neighbourhoods and professions could not renew the electoral coalition which made it politically possible in the first place.

The transformations which Thatcherite policies imposed on British institutions always risked engulfing its political vehicle, the Conservative Party. Political parties that impose revolutionary changes on nearly every aspect of social and economic life cannot escape their consequences for themselves.

The Conservative Party has been in decline since the 1950s. That process of decline quickened dramatically during its period of unchallenged power in the 1980s, with old members dying off and not being replaced by new recruits. It is a telling postscript to the glory years of Thatcherite supremacy that the average age of the Conservative Party's membership when it suffered its catastrophic defeat in May 1997 was somewhere in the mid-sixties.

Despite Thatcher's own rigidly hostile attitude to constitutional reform, the institutions of the British state could not escape deep changes arising as unintended side-effects of Thatcherite policies. Chief among these was a sweeping centralization of power in the institutions of national government. As A. V. Dicey observed of the original, nineteenth-century experiment in *laissez-faire*, 'Sincere believers in *laissez-faire* found that for the attainment of their ends the improvement and strengthening of governmental machinery was an absolute necessity.'[3]

This was not a peculiarly British aberration. It was the local expression of a universal paradox. In the normal course of things markets come embedded in social life. They are circumscribed in their workings by intermediary institutions and encumbered by social conventions and tacit understandings. Among these intermediary institutions, trade unions and professional associations have long been central in standing between individuals and market forces. Constructing a free market demands that these social institutions be weakened or destroyed. They must be defeated as particular producer interests that stand in the way of the universal consumer. Only a strong centralized state can wage war on such powerful intermediary institutions.

The centralization of the British state in the Thatcherite period was not an error of policy that might have been avoided. It was an integral part of engineering the free market.

The British constitution which Thatcher inherited in 1979 was soon deformed beyond recognition. The barriers between the institutions of the British state, the government and the Conservative Party that were embodied in the tacit understandings and unwritten conventions of the pre-Thatcher constitution were blurred or weakened. Once taken for granted, the political neutrality of the Civil Service began to seem doubtful. The institutions of the quango state were colonized by Tory placemen and women. Intermediary bodies that were once autonomous institutions became the property of a caste of Tory nomenclaturists. The relationship of trust between rulers and ruled that was an indispensable condition of legitimacy in an unwritten constitution became a mere memory. The upshot was a radically unbalanced constitution that could not outlast a Conservative electoral defeat.

Thatcherite policies effected many significant changes in British society and institutions, some of them irreversible. Of these the many privatizations may not turn out to have the deepest or most lasting importance. The first privatization was not even initiated by the Tories; it was implemented by Labour, when Denis Healey announced the selling off of part of the state's share in the ownership of British Petroleum. In fact, privatization figured only slightly in early Thatcherism. It did not appear at all in the 1979 election manifesto and first featured in a Tory administration in 1982, when the lack of funds needed for the modernization of the British telecommunications industry forced the government to consider what was then a revolutionary step – the privatization of a major pubic utility.

That seminal privatization was driven not by doctrine but by the logic of events. An industry that needed urgently injections of capital that it knew it could not get from public, Treasury-controlled funds had no option but to go to the capital markets for them. To do that it needed to be privatized. In one of the ironies that abound during this period, the privatization of British Telecom was so successful that in the event it was able to fund its technological modernization from its own resources.

Privatization appeared for the first time in a Tory election manifesto in 1983. The list of state assets privatized during the following years of neo-liberal policy is long and substantial. In 1979 government institutions owned much or all of coal, steel, gas, electricity, water, railways, airlines, telecommunications, nuclear power and shipbuilding, and had a significant stake in oil, banking, shipping and road haulage. By 1997 nearly all of this was in private hands. In addition, well over a million former tenants in municipal housing owned their own homes.

Running alongside this privatization of state assets there was a comprehensive nationalization of local government and intermediary institutions. The National Health Service, the schools, former poly-technics and universities, prisons, the administration of justice and the authorities regulating the police forces were all reorganized. They were removed from the control of democratically elected local authorities and placed under the control of unelected quangos and Next Steps Agencies which were accountable, if at all, only to central govern-ment. By 1995 such quangos employed more people and spent more money than did local government. Finally, market mechanisms – com-pulsory competitive tendering, performance-related and profit-related pay and similar devices – were injected into all public services.

The diverse institutions of governance through which power had long been dispersed in Britain were centralized in the state as never before in peacetime history. Market mechanisms, or simulacra of mar-kets, were imposed on all of them.

The Thatcherite 'nationalization of Britain'[4] paralleled the changes imposed on the labour market. Reducing trade union power, and approaching a more individualist labour market were among the few unequivocally clear objectives of the first Thatcher government. In combination with the monetarist commitment to price stability achieved at any social or economic cost, they sealed the fate of the post-war settlement in Britain.

The Keynesian–Beveridgean consensus not only assumed full employment as the most indispensable precondition of a sustainable welfare state, it also imposed an overriding obligation on national government to promote it. The explicit abandonment under Thatcher of government responsibility for full employment marked not only a change in economic doctrine from Keynes to Friedman. It effected a fundamental shift in understanding the functions of the state. In this shift the decisive text was not Hayek's *Constitution of Liberty*, or any other crib for neo-liberal ideologues, but *Stepping Stones* by John Hoskyns, a guide to dealing with trade union power and creating a free market in labour (it was never published).[5]

According to the Thatcherite understanding of the role of the state, its task was to supply a framework of rules and regulations within which the free market – including, crucially, the labour market – would be self-regulating. In this vision the role of trade unions as intermediary institutions standing between workers and the market had to be altered and weakened. Employment law was reshaped. The contemporary model that informed these changes throughout was the American labour market, with its high levels of mobility, downward flexibility of wages and low costs for employers.

Partly as a result of these policies, there was an explosive increase in part-time and contract work. The bourgeois institution of the career or vocation ceased to be a viable option for an increasing number of workers. Many low-skill workers earned less than the minimum needed to support a family. The diseases of poverty – TB, rickets, and others – returned.[6] The former middle classes were exhorted to become 'portfolio persons', attached to no particular company or institution. As a survey concluded in 1996, 'The traditional career has ended and become just a memory.'[7]

At the same time, entitlements to welfare benefits were restricted across the board, with unemployment benefits (such as the Job Seekers Allowance of 1996) designed specifically to compel recipients to accept work at market-driven rates. It may not be fanciful to hear an echo here of the Poor Law reforms of the 1830s. In both cases the result was a large shift in economic bargaining power away from employees.

The innermost contradiction of the free market is that it works to weaken the traditional social institutions on which it has depended in the past – the family is a key example. The fragility and decline of the traditional family increased throughout the Thatcherite period. The proportion of women aged eighteen to forty-nine who were married fell from 74 per cent in 1979 to 61 per cent, while the proportion cohabiting increased from 11 per cent to 22 per cent during the same period. Births outside marriage more than doubled during the 1980s. One-parent families increased from 12 per cent in 1979 to 21 per cent in 1992, with the biggest single increase being in single mothers who had never been married.

By 1991 there was one divorce for every two marriages in Britain – the highest divorce rate of any EU country, and comparable only with that in the United States.[8] Is it coincidental that no EU country apart from Britain has imposed American-style deregulation on its labour market? In those British cities in which Thatcherite policies of labour market deregulation were most successful in lowering rates of unemployment, rates of divorce and family breakdown were correspondingly highest.[9]

Still more striking was the growth of an underclass. The percentage of British (non-pensioner) households that are wholly workless – that is, none of whose members is active in the productive economy – increased from 6.5 per cent in 1975 to 16.4 per cent in 1985 and 19.1 per cent in 1994.[10] This increase continued, perhaps even accelerated, under the government of John Major. Between 1992 and 1997 there was a 15 per cent increase in unemployed lone parents.[11]

To spell it out: in Britain today around one in five households (not counting pensioners) contains not a single working person. This represents a magnitude of social exclusion unknown in any other European country, but long familiar in the United States. This dramatic growth of an underclass occurred as a direct consequence of neo-liberal welfare reforms, particularly as they affected housing. The selling-off of council houses to their tenants is often praised as a Thatcherite success story. Certainly it was electorally significant as a source of support for Thatcherism in the 1980s – though it may well have worked against the Conservatives in the 1990s. In social and economic terms, the decimation of municipal housing was one of the chief elements in the emergence of a neo-liberal dependency culture. Spending on housing benefit during 1996–7 was estimated at over £11 billion. This is 1.5 per cent of Britain's gross domestic product and over ten times the total cost of housing benefits in 1979–80.[12] Public expenditure on social housing was replaced, many times over, by rent rebates and assistance with the payment of mortgages. The price of privatizing municipal housing in Britain has been a colossal increase in welfare dependency.

What is more significant in these developments is the difference between British experience and that of other European countries, that have not undergone a prolonged period of neo-liberal public policy and the striking similarities they exhibit with trends in the United States. Even in penal policy there is a remarkable correlation. Britain's incarceration rate is far higher than any other EU country (though still much lower than that of the US) and rising fast. Between 1992 and 1995 Britain's prison population increased by nearly a third (to over 50,000).

Figures on rates of crime are harder to come by, and notoriously tricky to interpret. Nevertheless there can be no mistaking the overall trends. In 1970 there were under 1.6 million serious crimes known to the police in England and Wales; in 1981 there were 2.8 million.[13] At the end of 1990 the figure of recorded crime stood at 4.3 million; for 1992 the corresponding figure was 5.6 million. Moreover, the 1992 British Crime Survey suggested that the real figure was nearer three times the official figure.[14]

At the same time, state expenditure on law enforcement in Britain increased steadily. Between 1978/9 and 1982/3 spending on the police forces increased by nearly a quarter in real terms. The number of police rose by nearly 10,000 to over 120,000 in Margaret Thatcher's first term in office.[15] (Such increases in the pay and numbers of police were not a feature of John Major's administrations.) Overall, the trends were for crime of all kinds and most forms of state expenditure on law enforcement to rise throughout the Thatcherite period – a trend paralleled in the New Zealand experiment and in Ronald Reagan's America.

A recent sociological assessment offers a good summary of Thatcherism's consequences for crime and social order:

As far as crime in general is concerned, the evidence suggests that both the predominant types of crime and the increased lawlessness of the last decade are best understood in terms of the long-term changes in British society that have been taking place for almost twenty years . . . the progressive weakening of the traditional social bonds of family and community and the final transformation of the traditional function of state primary and secondary schools from one of pedagogically oriented social control to one of competitively – and socially divisive – oriented acquisition of knowledge and skills. The role of the Victorian Board School, which persisted as a model for primary education well into the present century, has been forgotten . . . It is the virtual disappearance of a range of auxiliary agents of social control from park keepers to bus conductors and school attendance officers which has left the police overexposed and inadequately resourced to deal with the problem of crime . . . increasing resort to carceral solutions for social problems is equally lacking in effect but ruinously expensive . . . crime of the kind that afflicts Britain and much of the post-industrial world reflects an altogether deeper malaise.[16]

The connection between free markets and 'law and order' policies has never been inadvertent. As intermediary social institutions and the informal social controls of community life are weakened by market-driven economic change the disciplinary functions of the state are strengthened. The endpoint of this development comes when the sanctions of the criminal law become the principal remaining support of social order. In the United States this point may not be far off.

The self-undermining effect of Thatcherism as a political project came from its unintended social consequences. An economic policy that speeds the disappearance of industries and neighbourhoods encourages voters to question their loyalties. This was especially true in Britain, where electoral allegiances and class culture have always been closely and deeply connected. In accelerating the dissolution of the old class culture, Thatcherite policies weakened long-established party support. Initially, this worked to Thatcher's political advantage, as long-standing Labour voters switched to the Tories. Over a longer run, as it corroded Tory support in the middle classes, it made Conservative rule impossible to sustain.

Thatcherite policies also promoted a striking growth in economic inequality. According to the authoritative Rowntree Report on Income and Wealth, inequality increased in Britain between 1977 and 1990 faster than in all but one other comparable country. After 1979 the lowest income groups ceased to benefit from economic growth. Since 1977 the proportion of the population with less than half the average income more than trebled.[17] By 1984–5 the richest fifth's share of after-tax income – 43 per cent – was higher than at any time after the war.[18]

Though several measures of inequality have risen in many First World countries, the speed and magnitude of economic inequalities in Britain is far ahead of nearly all others. Only in New Zealand, where neo-liberal policies were even more radical and the egalitarian inheritance more pronounced, did inequality grow faster.

In the general election of May 1997 the Conservative share of the popular vote was lower than it had been at any time since the Great Reform Act of 1832. The Conservative party was shipwrecked by the Thatcherite revolution. The Tory débâcle had many causes. Some lay in policy errors that might have been avoided, others in historical accidents that need not have happened. The poll tax was a prime example of avoidable error. Thatcher's stridently nationalist rhetoric about the

European Union in the period immediately before her downfall may not have augured any basic shift in policy on her part; but it alarmed pro-European opinion in her party and in the business world. The BSE crisis that haunted the dying administration of John Major was a consequence of misguided policies, though it happened when it did by accident.

As always in political life, luck played a role that was sometimes decisive. Thatcher very nearly came unstuck in the Westlands crisis, at which point the free-market experiment might have ended in Britain.[19] A major military setback in the Falklands War with Argentina could also have had disabling political repercussions. Like all politicians Margaret Thatcher depended on her luck holding. Until 1990, when she was brought down by a Tory coup against her, it did.

Thatcherism was granted another lease of life by John Major's surprise victory in the general election of 1992. By then the electorate had come to accept that the performance of the economy was not a result of skilful management by government but a by-product of world markets. Until the 1980s the governments in Britain sought to align the business cycle with the electoral cycle. They tried to manage the economy to their own advantage by 'stop–go' policies. A major goal of the New Right was to separate governments from economic fluctuations in the judgement of voters. They shaped a public culture in which governments could shift responsibility for the economy to world markets.

The result of the 1992 election showed that the New Right had succeeded in its strategy of decoupling the economy's performance from the voter's perception of the competence of the government. But this victory was short-lived and paradoxical in its consequences. When Britain was driven out of the ERM in 1993, the link between the competence of government and the performance of the economy was re-established in the perception of the voters.

For the Conservatives this recoupling was disastrous. Yet the split between economic performance and the competence of government produced by New Right policy in the 1980s lingered on in voters' minds. The Conservatives got little credit for the economic boom of the mid-1990s.

British public opinion takes a market economy for granted. If it was ever sympathetic to socialist projects of economic planning, it is so no longer. But it is also hostile to the sway of unfettered markets over the life of society. It wishes to see some goods – basic medical care, schooling and protection from crime – provided to all as a mark of citizenship. It regards the privatization of public utilities such as water with suspicion and it resists the further marketization of public services such as the care of the elderly. It will not accept American labour mobility: 60 per cent of British adults live within five miles of where they were born – a higher proportion than in the nineteenth century.

Thatcherism has signally failed to alter these British attitudes. Deep-rooted values of fairness and mutual aid block the full reinstatement of the free market in Britain. The public legitimacy of the free market has waned with the modernization of society that Thatcher's policies promoted. The beliefs and practices on which free markets could trade in the mid-Victorian period were weak or absent in 1979, and weaker still when the Conservatives lost power in 1997. The free market worked to dissipate what remained of them. In Britain, as elsewhere, the social dislocations produced by the free market have evoked a powerful political revulsion that has partly thwarted its political ambitions.

In its larger outlines, the economic restructuring which Thatcherite policies effected in Britain is not reversible by any subsequent government. It has not overcome Britain's long economic decline. Nor, save perhaps in one or two sectors such as telecommunications and the entertainment industries, has it generated the 'enterprise culture' of which its ideologues spoke and wrote. Yet, precisely because of Britain's continuing economic weakness – its dependency on foreign investment and world capital markets – no government can now roll back policies of privatization, or act decisively through the tax system to remedy the increase in economic inequalities.

History has imposed on the Labour government elected in May 1997 the task of promoting social-democratic values at a time when the historic institutions and policies of social democracy have disappeared.[20] As Europe's first post-social-democratic administration, Tony Blair's government must strive to reconcile a deregulated market economy with social cohesion. It must do so in an environment that has been marked indelibly by free-market policies and by the irreversible advance of economic globalization during the long Thatcherite period.

The undoing of conservatism

Thatcherite economic policies strengthened and accelerated most of the social and economic forces that have subsequently resulted in the dissolution of traditional families and communities. They set British society on a forced march into late modernity.

The role of Thatcherism as a modernizing project is rarely understood. The backward-looking character of market liberal ideology can be deceptive. Re-engineering the free market in late modern Britain dissolved the last remnants of the social order that had sustained it in the nineteenth century. Not only the traditional family but the class culture of deference and respectability which had been indispensable to the free market have been largely swept away.

Unperceived and never comprehended by Thatcherism's vociferous ideologues and their blinkered disciples, one effect of Thatcher's policies was to subject Britain's deformed class culture to a modernization more far-reaching than any that Labour had ever attempted.

In imposing a forced modernization on many aspects of life in Britain, Thatcherism made the projects of its chief political rivals obsolete. It marginalized One Nation Toryism in the Conservative Party and the Social Democrats who broke away from the Labour Party in the early 1980s. Neither had a clear sight of the scale of the changes that were afoot in Britain. In different ways each depended on a class culture that Thatcherism was eroding. The rout of these contending political projects was one of the New Right's signal successes in Britain. But in displacing these tendencies from the political centre ground in Britain, Thatcherism created some of the conditions for its own demise.

One of Thatcherism's many ironies was its relationship with the nation-state. Neo-liberal economic policies stripped the nation-state of most of its leverage over national economic life, while Thatcherite public rhetoric clothed this denuded institution with an archaic veil of authority. The nation-state was held to be supremely important. National culture was claimed to be vital to social order. Yet neo-liberal economic policies prised open the British economy to world markets as never before.

A rhetoric of inexorable economic globalization was combined with the assertion of the unique authority and indispensable utility of a common national culture. Britain's relationship with the European

Union was condemned as a fetter on its national sovereignty by Tory neo-liberals who held that no national government could hope to buck world markets. The sovereign nation-state was glorified at just the historical moment when those who elevated it declared it to be economically redundant.

In the mass media Thatcherite policies positively promoted the fragmentation of the common national culture by globalization. Genuinely national institutions such as the BBC were attacked relentlessly, while commercial internationalization of the media was actively begun. The nation-state was denied any central role even in the renewal of the national culture.

The intermediary social institutions on which the free market depended in mid-Victorian England became hindrances to its reconstruction in the late twentieth century. Professional associations, local authorities, mutual societies and stable families were impediments to the mobility and individualism that are required by unfettered markets. They limit the power of markets over people. In a late modern context re-engineering the free market cannot avoid weakening or destroying such intermediary structures, and such was their fate in Britain.

It is odd that there are still those who find the association of free markets with social disorder anomalous. Even if it could itself be rendered stable the free market is bound to be destructive of other institutions through which social cohesion is preserved. No society can opt for the free market and hope to avoid these consequences.

Re-engineering the free market is hardly a conservative political project. Its effect is to sever cultural and institutional continuities, not to renew them. The Right's project in present circumstances cannot be the conservation of cultural traditions. It claims to want progress – but progress without any fixed goals. The most clear-sighted and candid of the New Right's thinkers defined progress as 'movement for movement's sake'.[21]

Any genuine conservative must regard this as a prescription for purposeless change – in other words, as an expression of nihilism. In its more concrete uses, which are doubtless the ones that matter to neo-liberals, 'progress' denotes the incessant social change forced on people by the imperatives of free markets. From these necessities arise the insoluble contradictions on which the project founders.

The permanent revolution of the free market denies any authority to the past. It nullifies precedent, it snaps the threads of memory and scatters local knowledge. By privileging individual choice over any common good it tends to make relationships revocable and provisional. In a culture in which choice is the only undisputed value and wants are held to be insatiable, what is the difference between initiating a divorce and trading in a used car? This logic of the free market, which is that all relationships become consumer goods, is denied indignantly by its ideologues. However, it is all too clearly evident in the daily life of societies in which the free market is dominant.

'If democracy and capitalism work best when they are leavened with cultural traditions that arise from nonliberal sources, then it should be clear' opines Francis Fukuyama blandly, 'that modernity and tradition can coexist in stable equilibrium for extended periods of time.'[22] Of course, as both Karl Marx and Max Weber recognized, modernity and tradition cannot be so smoothly reconciled. In late modern times globalization works against the traditions it inherits from the early modern age. When a late modern state throws its weight behind the world market it acts to scatter those inherited traditions to the winds. No amount of Tory social engineering can put together the delicate spider's web of traditions that new technologies and unfettered markets have blown away.

It was perhaps predictable that governments dominated by avowed Conservatives should have acted in our time as pace-makers for the forced modernization of the societies they rules. No less predictable was the inability of neo-conservative ideologues to comprehend the dilemma in which societies dominated by the free market are trapped.

That individualist capitalism subverts cultural traditions more successfully than any government is a tribute to the powers of the market and a comment on the limits of state action. It is curious that the same Right-wing thinkers who affirm the impotence of states in economic life should have such large hopes of them as social engineers. It is even more incongruous that New Right thinking, which like vulgar Marxism imagines that economic changes determine behaviour, should so systematically disregard the effects of freeing up markets on marriage, the family and the incidence of crime.

The dilemma of the Right today is that cultural conservatism is not among the options open to it. It is doomed to waver between promoting the free market at any cultural cost and taking up quixotic postures of cultural elitism. It cannot settle in a stable equilibrium any more than the free market can. It oscillates, uncertainly but incessantly, between unreasonable pessimism about the recent historical past and wild optimism about the near future.

The Right today likes to imagine that it is the voice of the past. In truth, its ranting radicalism and its decadent nostalgias tie it unmistakably and irrevocably to the chaos of the present.[23]

The reactionary utopianism of the Right is a costly and hazardous venture. Peace and stability are the last things to be expected in societies which allow themselves to be ruled by it. Policies of buttressing traditional forms of family life and repressing the worst symptoms of crime can do little to restore the institutions and communities which the free market has desolated. The fate of the Right in the late modern age is to destroy what remains of the past in a vain attempt to recover it.

Few visions of the future have ever been so delusive as Herbert Marcuse's or Michel Foucault's perennially fashionable vision of perfected capitalist control of society. Late modern capitalism may incarcerate people in high-tech prisons and monitor them by video surveillance cameras at their work-place and in the high street; but it does not box them into an iron cage of bureaucracy or imprison them forever within a minute niche in the division of labour. It abandons them to a life of fragments and a proliferation of senseless choices.

The dystopia we face is not a nightmare of totalitarian control. Intermingling the ephemera of fashion with an ingrained reflex of nihilism, *American Psycho* is a truer approximation to the late modern condition than Kafka's *The Castle*.

Free markets are the most potent solvents of tradition at work in the world today. They set a premium on novelty and a discount on the past. They make of the future an infinite rerun of the present. The society they engender is antinomian and proletarian.

Free markets are often attacked for their short-term approach to investment in industry.[24] But the free market is most recklessly short-termist in its demolition of the virtues that it once relied upon. These virtues – saving, civic pride, respectability, 'family values' – are now profitless museum pieces. They are bits of bric-à-brac, dusted off for public display from time to time by the Right-wing media, but having few uses in an economy founded on ephemera.

The most enduring icon of the free market in the late twentieth century will not be Margaret Thatcher. It may well turn out to be Madonna.

The New Zealand experiment: a second Great Transformation in miniature

The neo-liberal experiment in New Zealand is the most ambitious attempt at constructing the free market as a social institution to be implemented anywhere this century. It is a clearer example of the costs and limits of reinventing the free market in a late-twentieth-century context than the Thatcherite experiment in Britain. Among the many novel effects of neo-liberal policy in New Zealand has been the creation of an underclass in a country that did not have one before.

The New Zealand experiment is the free-market project in laboratory conditions: uncompromising neo-liberal ideology animated a programme of radical reform in which no major social institution was left unreconstructed. The reforms were initiated by a social-democratic party before they became bipartisan and, for a while, they were politically unchallengeable. A Westminster-style constitutional tradition in which a unicameral parliament enjoyed an authority and freedom of action unfettered by any constitutional restraints allowed the most far-reaching transformation of a hitherto interventionist state we have yet to witness.

One of the world's most comprehensive social democracies became a neo-liberal state. New Zealand society underwent a correspondingly profound metamorphosis. The consequences and hazards of the New Zealand experiment are instructive, not to say ominous.

The experiment in which the free market was re-engineered in New Zealand has many similarities with the structural adjustment programmes forced on the governments of developing countries as a condition of credit from transnational international institutions. But New Zealand was not a Third World country – it was an advanced social democratic state. Traditions of state intervention in the economy to protect social cohesion were more deeply entrenched in New Zealand than in any other western country, with the exception of social-democratic Sweden.

By the early 1980s a major shift in policy may have been unavoidable. It was not unreasonable to fear that New Zealand might slip from its status as a First World economy. As with Thatcherism in Britain, the initial impetus to the experiment was not doctrinal, it was pragmatic. It did not originate within New Zealand's political class, it was conceived among its civil servants. It came from the perception in the Treasury that New Zealand's position as a First World country was becoming economically untenable. That, in turn, was a by-product of ongoing economic globalization, particularly the emergence of highly successful modernized economies in hitherto Third World countries such as Singapore.

A programme of neo-liberal restructuring was not the only, or the most promising response to New Zealand's quickening relative economic decline. Yet, as in other countries, New Right thought seemed compelling in having radical solutions for economic problems that could not go untreated for much longer.

As a result of this, undertaken by Labour administrations from 1984 to 1990 and carried on by the National Party thereafter, New Zealand's inheritance as an egalitarian social democracy and a socially cohesive Keynesian managed economy has been uprooted. At present, New Zealand approximates, more closely than any other western country, to the pure neo-liberal model of lean government and a free market economy.

Immediately or shortly after the Labour government took office in July 1984, exchange controls were abolished and the currency floated, controls on prices, wages, interest rates, rents and credit scrapped. Subsidies to exports were removed, import licenses abolished and all tariffs massively reduced. Most state-owned enterprises and assets were privatized. In a decisive break with New Zealand's long-standing Keynesian inheritance, full employment was abandoned as an objective of public policy in favour of the monetarist goal of price stability. These were measures of deregulation and 'rolling back the state' that corresponded closely with those adopted by other New Right governments, particular Mrs Thatcher's in Britain.

Uniquely in New Zealand, farming was defunded, with nearly all state assistance and protection being withdrawn in the years from 1984–7. No less exceptional was the deregulation of the labour market, which went far beyond the limitations on trade union power introduced in Thatcherite Britain. By 1991 the system of national collective bargaining had been comprehensively replaced by individual employment contracts in both the public and the private sectors. This created a labour market more market-driven and more thoroughly individualist than any other. An independent central bank was created, with price stability as its sole objective.

The state in New Zealand relinquished responsibility for overall levels of employment in the economy. Indeed, the goal of free marke-teers in New Zealand was to remove from the state the levers to pursue that or any other macroeconomic policy. That goal was largely achieved.

Equally, the imposition of a neo-liberal model on public services was more far-reaching than in any other country (save perhaps Chile). Public hospitals were converted into commercial enterprises and compelled to compete with private suppliers of medical care. Education was restructured, with responsibility for the delivery of educational services devolved to local school boards. Schools levied fees for their services and were required to supplement their budgets by commercial activities. Entitlement to welfare benefits of all kinds was rigorously pruned, with the population being stratified into economic categories which determined their levels of subsidy for state services. All state services were marketized, and all of the state's welfare functions reduced. At the same time, as Kelsey notes drily, 'Expenditure on police, courts and prisons continued to grow.'[25]

Kelsey summarizes the upshot of the New Zealand experiment by observing 'The result of a decade of radical structural adjustment was a deeply divided society.'[26] More generally, she comments that 'In less than a decade, New Zealand had gone from a bastion of welfare interventionism to a neo-liberal's paradise. Real economic and political power had shifted outside the realms of the central state. In this process of what might be termed "the privatization of power", citizens were reduced to consumers in the economic rather than the political market-place.'[27] There is much evidence to support these assessments. One estimate put 17.8 per cent of the New Zealand population under the poverty line in 1991.[28]

In a crucial coincidence, the increase in the numbers of unemployed following the abandonment of Keynesian for monetarist goals in macroeconomic management occurred alongside the adoption of targeting and selectivity and large-scale reductions in welfare entitlements. As the end of full employment forced more and more people into dependency on welfare, the welfare state was itself rolled back. The result has been the emergence in New Zealand of a social stratum that never existed when the country was burdened by a universal welfare state – an economically marginalized, socially excluded underclass of welfare dependents.

For anyone familiar with the American Right-wing theories and rhetoric which were the dominant inspiration of New Zealand's neo-liberal revolutionaries, the unprecedented growth in that country of an underclass is richly ironic. The message of the American New Right has always been that poverty and the underclass are products of the disincentive effects of welfare, not of the free market. And so, the moral hazards of the welfare state are universal, arising from invariant laws of human psychology – as are the benefits and virtues of the free market.[29]

To be sure, this universal claim has always had trouble accounting for the experience of those anomalous areas of the world beyond the borders of the United States. It has never squared with the experience of the countries of continental Europe, where levels of welfare provision far more comprehensive and generous than those of the United States have long coexisted with the absence of anything resembling an American-style underclass. It does not touch at virtually any point the experience of other Anglo-Saxon countries. Where are the lawless underclasses of Austria or Norway, where welfare provision is generous? Where is the underclass in Canada? Where was the underclass in the old, pre-reform New Zealand? In the Americocentric world of the New Right, such questions are never asked – let alone answered.

In New Zealand, the theories of the American New Right achieved a rare and curious feat – self-refutation by their practical application. Contrary to the New Right's confident claims, the abolition of nearly all universal social services and the stratification of income groups for the purpose of targeting welfare benefits selectively created a neo-liberal poverty trap.

The underclass of the late 1990s is not the product of the moral hazards of universal welfare. Certainly, it is incubated in a culture of dependency; but that culture was partly created by neo-liberal welfare reforms and unregulated labour markets. In New Zealand, as in the United Kingdom, the sudden growth of the underclass is a textbook example of the manufacture of poverty by the neo-liberal state.

Beyond the growth of the underclass, New Zealand has experienced an astonishing growth in economic inequalities of all kinds. The bargaining power of employees in relation to employers was considerably reduced by legislation imposing individual contracts on the labour market. At the same time, reductions in marginal levels of income taxation were implemented, affecting particularly those at the top. The result was that income inequalities increased in New Zealand more than in any other western country.[30]

The shift of power in New Zealand from the institutions of the central state to the institutions of the market did not occur spontaneously. As in mid-Victorian England, it occurred as a consequence of a systematic, comprehensive and far-reaching exercise of state power. New Zealand's variant of British parliamentary absolutism was deployed to remodel New Zealand's economy and social life. Kelsey writes that 'In the space of a decade a strong central state authority, operating with almost total disregard for democratic process and pluralist politics, and abetted by a private sector elite, revolutionized New Zealand's economy and its people's lives.'[31]

The phases of this revolution included the infiltration of the social-democratic Labour Party by neo-liberal ideologues, the acceptance after 1990 of neo-liberal public policy as a bipartisan consensus framing the limits of what was politically possible, the removal in 1989 of the country's Reserve Bank from democratic accountability and the imposition on it of an inflexible duty to stabilize price levels regardless of broader economic conditions, and the locking in of neo-liberal domestic economic policy beyond any possibility of political opposition by tying it into New Zealand's conformity to the provisions of GATT and the WTO.

Most decisively, the restructuring of New Zealand's economy which opened it to unregulated capital flows conferred on transnational capital an effective veto power over public policy. Wherever public policies might be perceived as impacting upon competitiveness, profits and economic stability they could be quashed by the threat of capital flight. Neo-liberal reforms thereby became politically irreversible. The social democratic objectives of earlier periods of public policy in New Zealand were not merely dismantled, abandoned or reversed, they were removed as options in democratic practice. The goal of this revolution was to insulate neo-liberal policy irreversibly from democratic accountability in political life.

The neo-liberal statecraft that was deployed in New Zealand could not have been effective in a state in which powers were extensively devolved. It is hard to envisage such a transformation occurring in Germany, where public policy is constrained severely by the powers of regional governments. In this the New Zealand experiment resembles most closely the Great Transformation in nineteenth-century England – as well as in the Thatcherite 1980s and 1990s.

Many of the changes effected in New Zealand's social and

economic life during the neo-liberal period are – as those who engineered them meant them to be – irreversible. In strictly economic terms, the neo-liberal experiment achieved many of its objectives. It forced a restructuring of the economy which, though it could have been achieved without some of the social costs imposed by neo-liberal policies, would have been necessary in any case

The principal cost of New Zealand's experiment has been a loss of social cohesion. Its political aftershock has been a meltdown in which the electoral system was repudiated and all the major parties have fragmented. In the 1996 general election the Conservative National party retained power at the price of entering into an unstable coalition with the anti-immigrant, Nationalist party of Winston Peters.

In this new political context the democratic legitimacy of the free-market project in New Zealand is bound to be challenged. Yet it is highly doubtful that the neo-liberal reforms of the 1980s and 1990s will be overturned – New Zealand's dependency on the world's capital markets rules that out. The extremity of neo-liberal policies in New Zealand means that a government wishing to respond to popular discontents would have – at least in the near future – a margin of freedom in which to act.

The effects of market fundamentalism in New Zealand may well be tempered over the next few years. Neo-liberal rhetoric will be publicly abandoned by nearly all New Zealand's political parties. The disregard of economic fundamentalists for social stability will be repudiated by politicians. Criticism of the excesses of the neo-liberal experiment in New Zealand will become an integral component of a new political consensus.

Yet the basic structures will remain in place. There will be no rollback of New Right policies in New Zealand. Popular nostalgia for the old New Zealand will be pervasive; but it will be ineffectual and politically impotent. The country and the world in which it must live have changed too much for any reversion to pre-reform New Zealand to be feasible or to be seriously attempted.

Market reform versus economic development in Mexico

Within weeks of the débâcle in which its currency was devalued and Mexico was in danger of defaulting on its foreign debt, President

Clinton assembled a $40 billion bail-out for the Mexican government. It included around $20 billion in American loan guarantees – a financial aid package larger by far than any that the United States had ever considered for the transitional countries of the post-communist world. In addition, the United States insisted that the international Monetary Fund advance Mexico $18 billion – the largest IMF rescue operation ever mounted in the world. In January 1997 President Clinton hailed the bail-out as an unprecedented success. On 15 January 1997, Mexico paid back the remaining portion of the emergency loan of $12.5 billion it received in February 1995. At the same time the Mexican Finance Minister, Mr Guillermo Ortiz, announced that Mexico was negotiating a new three-year borrowing programme with the IMF.[32]

The reasons for the huge and uncharacteristically expeditious American commitment put together by President Clinton in January 1995 were four-fold. In the first place it was considered necessary to prevent the 'tequila' effect of stock-market crashes and financial crises reaching beyond Latin America to eastern Europe and Southeast Asia. Assisting Mexico was perceived to be vital in order to defuse a serious risk to the world's financial institutions. Second, the bail-out may have forestalled substantial further losses by Americans whose pension savings had been invested in Mexico. It thereby limited the damage to American firms such as Salomon Brothers. Third, the salvage operation was judged to be unavoidable if deepening political instability in Mexico was to be prevented. Because President Clinton had staked his political fortunes on the success of NAFTA, the North American Trade Agreement signed between the US and Mexico in 1992, political upheaval in Mexico posed a major threat to his prospects in the 1996 presidential campaign. Mexico had an enormous strategic importance to the United States. According to the US Commerce Department, one year after the ratification of NAFTA Mexico had become one of America's three largest trading partners, standing somewhere between Canada and Japan. It bought as many American goods as Russia, China and most of Europe together.

Mexico has a highly porous 2,000-mile-long border with the United States. It is the largest single source both of illegal immigration and of the importation of illegal drugs into the United States. American policy-makers feared that economic collapse in Mexico could trigger an increase in illegal Mexican immigration, with grave and unmanageable political repercussions in the US. In fifteen or twenty years, Mexicans living in the United States will overtake American Blacks in numbers and become America's largest ethnic minority. Even as things stand now they are a powerful political force.

Mexico has long been viewed from the North as a Latin American country of unique political stability in which 'nothing ever happened'. The rebellion of Mayan indigenous peoples in Chiapas which began on New Year's Day 1994, posed a question mark over this legend of Mexican quiescence. An economic meltdown in Mexico might be a catalyst for further revolts. It could trigger a rerun of the Latin American debt crisis of 1982, perhaps on a larger and less controllable scale. A full-scale political collapse in Mexico would have incalculable implications for the US.

A fourth reason may have been weightier than any of the others. Mexico was a show-case of neo-liberal market reform. It was the prime site for the American project of engineering the free market throughout the world. Since the early 1980s it had a political elite obedient to the transnational financial organizations in which American free-market doctrines were institutionalized. Acting under the auspices of the International Monetary Fund, the government of Miguel de la Madrid (1982–8) had launched a neo-liberal austerity programme of reduced government expenditure, wage and price controls and privatization.[33]

Mexico's accession to GATT in 1985 signalled that the modernizing faction of the governing PRI – the Institutional Revolutionary Party that had ruled Mexico for over six decades – had overridden its 'dinosaurs'. Mexico's modernizers had accepted that the quasi-autarchic economic policies of the past would be increasingly costly in the global economic climate they foresaw. The government of President Carlos Salinas de Gortari (1988–94) was hailed as a model of successful modernization by all sectors of American opinion. In its aptly named 'Conventional Wisdom' section the American magazine *Newsweek* portrayed Mexico at the end of 1993 as having been transformed by NAFTA into a 'US sunbelt state'.[34]

American business and political elites were confident that Mexico had modernized. It did not occur to them that economic modernization for Mexico could mean anything other than assimilation into American business culture. They saw the devaluation crisis of 1994–5 as a temporary setback in a coupling of two countries under an

American free-market regime. Mexico became a neo-liberal experiment that could not be allowed to fail.

In setting aside generations of nationalism and protectionism in Mexico for a free-trade agreement with the United States, the Salinas government was not only recognizing the reality that Mexico's semi-autarchy had become unsustainable. In staking its own political fortunes on a wager that the neo-liberal model of economic development was workable in Mexico, it was also gambling with Mexico's political stability. The quintessentially absurd notion that a country which is, in the words of one of Mexico's most acute political thinkers, 'radically, substantively, ferociously different from the United States'[35] could in less than a decade be modernized on an American model had become accepted as an established fact.

According to one account,[36] newly established Mexican branches of the American video store Blockbusters shelved American films along with Mexican films. Only Latin American and European films were categorized as foreign, neatly capturing the American belief that Mexico and the United States had, for all practical and cultural purposes, fused into one.

The political risks of neo-liberal economic reform cannot be perceived by those who imagine that the institutions of the free market and democratic government operate in a natural equilibrium. Hardly glimpsed in the United States, these risks had long been understood in Mexico. They were clearly grasped by the principal architect of the free market in Mexico, President Carlos Salinas.

In an interview published in late 1991, Salinas drew attention to the misguided linkage between economic restructuring (*perestroika*) and political liberalization (*glasnost*) in the reform programme of Soviet President Gorbachev, implying that it may have been responsible for the Soviet collapse: 'Freedoms of what you call the *glasnost* kind have existed for decades in Mexico . . . When you are introducing strong economic reform, you must make sure that you build the political consensus around it. If you are at the same time introducing additional drastic political reform, you may end up with no reform at all. And we want to have reform, not a disintegrated country.'[37] These remarks may explain why until late 1989 Salinas opposed the free trade pact which in February 1990 he announced he would seek with the United States.[38] Evidently, Salinas understood well the political risks of market reform in Mexico. His American mentors did not.

They were risks that did not exist in the economic philosophy that underpinned American policies towards Mexico.

Yet Salinas's fears were well founded. As in other countries in which an attempt was made to engineer free markets the regime which sponsored the experiment became one of its casualties. In the elections of July 1997 the PRI not only lost control of the country's capital city to Cuauhtemoc Cardenas of the Leftwing PRD (Party of the Democratic Revolution) but also its majority in the lower house of Congress. In the country as a whole the PRD mounted a powerful challenge to the Conservative PAN (National Action Party) for the status of the main opposition party. The PRI still controlled the senate and remained the largest single party but it lost as many seats as it had done in all of its sixty-eight years in power. The PRI regime was consumed by the policies of economic insecurity that its free market policies had fuelled.

Engineering the free market in Mexico enhanced economic and social inequalities in what had long been one of the world's most unequal societies. In 1992, the richest 10 per cent of Mexicans received 38 per cent of the country's income, the poorest half only 18 per cent. Two-thirds of all income is distributed to 30 per cent of the population. This compares poorly even with post-Reagan America, in which the top 20 per cent of the population received around 55 per cent of the national income. The lowest 30 per cent of the Mexican population receives only 8 per cent of national income. The minimum wage in 1993 was less than half of what it was in 1975.[39] Many surveys rank Mexico as one of the three or four countries containing the highest concentration of the world's wealthiest individuals. The combined fortunes of a dozen individual Mexicans have been estimated to amount to about 10 per cent of Mexico's gross annual product.[40]

What is more significant than the wealth of the super-rich is the small size of the middle class in Mexico – and the fact that neo-liberal policies have made it even smaller over the past fifteen years. Between 1940 and 1980, steady economic growth in Mexico allowed a gradual expansion of the middle classes. As the Mexican political thinker Jorge Castaneda has written:

There is, of course, a middle class in Mexico ... but it constitutes a minority: somewhere between a quarter and a third of the population. The majority – poor, urban, brown and often excluded from the characteristics of modern life in the United States and other industrialized countries (public education, decent health care and housing, formal employment, social security, the right to vote, hold public office, and serve on a jury, and so on) – mingles with itself. It lives, works, sleeps, and worships separately from the small group of the very wealthy and the large but still restricted middle class . . . The decades after the Mexican Revolution – through the 1950s, perhaps – provided some upward mobility, some mingling, certainly the advent of a new business elite and an emerging middle class. By the 1980s, Mexico was once again a country of three nations: the *criollo* minority of elites and the upper-middle class, living in style and affluence; the huge, poor *mestizo* majority; and the utterly destitute minority of what was in colonial times called the Republic of Indians – the indigenous peoples of Chiapas, Oaxaca, Michoacan, Guerrero, Peubla, Chihuahua, and Sonora, all known today as *el Mexico profundo*: deep Mexico.[41]

Market reform in Mexico from the early 1980s onwards has tended to widen economic inequalities and reverse the growth of the middle class that occurred in the previous forty years. This process accelerated with NAFTA, and moved into a new gear with the austerity programme instituted in the wake of the devaluation crisis of 1994. As Ai Camp has commented: 'One social issue with important ramifications is the ability of a country's economy and its economic model to produce upward social mobility and to increase the size of the middle class. A great danger in the austerity programme introduced by President Zedillo is that . . . many Mexicans may lose their status as members of the middle class and, even more likely, will be unable to move from the working class into the middle class.'[42]

The socially destabilizing effects of neo-liberal policies in Mexico have not been restricted to the shrinkage of the middle class. They have significantly worsened the lot of the poorest. In 1984, before the neo-liberal project was really underway, the poorest half of the population received 20.7 per cent of national income; by 1992 that had fallen to 18.4 per cent.[43] There is little doubt that the share of the poorest in the static or declining Mexican national income of 1995–6 fell yet further, though figures are unavailable.

The trade opening promoted by NAFTA resulted in about 40 per cent of grocery shopping being concentrated in American-style supermarkets by the mid-1990s. The arrival of American retailers such as Wal-Mart and K-mart drove small Mexican 'mom-and-pop' stores out of business in their thousands.[44] Policies of economic liberalization such as the privatization of traditional land-tenure arrangements and the dismantling of price-supports for agricultural products made rural workers and communities more vulnerable to market fluctuations, such as a collapse in the price for coffee.

The austerity programme imposed after the abortion of the neo-liberal project in the devaluation of 1994 made the situation even worse for both the rural and the urban poor. In 1995 the Mexican economy contracted by 7 per cent. A million jobs were lost – in a country where, because of the growth of the population and its age structure, around a million new workers enter the labour market every year. According to the American credit-rating agency Standard and Poor's, the banking crisis following the devaluation cost 12 per cent of the country's gross domestic product in 1996, more than twice the sum realized when the banking system was privatized in 1991–2. According to unofficial estimates, open and hidden unemployment may have affected a quarter of the workforce.[45]

The absurdity of neo-liberal reform in Mexico arises partly from the fact that around half of the population constitutes an excluded underclass. Increases in wealth that have arisen from market reforms have not trickled down even to the middle classes, still less into the underworld of the poor. 'Trickle-down' theories of prosperity are implausible enough in advanced countries such as the United States and Britain. They are Borgesian fictions in Mexico.

The Indian and peasant revolt in Chiapas which began on 1 January 1994 with guerilla attacks on the colonial city of San Cristobal de las Casas had many local causes. Its central demands were reformist, not revolutionary. They concerned injustices in land tenure suffered by various indigenous Mayan peoples. The New Year's Day revolt of the Zapatista Army for National Liberation (EZLN) – so called because it revered the memory of the Mexican revolutionary Emiliano Zapata – was at the same time an act of resistance against neo-liberal hegemony in Mexico.

Yet the EZLN lacked any coherent programme for Mexico as a whole. Their leader, the enigmatic Subcommander Marcos (later identified as a university professor, Rafael Sebastian Guillen) espoused a hybrid of Maoist and post-modern ideas. Nevertheless, the movement has proved itself capable of disrupting the power of the Mexican state – though not of displacing it.

In this the Zapatistas are no different from guerilla movements in other Latin American countries over the past twenty years. On 29 December 1996, the guerillas of the Guatemalan National Revolutionary Unity army (URNG) signed a peace treaty with the government of President Alvaro Arzu. With that they ended a war that had lasted since November 1960, at a cost of between 150,000 and quarter of a million lives and the displacement of around one million people. The end of Latin America's last full-scale guerilla war did not signify that the grievances which fuelled it had been removed. It meant that the scorched-earth policy of the Guatemalan dictator General Efrain Rios Montt in the early 1980s had succeeded. Few observers believe that the peace accords will be followed by effective action to counter discrimination against the Mayan majority in Guatemala. It is unlikely that the fate of the Zapatista movement of Subcommander Marcos will be much different.

In conjunction with a stagnation in living standards that has been nearly continuous since 1982, the attempt to construct a free market in Mexico has fragmented the oligarchies which ruled the country for sixty years without establishing properly functioning democratic institutions. The opposition victories of July 1997 are symptoms of the PRI's weakness. They are not yet proof of democracy's strength. What's more, the corruption of state institutions during the neo-liberal period has created formidable obstacles to functioning democracy in Mexico.

The series of assassinations of public figures that occurred under the presidency of Carlos Salinas were a symptom of the breakdown of the tacit conventions which in the past governed Mexican political life. It cannot be known whether these killings – of the Catholic Cardinal Posadas at Guadalajara airport in May 1993, of Luis Donaldo Colosio, the PRI presidential candidate hand-picked by Salinas, in Tijuana in March 1994, of José Francisco Ruiz Massieu, the brother-in-law of President Salinas and general secretary of the PRI who was earmarked as a new majority leader of the Congress when Ernesto Zedillo's government took office in September 1994 – were the work of PRI 'dinosaurs' who opposed tentative moves to political liberalization or of drug cartels in revenge for the Salinas government's reneging on a secret non-aggression pact with them.[46]

The jailing of Raul Salinas, the brother of the former President in February 1995, on charges of complicity in the murder of José Francisco Ruiz Massieu, and the detaining of Raul Salinas's wife in November 1995 by Swiss police as she tried to withdraw over $80 million from an account held by her husband under an alias, have fuelled suspicions among many Mexicans that the former President and his brother rigged privatization bids to their own benefit. Papers published in February 1997 by *Proceso*, the respected Mexico City weekly journal, claimed to establish links between Raul Salinas, former Mexican Deputy Attorney-General Mario Ruiz Massieu, brother of the murdered José Francisco Ruiz Massieu, and Mexican drug cartels. The authenticity of the documents published by *Proceso* has been strongly denied by lawyers acting on behalf of the former President.[47] It is doubtful if the full truth will ever be established.

There may also be a risk of the Mexico's becoming a 'narco-democracy': the Mexican government's top narcotics officer was arrested in February 1997 for allegedly being in the pay of Mexico's most powerful drug baron; it has also been claimed that other senior Mexican figures, including the governor of the northwest Mexican state of Sonora, are implicated in the drug trade. The 'Columbianization' of Mexican political life is a very real danger.[48]

Neo-liberal economic policies that were implemented as part of a programme of modernization of the PRI regime have instead undermined it. This is the political risk which former President Carlos Salinas de Gortari acknowledged when he compared neo-liberal reform in Mexico with *perestroika* in Gorbachev's Soviet Union.

The American policy of promoting neo-liberal economic reform in Mexico appears to have been based on the conviction that a genuine exponent of free markets had been found in Carlos Salinas. It is hard to know what supported this belief. How could anyone believe that, in a political culture in which deception is a virtue, Carlos Salinas had become a born-again neo-liberal, a fiscal Quaker of the Chicago persuasion? Yet Salinas was consistently promoted by the United States when he was in office and briefly thereafter as potential head of the World Trade Organisation.

American policy-makers were blind to the opacity of the political culture they imagined they could transform. They must have believed that, despite all appearances, they were dealing with a culture that was not radically different from their own. They did not understand that, as Mexico's great writer Octavio Paz has stated, 'the core of Mexico is Indian. It is non-European.'[49]

Paz might have added that, insofar as it is European, Mexican culture and society can be expected to be no less resistant to American values than other European countries. If they noticed these facts at all, American policy-makers interpreted them as evidence of Mexico's chronic underdevelopment. The Washington consensus was confident that Mexico, along with the rest of the world, would soon 'become like us'.

The effects of market reform in Mexico have been perverse even from an American standpoint. It must be presumed that the overriding American interest in Mexico is in maintaining its political stability. Yet neo-liberal policies have worked to transform Mexico from an exceptionally stable Latin American country into one facing a highly problematic future. In this sense the economic philosophy guiding recent American policy has worked against the United States' strategic interests.

The fund managers who invested in Mexico before the devaluation understood that their large profits came from taking a big risk. (One result of the bail-out was to transfer the cost of that risk to the Mexican economy.) They did not understand that much of that risk derived from the inherent absurdities of a programme of modernization which aimed to re-engineer Mexican economic life as a variant of the American free market.

Where the Mexican state will go in the wake of neo-liberalism cannot be known. A return to the economic nationalism of the past is not on the cards. In Mexico, perhaps more clearly than anywhere else, free market policies have manifestly failed; but they have left the society which they desolated with few positive options.

The consequences of engineering the free market

The many resemblances between the effects of free-market policies in the three very different countries of Mexico, New Zealand and the United Kingdom are hardly accidental. In each country the free market acted as a vice within which the middle classes were squeezed. It enriched a small minority and increased the size of excluded underclasses. It inflicted serious damage on the political vehicles through which it was implemented. It used the powers of the state without scruple, but corrupted and in some measure delegitimated the state's institutions. It scattered or destroyed its initial coalition of political support. It fractured societies. In its aftermath it set the terms within which oppositional parties were compelled to operate.

The effects on economic performance differed in the three countries, however. In the case of Britain, the deep restructuring that free markets effected made the British economy more competitive, but that improvement did not reverse nearly a century's economic decline, and its cost in social exclusion was high. Similarly in New Zealand neo-liberal policies achieved a restructuring of the economy, but with much damage to social cohesion. In Mexico they inflicted massive social and political damage with little, if any, benefit to the economy as a whole.

In each of the three countries the political parties that implemented neo-liberal policies have lost power or broken apart. In New Zealand popular discontent with bipartisan support for free-market policies triggered a meltdown of the electoral system and the fracturing of both major parties. In Mexico the PRI regime is losing its hold on power. In Britain major constitutional reforms are a key part of Labour's agenda.

At the same time neo-liberal control of policy has removed contending political projects from serious contention. One-Nation Toryism and social democracy in Britain, economic nationalism and protectionism in Mexico, all varieties of the Keynesian managed economy in New Zealand – these are political projects that belong irrecoverably in the past. The free market transformed each of these economies and polities beyond any possibility of retrieval, helped by the vast changes in technology and the world's economies that, for a short while, it seemed to have harnessed to its own purposes.

The New Right was able to sustain itself in power by working with the grain of economic and technological changes in the world at large. In its heyday, supporters of the free market were able to mobilize the forces of economic globalization to tighten their hold over policy in many countries. As globalization enters its next phase, the global free market itself will surely be consumed.

3   What globalization is not

Capitalism, while economically stable, and even gaining in
stability, creates, by rationalizing the human mind, a mentality
and a style of life incompatible with its own fundamental
conditions, motives and social institutions.

JOSEPH SCHUMPETER, 'The Instability of Capitalism'[1]

'Globalization' can mean many things. On the one hand, it is the
worldwide spread of modern technologies of industrial production
and communication of all kinds across frontiers – in trade, capital,
production and information. This increase in movement across frontiers is itself a consequence of the spread to hitherto pre-modern
societies of new technologies. To say that we live in an era of globalization is to say that nearly every society is now industrialized or
embarked on industrialization.

Globalization also implies that nearly all economies are networked
with other economies throughout the world. There are a few countries,
such as North Korea, which seek to cut their economies off from the
rest of the world. They have succeeded in maintaining independence
from world markets – but at great cost, both economic and human.
Globalization is an historical process. It does not require that economic life throughout the world be equally and intensively integrated.
As a seminal study of the subject has put it, 'Globalization is not a singular condition, a linear process or a final end-point of social change.'[2]

Nor is globalization an end-state towards which all economies are
converging. A universal state of equal integration in worldwide

economic activity is precisely what globalization *is not*. On the contrary, the increased interconnection of economic activity throughout the world accentuates uneven development between different countries. It exaggerates the dependency of 'peripheral' developing states such as Mexico on investment from economies nearer the 'centre', such as the United States. Though one consequence of a more globalized economy is to overturn or weaken some hierarchical economic relationships between states – between western countries and China, for example – at the same time it strengthens some existing hierarchical relations and creates new ones.

Nor does the claim that we are undergoing a rapid advance in the further globalization of economic life necessarily mean that *every* aspect of economic activity in any one society is becoming significantly more sensitive to economic activity throughout the world. However far globalization proceeds, it will always be true that some dimensions of a society's economic life are not affected by world markets, though these may shift over time.

The emergence of world market prices for some commodities is only the beginning of globalization. There are few societies today in which much of life is not interwoven with economic activities in distant parts of the world. Yet throughout the nineteenth century, and for much of the twentieth century, global markets left most societies virtually untouched. Most of those traditional societies have now disappeared, or else they have been drawn irresistibly into the network of global market relationships.

In China, until the past few decades, hundreds of millions of people lived in peasant communities whose relations with world markets were slight and intermittent. Having survived forced collectivization and the Cultural Revolution, these communities are now breaking up as the forced introduction of markets compels poor peasants to seek subsistence in cities or distant regions of China. Market reforms in India are challenging traditions of marriage and caste which had survived almost unchanged for forty years following the end of the British Raj. At the same time, these changes are provoking radical Hindu movements which contest the belief that modernization in India must mean further westernization. In the former Soviet Union, marketization is succeeding, where communism failed, in imposing a kind of modernity – even if it is only the modernity of poverty and cultural fragmentation – on social life. Socialist and traditional societies that in the past stood outside the world market can do so no longer.

Yet in another sense, globalization is shorthand for the cultural changes that follow when societies become linked with, and in varying measures dependent upon, world markets. The advent of modern information and communication technologies has meant that cultural lives are far more deeply influenced than ever before.

Brands for many consumer goods are no longer country-specific but global. Companies produce identical products for worldwide distribution. The popular cultures of virtually all societies are inundated by a common stock of images. The countries of the European Union share the images they all absorb from Hollywood movies more than they do any aspect of each other's cultures. The same is true of East Asia.

Behind all these 'meanings' of globalization is a single underlying idea, which can be called *de-localization*: the uprooting of activities and relationships from local origins and cultures. It means the displacement of activities that until recently were local into networks of relationships whose reach is distant or worldwide. Anthony Giddens sums this up: 'Globalization can . . . be defined as the intensification of worldwide social relations which link distant realities in such a way that local happenings are shaped by events occurring many miles away and vice versa.'[3]

Thus, domestic prices – of consumer goods, financial assets such as stocks and bonds, even labour – are less and less governed by local and national conditions; they all fluctuate along with global market prices. Multinational corporations break up the chain of production of their products and locate the links in different countries around the world, depending on which appears at any time to be the most advantageous to them. The products sold by multinationals are identified less and less with any single country and increasingly with a world brand or with the company itself; the same images are recognized – in advertising and entertainment – in many countries. Globalization means lifting social activities out of local knowledge and placing them in networks in which they are conditioned by, and condition, worldwide events.

Globalization is often equated with a trend towards homogeneity. That, again, is just what globalization is *not*. Global markets in which capital and production moves freely across frontiers work precisely because of the *differences* between localities, nations and regions. Had wages, skills, infrastructure and political risks been the same throughout the world, the growth of world markets would not have occurred. There would not be profits to be made by investing and manufacturing worldwide if conditions were similar everywhere. Global markets thrive on differences between economies. That is one reason why the trend to globalization has such an irresistible momentum.

If highly mobile, quicksilver capital avoids a given region or country because it lacks infrastructure, a skilled workforce or political stability – as private investment capital has avoided Central and West Africa over the past few decades – those parts of the world will grow poorer, and their differences from areas that are attractive sites for productive capital will be exaggerated. If new technologies spread from the western countries in which they originated to East Asia, they will not carry with them the economic cultures – the varieties of capitalism – that produced them. On the contrary, they will fertilize and strengthen the indigenous economic cultures of those regions. When new technologies enter economies from which in the past they were shut out, or which lacked market institutions that could exploit them effectively, they will interact with indigenous cultures to generate types of capitalism that have hitherto not existed anywhere.

Consider China. The entry into world markets of mainland China does not mean that Chinese economic life will come to resemble that of any other industrialized country. It is already very different from the capitalism that has grown up in post-communist Russia, in which family relationships are much less central. Chinese capitalism resembles most closely that practised by the Chinese diaspora throughout the world. But it has many distinctive and peculiar features arising from the turbulent and terrible history of the nation over the past two generations.

In China, as in all other societies, the life of markets expresses the larger and deeper culture of which markets are only the visible tip. The place that relationships of trust have in families and markets in different societies in itself guarantees that their economic cultures – the size of firms, the concentration or diffusion of holdings of capital, and so on – will vary considerably.

Since, in China, trust does not extend easily beyond family members, businesses are unlikely to take the form they have assumed in Japan, where relationships of trust that reach well beyond the network of kin are common. A fully capitalist market economy in mainland China would be as different from Japanese as from western capitalism. It would probably contain many flourishing small family businesses and few large companies of the sorts that are common in Japan. It would not rest upon, or necessarily produce, a middle class of the kind that has long existed in Japan. In fact, this kind of capitalism does indeed seem to be emerging as a consequence of rapid market reforms in several regions of China.

It has many precursors in the Chinese diaspora. As Micklethwaite and Wooldridge have noted:

> the entrepreneurial 'bamboo network' of family businesses created by the overseas Chinese is not just another interesting variant but a fully-fledged alternative model – and one which looks increasingly powerful . . . In the Philippines, the overseas Chinese make up only one per cent of the country's population but control over half of the stock market. In Indonesia, the equivalent proportions are 4 per cent and 75 per cent, in Malaysia 32 per cent and 60 per cent . . . by 1996 the 51 million overseas Chinese controlled an economy worth $700 billion – roughly the same size as the 1.2 billion mainlanders.[4]

The growth of global markets does not mean, either, that American business culture will be copied throughout the world. The American belief that corporations are above all else vehicles of shareholder profits is not shared in most other types of capitalism.

In Germany, the interests of many other 'stakeholders' in addition to the shareholders are represented on boards of companies. It is inconceivable that any large enterprise would withdraw from its indigenous labour market as suddenly and comprehensively as American companies did when relocating from California to Mexico. A global market framed to reflect American business practice will undermine social markets built on the post-war German model; but it will not turn German capitalism into a variation of American market individualism. Instead it will result in a transmutation of capitalism in both Germany and America.

No economic culture anywhere in the world can resist the changes forced on it by the existence of global markets. In every case, including the United States itself, the result will be to engender novel types of capitalism. Global markets impose a forced modernization on economies everywhere; they do not create replicas of old business cultures. New capitalisms are created, and old ones destroyed.

Nor does the spread of global communications produce anything resembling convergence among cultures. The American world view that is purveyed through CNN – according to which, contrary to appearances and all underlying realities, American values are universal and American institutions the solution for the world's most intractable problems – is an ephemeral artefact of America's present lead in communications technologies. It is not a signpost on the road to a universal civilization. Media companies which vary their product to suit different cultures, such as MTV, may expect to remain global. If CNN remains fixed in its Americocentric world view, it is likely soon to be no more than one national media company among many others.

By enabling practitioners of different cultures who are geographically scattered to interact through new communications media, globalization acts to express and to deepen cultural differences. The South Asian populations that are scattered across European countries reinforce their cultural ties when they watch satellite television channels that broadcast in their languages and embody their history and values. The Kurds exiled in European countries preserve their common culture through a Kurdish television channel.

The universal proliferation of similar images is a surface effect of global communications media. They break up common cultures and replace them with traces and fragments. Yet modern communications media can also – as in Japan, Singapore, Malaysia and China – enable cultures to assert their identity and differences from western late modernity and from each other.

Economies *may* become more integrated with one another – as those of Japan and the United States have in recent decades – without significantly converging in the way they do business. Despite much increased levels of trade between the two countries, the corporate culture of Japanese companies remains very different from that of any American company. No Japanese company has had a downsizing or delayering of the sort that has become routine in nearly all key American corporations. These differences between American and Japanese companies reflect divergences between their parent cultures that show no signs of narrowing.

Globalization before 1914, and today

The world before 1914 resembled a global market. There were few borders that mattered. Money, goods and people flowed freely. The technological foundations of the nineteenth-century global market had been laid in the submarine intercontinental telegraph cables and steamships of the second half of the century. From then on the world's ports were linked together and world prices for many commodities came into being. Again, by the latter part of the nineteenth century (roughly from 1878 to 1914) an international financial system came into existence which limited the economic autonomy of national governments. In that *belle époque* sovereign nation-states were as effectively constrained in the economic policies which they could pursue by the Gold Standard that was then in operation as they are now by the mobility of capital. In all these ways we can recognize in the pre-1914 world a precursor of today's global market.

Yet it is a fundamental mistake to conclude that we have returned to the international economy of the nineteenth century. All the magnitudes of economic globalization today – the speed, size and interconnections of the movements of goods and information across the globe – are enormously greater than any that have existed in any previous period of history. Consider a few of these magnitudes. During the post-war period world trade has grown twelve-fold. At the same time, output has grown only five-fold. In nearly all countries, imports and exports constitute a far larger proportion of economic activity than in the past. One academic assessment estimates that trade links between a fixed sample of 68 countries have grown from 64 per cent in 1950 to 95 per cent in 1990.[5] Even in the vast American market in which purely internal trade is common for small companies, a fifth of firms having less than 500 staff exported goods or services in 1994, and that proportion is rising.[6]

There can be little doubt that, at least since the 1980s, the ratio of world trade to gross domestic product has exceeded that occurring at any time in the open international economy which existed before the First World War.[7] There has been a vast and unprecedented expansion in the volume of trade.

There is now a world market in capital as never before, and strong evidence that investors in many countries are diversifying their holdings of both equities and bonds globally and that, as a consequence, returns on capital have tended to converge in the 1980s and 1990s.[8] This is a trend far more advanced in regard to government bonds than it is in respect of equities, but it is unmistakeable.[9] Increasingly, interest rates in all countries are being set by worldwide conditions, not by circumstances or policies in any one country. Private investment flows from advanced industrial countries to newly industrialized countries grew twenty-fold in the years from 1970 to 1992.[10]

Most significantly, perhaps, transactions in foreign exchange markets have now reached the astonishing sum of around $1.2 trillion a day – over fifty times the level of world trade. Around 95 per cent of these transactions are speculative in nature, many using complex new derivative financial instruments based on futures and options.[11] According to Michel Albert, 'the *daily* volume of transactions on the foreign exchange markets of the world totals some $900 billions – equal to France's *annual* GDP and some $200 million more than the total foreign currency reserves of the world's central banks.'[12]

This *virtual* financial economy has a terrible potential for disrupting the underlying *real* economy, as seen in the collapse in 1995 of Barings, Britain's oldest bank. Together with the accelerating development of global capital markets on which it stands, the virtual economy is a phenomenon unknown in the world's economic history. Nothing like it existed pre-1914.

The growth and power of multinational corporations is enormous and also unprecedented. Multinationals now account for about a third of world output and two-thirds of world trade. Most significantly, around a quarter of world trade occurs *within* multinational corporations.[13] In 1993, according to a United Nations survey, the combined output of multinationals was around $5.5 trillion – roughly as much as that of the United States as a whole.[14]

It is true that companies which trade and invest internationally also existed centuries ago – the Hudson Bay Company and the East India Company are examples. In that broad sense multinationals began life with European colonialism. But the role of multinationals in the world today is on a completely different scale. They are able to divide the process of production into discrete operations and locate them in different countries throughout the world. They are less dependent than ever before on national conditions. They can choose the countries whose labour markets, tax and regulatory regimes and infrastructures they find most congenial. The promise of direct inward investment, and the threat of its withdrawal, have significant leverage on the policy options of national governments. Companies can now limit the politics of states. There are few historical precedents for this kind of private power.

This is not to say that multinationals are homeless transnational institutions which move across borders without cost and express no particular national business culture. They are often companies which retain strong roots in their original economies and cultures. In a systematic and comprehensive survey Ruigrok and van Tulder concluded that few, if any, of the world's biggest companies are fully global. Even companies such as British Aerospace, most of whose business is done abroad, keep most of their assets at home.[15] Hirst and Thompson note that multinational companies 'typically have about two thirds of their assets in their home region country, and sell about the same proportion of their goods and services in their home region/country'.[16]

Again, very few multinationals are genuinely cross-cultural organizations. One of the rare examples is ABB, a Swiss–Swedish corporation which consists of 1,300 separate companies.[17] ABB may well be more truly cross-cultural than any other corporation: in this it may be unique. Nearly all multinationals express and embody a single parent national culture. This is true especially of American firms.

It is fashionable to see multinational corporations as constituting a kind of invisible government supplanting many of the functions of nation-states. In reality they are often weak and amorphous organizations. They display the loss of authority and the erosion of common values that afflicts practically all late modern social institutions. The global market is not spawning corporations which assume the past functions of sovereign states. Rather, it has weakened and hollowed out both institutions.

Scepticism about globalization

There is an influential body of opinion which denies that today's trends signify anything really new. It argues that, because the historical movement we call globalization began several centuries ago and because by most measurements the global openness of the international economy was high in the pre-1914 liberal economic order, late twentieth-century globalization is not a new phenomenon. There is truth and error in this revisionist view. It is a useful corrective for a Utopian view of globalization advanced by some business thinkers. Kenichi Ohmae gives a canonical statement of what might be called the McKinsey worldview – the view of things propagated by American business schools – when he writes: 'with the ending of the Cold War, the long familiar pattern of alliances and oppositions among industrialized nations has fractured beyond repair. Less visibly, but arguably far more important, the modern nation-state itself – that artifact of the eighteenth and nineteenth centuries – has begun to crumble.'[18] In criticizing such theorists of hyper-globalization revisionists make a contribution to understanding the present; but they are attacking a straw man.

No one except a few Utopians in the business community expects the world to become a true single market, in which nation-states have withered away and have been supplanted by homeless multinational corporations. Such an expectation is a chimera of the corporate imagination. Its role is to support the illusion of an inevitable worldwide free market.

Sceptics about globalization are right to point to the ideological role of these fantasies. They reinforce the belief that national governments nowadays have no real options. As Hirst and Thompson put it, 'Globalization is a myth suitable for a world without illusions, but it is also one that robs us of hope . . . for it is held that Western social democracy and socialism of the Soviet bloc are both finished. One can only call the political impact of "globalization" the pathology of over-diminished expectations.'[19]

Yet Hirst and Thompson's scepticism about globalization itself serves a political purpose. By arguing that today's world market is not unprecedented they are able to defend as still viable political responses to globalization – such as European social democracy – that belong in the past.

They argue that 'the international economy was in many ways more open in the pre-1914 period than it has been at any time since . . . International trade and capital flows, both between the rapidly industrializing economies themselves and between these and their various colonial territories, were more important relative to GDP levels before the First World War than they are today . . . Thus the present period is by no means unprecedented.'[20] This view neglects some of the most decisive contrasts between the pre-1914 international economy and today's global market.

As the British political theorist David Held and his colleagues have noted, 'Measured in constant prices the classical Gold Standard ratios (of trade as a proportion of GDP) had been surpassed by the 1970s and ratios are now significantly higher . . . Further, much of postwar GDP growth has been in non-tradable services, particularly public services . . . Tariff levels (as well as transport costs) have been lower than classical Gold Standard levels since the 1970s, thus indicating that markets are now more open.' They conclude: 'A global trading system emerged at the end of the nineteenth century, but it was less extensive than today and was often less enmeshed with national markets and production.'[21] This seems a reasonable assessment.

A key difference between the international economy now and as it was before 1914 is that power and influence are flowing away from the western powers. The terms of world trade, the functioning of the financial system via the Gold Standard, and every other significant aspect of the pre-1914 economy were imposed and maintained by European states.

It is true that trade has grown mainly between the western industrialized countries – if, absurdly, in 'the West' we include Japan. Yet the pattern of trade today is very different from what it was. As David Held et al. observe:

Trade has continued to grow relative to income, and has continued to be concentrated between industrialized countries, in contrast to the classical Gold Standard era when exchange of products between developed and developing countries accounted for half or more of total trade . . . intra-industry trade led to relative growth in industries with scale economies and technological dynamism, whilst rising income levels increased demand for variety so that demand for imported differentiated products rose, largely between industrialized countries . . This . . . has significantly increased the import content of manufactured goods in developed countries, except Japan.

What is more, newly industrializing countries can no longer be considered an homogenous bloc. Incomes and wages in some of them – South Korea, Taiwan, Singapore – are actually higher than in the deskilled countries of the industrialized west, such as Britain. The balance of advantage, which in the pre-1914 era was fixed in favour of the European countries, is now shifting away from western countries in many areas of economic activity.

If the pre-1914 open economy was an artefact of European control over the territories and economies of nearly every other society in the world, the global market whose chaotic infancy we have witnessed is based on no such hegemony. Which western power can now claim plausible to exercise significant leverage over China? Not even the United States now exercises over China anything like the influence that was commonplace for the imperial powers in the pre-1914 period.

In this, the period of advancing globalization in which we live is genuinely unprecedented. It is indeed partly because it contains no hegemonic power akin to Britain before 1914 or the United States after the Second World War that the stability in times of crisis of the global market today cannot be taken for granted. If there is a recent historical analogy for our world since 1989, it is not the world before 1914. It may be the volatile interwar period after 1919.

The world economy today shows many features which, on Hirst and Thompson's own account, bring it closer to a disorderly globalized market than to the comparatively orderly international market that existed before 1914. They capture accurately aspects of today's realities when they tell us that 'The international system becomes autonomized and socially disembedded, as markets become truly global. Domestic policies, whether of private corporations or public regulators, now have routinely to take account of the predominantly international determinants of their sphere of operations.'[22]

Sovereign states today do not confront the predictable disciplines of a quasi-automatic Gold Standard. They are constrained instead by the risks and uncertainties, the perceptions and reactions of global markets. The policy options open to nation-states in the 1990s are not delivered to them as a menu with fixed prices. The governments of sovereign states do not know in advance how markets will react. There are few, if any, rules of monetary or fiscal rectitude whose violation will result in predictable penalties. At the margin, no doubt, policies that are ultra-risky in terms of inflation or government debt, say, will be punished by watchful bond markets; but the scale of severity of such market responses cannot be known in advance. National governments in the 1990s are flying blind.

The view of globalization advanced by academic sceptics such as Hirst and Thompson underestimates the novelty of late twentieth-century conditions. Today's world economy is inherently less stable and more anarchic than the liberal international economic order which collapsed in 1914. Like the hyperglobalizers, whose Utopian fantasies they effectively criticize, globalization sceptics are trading in illusions. They cannot accept that globalization has made the world economy today radically different from any international economy that has existed in the past; that would spell death to their hopes of a revamped social democracy. They are right in their belief that a more radically globalized world is less governable – such a world economy makes their vision of 'continental Keynesianism' unworkable.[23] In truth a much less governable world is the inevitable result of the forces that have been at work over the past two decades.

Hyperglobalization: a corporate Utopia

A rival school of thought recognizes the novelty of the global market. It holds that global markets have rendered nation-states practically irrelevant. It envisions the global economy as inhabited by powerless nation-states and homeless corporations. As the powers of sovereign states wither, those of multinational corporations wax. As national cultures become little more than consumer preferences, so companies become ever more cosmopolitan in their corporate cultures.

The writers of this school represent as inevitable what is, in fact, a highly unlikely outcome of the current drive to create a global free market. It conflates the end-state favoured by that project with the actual development of economic globalization. It represents an historical transformation that has no end-state, and which is subverting American capitalism as well as its rivals, as a process leading to universal acceptance of American free markets.

'Hyperglobalization' theories – as these views have been termed by Held and his colleagues[24] – represent global markets as embodying something akin to perfect competition. In this illusive vision, transnational corporations can move freely and costlessly around the world to maximize their profits. Cultural differences have lost any political leverage on governments and corporations. As in the perfectly competitive markets of economic theory, the participants in this model of the global economy – sovereign states and multinational corporations, for example – are presumed to have all the information relevant to their decisions.

In reality they are navigating in a fog of risks and uncertainties whose hazards they can only surmise. A borderless world ruled by homeless transnationals is a corporate Utopia, not a description of any present or future reality.

Kenichi Ohmae subscribes to this Utopian view: 'For more than a decade, some of us have been talking about the progressive globalization of markets for consumer goods like Levi's jeans, Nike athletic shoes and Hermes scarves – a process, driven by global exposure to the same information, the same cultural icons, and the same advertisements . . . Today, however, the process of convergence goes faster and deeper. It reaches well beyond taste to much more fundamental dimensions of worldview, mind-set, and even thought-process.' He concludes that this market-driven convergence of cultures renders the institution of the nation-state marginal in economic life: 'in a borderless economy, the nation-focused maps we typically use to make sense of economic activity are woefully misleading. We must . . . face up at last to the awkward and uncomfortable truth: the old cartography no longer works. It has become no more than an illusion.'[25]

Similarly, Nicholas Negroponte declares that 'Like a mothball, which goes from solid to gas directly, I expect the nation-state to evaporate . . . Without question, the role of the nation-state will change dramatically and there will be no more room for nationalism than there is for smallpox.'[26] Bryan and Farrell write: 'Increasingly, millions of global investors, operating out of their own economic self-interest, are determining interest rates, exchange rates, and the allocation of capital, irrespective of the wishes or political objectives of national political leaders.'[27] Robert Reich speaks of 'the coming irrelevance of corporate nationality' and counsels that 'as corporations of all nations are transformed into global webs, the important question – from the standpoint of national wealth – is *not* which citizens own what, but which citizens learn how to do what, so that they are capable of adding more value to the world economy and therefore increasing their own potential worth.'[28] John Naisbitt asserts: 'We are moving toward a world of 1,000 countries . . . The nation-state is dead. Not because nation-states were subsumed by super-states, but because they are breaking up to smaller, more efficient parts – just like big companies.'[29]

Neither states nor markets are orderly institutions of the kinds such a model envisages. There are few genuinely transnational corporations of the kind of which Ohmae and other business Utopians speak. Most multinational companies retain strong roots in particular countries and business cultures. Ownership, executive boards, management styles and corporate cultures remain thoroughly national. The American companies which most nearly approximate Ohmae's model do so because they exemplify local American values and an indigenous business culture, not because they are global.

The few companies in the world that consistently behave with regard to their indigenous economy as rootless multinationals do so not because of properties they share with other international corporations. They do so because their corporate culture is governed by American corporate values in which profits override social costs and national allegiances.

According to one extended study, only around 40 large firms worldwide generate at least half their assets abroad, while less than twenty maintain as much as half their production facilities abroad.[30] Moreover, as Hirst and Thompson have noted, key functions of firms, such as research and development, remain under tight domestic control: 'Japanese companies appear to have been reluctant to locate core functions like R&D or high value-added parts of the production process abroad'. They conclude: 'national companies with an international scope of operations currently and for the foreseeable future seem more likely than the true TNCs'.[31]

The model of hyperglobalization errs badly in writing off sovereign states as marginal institutions. For multinationals, sovereign states are not marginal actors in the world economy whose policies are easily circumvented. They are key players whose power is well worth courting. The leverage of sovereign states over business may actually be greater in some respects today than it has been in the past.

Corporations today do not have the protected relationships with governments that some enjoyed in the heyday of imperialism. If it is true that corporations can shop around the world for the tax and regulatory regime they want, it is also true that political risks have increased in many parts of the world. Where states are fragile it is harder to regulate mobile production and capital; but it is also harder for business to stitch up enduring corporatist relationships with governments. That is a limitation on the power of both states and corporations.

Today's competition between states for investment by multinational corporations allows them to exercise a leverage they did not possess in a more hierarchical world order. At the same time such competition limits the freedom of action of sovereign states. The leverage that states can exercise over corporations must be exercised in a global environment in which most of the competitive pressures that affect them work to limit the control of governments over their economies within a narrow margin.

Sovereign states remain the key arena of influence-seeking by corporations. Multinationals exercise influence over the policies of sovereign states as well as exercising their ingenuity in eluding their jurisdiction. This is the typical interaction of sovereign states and business in the late twentieth century.

There can be little doubt that NAFTA (the North American Free Trade Association between the United States, Mexico and Canada) prevailed over domestic political opposition in the United States largely because of the well-concerted lobbying activities of large American corporations.

Hyerglobalization theorists, like their sceptical critics, mistake today's world economy for a return to an earlier condition of orderliness. The reality of the late twentieth-century world market is that it is ungovernable by either sovereign states or multinational corporations.

Globalization and disordered capitalism

Both sets of theorists – the sceptics and the boosters – advance an unreal picture of the new global environment in which states must act. Sovereign states do not, as they did in the late nineteenth century, inhabit a familiar international environment that constrains their choices in predictable ways. They find themselves in an unfamiliar environment in which the behaviour of global market forces is decreasingly predictable or controllable. They are constrained not by institutions and conventions of international governance but by the risks and uncertainties that accompany an international market that tends to anarchy.

That multinational corporations expend considerable resources influencing the policies of governments contributes to the view that the sovereign state is not redundant. In most parts of the world, state institutions are a strategically decisive territory on which competition between corporations is waged.

Neither of the two main schools of thought have perceived that the emergence of a global economy is a decisive moment in the development of a late modern species of disordered, anarchic capitalism.[32] Capitalism today is very different from the earlier phases of economic development on which Karl Marx and Max Weber modelled their accounts of capitalism – and also from the stable, managed capitalisms of the post-war era.

The industrial working class has declined in size and economic significance. This has come about as manufacturing industries have shrunk and late modern economies become more comprehensively post-industrial. There has been a large-scale shift from Taylorist forms of work organization – mass manufacturing through factory-based wage-labour – to flexible labour markets. In these new labour markets the classical capitalist institutions of wage-labour and job-holding are restricted to a dwindling proportion of the population.

Much of the workforce now lacks even the economic security that went with wage-labour. It exists in the world of part-time and contract work and portfolio employment in which there is no stable relationship with a single identifiable employer. Along with these changes has gone a collapse of national collective wage-bargaining and greatly diminished leverage of trade unions in the productive process.

The economic basis of political parties has weakened. At the same time the leverage of single-issue pressure groups has been enhanced. The political ideologies that organized political life in the post-war period are obsolete. This transformation has been accentuated by the emergence of a new economic consensus. In this new orthodoxy the role of national governments in overseeing their domestic economies through policies of macroeconomic management has been reduced or marginalized. The central economic task of government is that of devising and implementing microeconomic policies, promoting yet greater flexibility in labour and production.

The corrosion of bourgeois life through increased job insecurity is at the heart of disordered capitalism. Today the social organization of work is in a nearly continuous flux. It mutates incessantly under the impact of technological innovation and deregulated market competition.

The effect of the new information technologies is not merely an increased scarcity of many kinds of less skilled or knowledge-intensive work. It is the wholesale disappearance of entire occupations. For much of the population traditional bourgeois institutions such as career structures and vocations no longer exist.

The result is a re-proletarianization of much of the industrial working class and the de-bourgeoisification of what remains of the former middle classes. The free market seems set to achieve what socialism was never able to accomplish – a euthanasia of bourgeois life.

The imperatives of flexibility and mobility imposed by deregulated labour markets put particular strain on traditional modes of family life. How can families meet for meals when both parents work on shifts? What becomes of families when the job market pulls parents apart?

There has been a hollowing out of the business corporation as a social institution. The growth of contracting-out of labour tends to reduce the permanent workforce of late modern companies to a small cadre. A limiting case of this development may be Microsoft, a global company which dominates markets in several new technologies but whose actual core workforce is in the low thousands.

In limiting cases, companies are becoming vehicles for bill collection and profit distribution, their few remaining employees often having a stake in its capital. Whole strata of former middle-management employees have been dispensed with in corporate downsizings which have an immediate beneficial impact on profit statements. Businesses everywhere, but especially in the English-speaking countries, are unloading the social costs of their remaining employees. They are doing this by transferring responsibility for pension provision, for example, back to them as individuals.

The weakening of companies as social institutions goes in tandem with the further commodification of work. Labour has become something that is sold in pieces to corporations. Businesses have shed many of the responsibilities that rendered the world of work humanly tolerable in the past. Some are not far from being virtual institutions.

The inherent instability of anarchic global markets has been enhanced by the growth of an enormous, highly leveraged virtual economy in which currencies are traded for short-term profits. There is no stable framework for the governance of the international monetary system. Since the breakdown of the post-war Bretton Woods arrangement for international monetary cooperation between 1971–3 there have been no agreements enforcing fixed exchange rates. Thus, the international monetary regime today is an anarchy of floating currencies. There are recurrent overshoots in the value of particular currencies and intermittent spasms of coordinated policy-making among the major powers (such as the Plaza Accords of 1985) in order to avert a breakdown of the system. Fluctuations in exchange rates can have such a profound destabilizing effect on economic activity that the present world monetary regime has been termed a system of 'casino capitalism'.[32]

We have seen a large shift from manufacturing and the provision of services as the central economic activities to the trading of financial assets. Financial engineering, not production, has become the most profitable activity.

These effects of disordered capitalism can be seen in societies as different as Italy, Sweden and Australia. Least advanced in Germany and Japan, they are most powerfully developed in the Anglo-Saxon economies. The United States, Britain, Australia and New Zealand stand out as standard-bearers of the new species of capitalism.

But the belief that capitalism everywhere will lead to similar disorder is a basic error. The ability to trade globally and rapidly tends to project these features of disorganized capitalism into every country; but how they impact on social and economic life varies deeply and widely.

In countries such as Spain, in which the extended family remains strong, the underclass of workless households that is so depressing a feature of Anglo-Saxon societies hardly exists. This is despite the fact that in Spain, to a greater degree even than in the other economies of continental Europe, unemployment has reached very high levels in recent times. This can partly be attributed to the fact that policy over the past two decades has not been dominated in continental Europe by objectives such as deregulation of the labour market. But this is unlikely to be the whole, or even the chief reason for the persistence of such differences.

None of the countries of continental Europe has ever had an age of *laissez-faire*; market institutions have not achieved the independence from constraint by other social institutions that characterizes the Anglo-Saxon free market. No European society has the long and deep experience of individualist forms of family life and property ownership that distinguishes England, the United States and other Anglo-Saxon societies.

In every country, the new and more volatile strain of capitalism is transforming economic life. The impact of anarchic global markets on the economic cultures of continental Europe institutionalizes high levels of structural unemployment. In these societies the principal source of social division is unequal access to work.

In the United States, a highly deregulated labour market, together with a roll-back in welfare provision and an experiment in mass incarceration that has left over a million Americans behind bars, may succeed in keeping unemployment rates low. The principal source of social division in America is less likely to be lack of access to work as such but inequalities of income and wealth, together with inequalities in health, education, security from crime and the types of work that are accessible to different sectors of the population.

The indigenous Chinese capitalism that is emerging in China is not based around the large corporations that have developed in Anglo-Saxon capitalism. Apart from state enterprises, Chinese firms are small and family-owned. The disorders of capitalism in China are not the hollowing out of corporations or the fragmentation of families but a lack of solidarity between different sections of society and a pervasive degradation of the environment. Russian capitalism exhibits similar disorders.

These differences arise from long-term historical divergences in cultures and economic institutions – together with their continuing reflections in the different public policies of nation-states. The impact of disordered capitalism is to limit the autonomy of national governments. It is certainly not to suppress differences between them.

Anarchic capitalism and the state

Nation-states must now act in a world in which all options are uncertain. It is not as though they have before them a list of choices with price tags attached to them. National governments find themselves in environments not merely of risk but of radical uncertainty. In economic theory, risk means a situation in which the costs of various actions can be known with reasonable probability, while uncertainty is a situation in which such probabilities cannot be known. Many of the policies which governments know they can pursue do not have consequences to which probabilities can be attached.

Worse, governments often cannot know whether the response of world markets to their policies will be merely to make them costly or to render them completely unworkable. Governments are in a situation in which even the span of options that is available to them is uncertain. This continuing radical uncertainty is the most disabling constraint on the power of sovereign states.

The reduction in the leverage of sovereign states is a symptom of a broader trend, in which the powers gathered by the institutions of the state in early modern times are becoming dispersed or weakened. Even the power to make and conclude wars by having an effective monopoly of armed force, which has defined the sovereign state since its inception, no longer belongs to it unequivocally. Whatever the horrors of war in the nineteenth century it had limited goals and could be terminated by the states that waged it. That was the kind of war classically theorized by Clausewitz.

Since the Second World War Clausewitzian war between the agents of sovereign states has been partly supplanted by wars between irregular armies, tribal and ethnic groups, and political organizations such as the Palestine Liberation Organisation (PLO) and the Irish Republican Army (IRA).[33] As the control of war has slipped in some measure from sovereign states the world has not thereby become more peaceful; it has become less governable and yet more unsafe.

Multinational companies have not gained the power and authority which sovereign states have lost and are as exposed to the vagaries of late modern societies as governments. Global corporations are not free agents that can defy public opinion without risk or cost. They are buffeted by shifts in the public cultures of the states in which they operate. Shell, a huge oil corporation, was deflected from use of an offshore platform at Brent Spar by a Greenpeace campaign that skilfully orchestrated media coverage. Shell proved as vulnerable a target for single-issue political action as any weak contemporary democratic state.

This does not mean that corporations will ever, as a matter of consistent policy, willingly bear the social and environmental costs of their activities. In a global free market they cannot. In addition to the unceasing pressures of global competition, multinational companies must now confront sporadic bursts of media attention which may deflect them from the single-minded pursuit of short-term profit.

Thus, in late modern contexts, power has leaked away from both states and corporations. Both institutions are mutating and evanescing, as global markets and new technologies transform the cultures from which each borrows its legitimacy and identity.

Sovereign states today act in an environment so transformed by market forces that no institution – not even the largest transnational corporation or sovereign state – can master it. In this environment the most unmanageable forces spring from a torrent of technological innovations. It is the combination of this unceasing stream of new technologies, unfettered market competition and weak or fractured social institutions that produces the global economy of our times.

As management gurus never cease reminding us, nation-states and multinational corporations can survive and prosper today only by using new technologies to achieve a competitive edge over their rivals. What most of them fail to note is that competitive advantage is inherently fleeting in the anarchic environment of disorganized global capitalism. In the late twentieth century there is no shelter – for corporations or for governments – from the global gale of creative destruction.

The decisive advantage that a multinational company achieves over its rivals comes finally from its capacity to generate new technologies and to deploy them effectively and profitably. In turn, this depends to a considerable extent on the ways in which companies enable knowledge to be conserved and generated. In the late modern competitive environment, business organizations which do not capture and exploit new knowledge, which waste the stock of tacit understandings among their employees or discourage them from acquiring new knowledge, will soon go under.

The global economy deskills people and organizations. It does so by making the environments in which they live and work unrecognizable to them. It thereby renders their stock of local and tacit knowledge less and less serviceable to them. A major problem that has not been solved by business organizations – except partially in Japanese companies[34] – is that of combining the institutional continuity needed, if the local knowledge of employees is to be harnessed, with the capacity for organizational innovation required to make the most of new technologies.

Sovereign states are not going to become obsolete. They will remain decisive mediating structures which multinational corporations compete to control. This pivotal role of sovereign states makes nonsense of the claims of hyperglobalists, business Utopians and populists who maintain that multinationals have supplanted sovereign states as the real rulers of the world. It explains why global markets seek leverage over states and why they cannot ignore them. It illuminates the narrow margin in which governments can act to help their citizens control economic risk. This protective function of states is likely to expand, as citizens demand shelter from the anarchy of global capitalism.

Sovereign states have yet another function – seizing control of the natural resources that are necessary for economic growth. In Central and East Asia, the struggle for the control of oil is a source of diplomatic rivalries as much today as it was in the nineteenth century. It could well be a cause of war. As scarcities of natural resources increase, sovereign states are being drawn into military competition for the necessities of existence.[35]

The waning of American power means the emergence of a truly multipolar world. In such a world competition among sovereign states will be more, not less, pervasive and intense.

4 How global free markets favour the worst kinds of capitalism: a new Gresham's Law?

a general law or principle concerning the circulation of money,
which Mr Macleod has appropriately named the Law or
Theorem of Gresham, after Sir Thomas Gresham, who clearly
perceived its truth three centuries ago. This law, briefly
expressed, is that *bad money drives out good money*, but that
good money cannot drive out bad money.

W. S. JEVONS[1]

In the monetary theory, Gresham's Law tells us that bad money drives out good. In a global free market there is a variation on Gresham's Law: bad capitalism tends to drive out good. In any competition that is waged with the rules of global *laissez-faire*, that have been designed to reflect the American free market, the social market economies of Europe and Asia are at a systematic disadvantage. They have no future unless they can modernize themselves by deep and rapid reforms.

Sovereign states are waging a war of competitive deregulation, forced on them by the global free market. A mechanism of downwards harmonization of market economies is already in operation. Every type of currently existing capitalism is thrown into the melting pot. In this contest the socially dislocated American free market possesses powerful advantages.

In economic theory Keynes recognized that the international mobility of financial capital would undercut the full employment policies of national governments. He could not have foreseen that the global mobility of capital would return governments to a world in which national economic management is feasible only at the margin.

National governments today can no longer implement the ambitious counter-cyclical policies that lifted their economies out of recession in the post-war period. Fiscal conservatism – the prudent management of government debt – is forced on them by world markets.

Few in the Keynesian era foresaw that worldwide mobility of capital and production would trigger a competitive downgrading of regulatory and welfare systems by sovereign states. Since the Soviet collapse, competition between central planning and capitalism has been replaced by a rivalry between different sorts of capitalism – American, German, Japanese, Russian, Chinese.

In this new rivalry American free markets work to undercut both European and Asian social market economies. This is despite the fact that the social costs of business are borne in different ways in European and Asian social markets. Both are threatened by the American model because each business bears social obligations that in the United States it has shed. At the same time, Chinese capitalism is emerging as a rival to the American version because it can go further than the American free market in undercutting social markets in Europe and the rest of Asia.

All the familiar models of market institutions are mutating as global competition is played out through the structures of sovereign states. It is a basic error to think that this is a contest that any of the existing models can win. All are being eroded and replaced by new and more volatile types of capitalism. The chief result of this new competition is to make the social market economies of the post-war period unviable while transforming the free-market economies that are its nominal winners.

How bad capitalism drives out good

The social costs which businesses carry in social market economies enable them to function as social institutions without undermining the cohesion of the larger societies in which they operate. At the same time these social costs must become burdens in any competition with enterprises operating in free markets. American firms have few such obligations.

The inherent advantages enjoyed by firms operating in free-market economies are neither incidental nor temporary. They are systemic. They cannot be fully compensated for by the superior education and skill levels that social market economies have often achieved, by better infrastructural investment in roads and other public goods and services, or by the social cohesion that such economic systems promote. The superior performance that social markets have displayed in these areas will not enable them to support the levels of welfare provision and the types of management and regulation that distinguished them in the past.

In the long haul of history, Europe's social markets may be as productive as American free markets. In the short run, in terms of rivalry in a global free market, they simply cannot be cost-competitive.

The conditions that confer a strategic advantage to the free market over the social market economies of the post-war period are unregulated global free trade in conjunction with unrestricted global mobility of capital.[2] In a free-trading global market the advantage lies (other things being equal) with firms whose costs are low. This is true whether they are labour costs, regulatory costs or tax costs.

Consider environmental costs. If, in one country, environmental costs are 'internalized' by a tax regime that forces them to be reflected in the costs of enterprises, but those enterprises are forced to compete in a global market with enterprises in other countries that do not carry such environmental costs, the countries that require businesses to be environmentally accountable will be at a systematic disadvantage.

Over time, either the enterprises operating in environmentally accountable regimes will be driven out of business, or the regulatory frameworks of such regimes will drift down to a common denominator in which their competitive disadvantage is reduced. This trade-off is an integral part of the global free market.

A global free market operates to 'externalize' costs that better regimes 'internalized'. In environmentally sensitive economies tax and regulatory policy is designed so that firms are required to pay for the costs their activities impose on society and the natural world. This has long been the case in the countries of continental Europe. Global free markets put heavy pressure on such policies. Goods produced by environmentally accountable firms cost more than similar goods produced by enterprises that are at liberty to pollute.

Global regulation of environmental standards, though an inspiring ideal, is a Utopian prospect. It is not enforceable where it is most needed – for example, there are few effective measures of environmental protection in Russia or China. In both countries, partly as an inheritance from the period of central economic planning and partly as a consequence of market reforms, environmental degradation is cataclysmic. Yet both countries are being induced to enter the global free market where their goods will have to compete with goods produced in environmentally accountable social markets.

Some of the world's advanced industrial economies are rich enough to resist the downward pressure on environmental standards. They may be able to compensate firms who are losing out in competition with businesses based in low-regulation economies. If advanced societies are able to protect their environments in this way it will be partly because they are able to export pollution by moving production to Third World countries where environmental standards are looser. The advanced countries will remain clean at the cost of other parts of the world becoming dirtier.

The overall effect of global free markets on the world environment will be unchanged. It will still work worldwide to unload costs that in an earlier, more accountable species of capitalism were borne by enterprises. More and more of the earth will, as a result, become less and less habitable. At the same time the price will rise for the few societies rich enough to be able to keep their local environments livable, and if, despite this, they persist in imposing the costs of pollution and other environmental social costs on businesses, profits will fall and capital will migrate.

Alternatively societies may adopt policies in which pollution control is paid for directly from public funds. By such measures they may succeed in protecting their local environments from some types of degradation, though they will not insulate themselves from the global impact of local pollution in poorer countries. As Chernobyl demonstrated, some kinds of pollution have a very long reach.

Unregulated global free trade and international mobility of capital

In the classical theory of free trade capital is immobile. Ricardo's doctrine of comparative advantage – which is still regularly invoked in defence of unregulated global free trade – says that when comparatively inefficient enterprises or industries shrink in any country, others will grow, absorbing the capital and labour released from the declining activities. Within each trading country capital will move to those economic activities in which it is most productive. Ricardian comparative advantage applies *internally* in trading nations, not externally between them. It implies that in a regime of unrestricted free trade the allocation of resources will be maximally productive within each trading nation, and thereby, by inference, throughout the world. Insofar as the world becomes a single market, efficiency and productivity in every country will be maximized.

Ricardo understood that this could be true only so long as capital is not to any significant extent internationally mobile:

> the fancied or real insecurity of capital, when not under the immediate control of its owner, together with the natural disinclination which every man has to quit the country of his birth and connections, and intrust himself with all his habits fixed, to a strange government and new laws, checks the emigration of capital. These feelings, which I should be sorry to see weakened, induce most men of property to be satisfied with a low rate of profits in their own country, rather than seek a more advantageous employment for their wealth in foreign nations.[3]

The contrast between this theoretical requirement of unrestricted global free trade and the realities of the late twentieth-century world needs little comment. When capital is mobile it will seek its absolute advantage by migrating to countries where the environmental and social costs of enterprises are lowest and profits are highest. Both in theory and practice the effect of global capital mobility is to nullify the Ricardian doctrine of comparative advantage. Yet it is on that flimsy foundation that the edifice of unregulated global free trade still stands.[4]

The argument against unrestricted global freedom in trade and capital movements is not primarily an economic one. It is, rather, that the economy should serve the needs of society, not society the imperatives of the market. In terms that are strictly and narrowly economic it is true that a global free market is incredibly productive. Equally, in the contest between free market economies and social market systems free markets are often superior in productivity. There is not much doubt that the free market is the most *economically efficient* type of capitalism. For most economists that ends the matter. Yet what social market economies do is in no sense irrational. The Japanese practice of employing workers who are not economically productive in a variety of low-skill occupations is neither unreasonable nor inefficient, provided that one of the criteria of efficiency by which such a policy is judged is the maintenance of social cohesion by the avoidance of mass unemployment.

As some economists have always recognized, the pursuit of economic efficiency without regard to social costs is itself unreasonable and in effect ranks the demands of the economy over the needs of society. That is precisely what drives competition in a global free market. The neglect of social costs, which is a professional deformation of economists, has become an imperative of the entire system.

The economic inefficiencies of restrictions on free trade are so nearly self-evident that anyone who is critical of unregulated global free trade is easily convicted of economic ignorance.[5] But the economic argument for unregulated global free trade involves a wild abstraction from social realities. It is true that restraints on global free trade will not enhance productivity; but maximal productivity achieved at the cost of social desolation and human misery is an anomalous and dangerous social ideal.

Global free markets and falling wages

When capital is as mobile as it is today, it will tend, other things being equal, to gravitate to countries whose workers have the lowest absolute wages. Of course things are rarely equal, especially the costs which enterprises incur on top of the costs of labour. The quality of infrastructure and services in different countries varies considerably. The costs and risks associated with political instability, the local rule of law and corruption, differ greatly from country to country. The education of the local workforce, location of plant, cost of transportation, political environment and many other factors are important.

Low wages in some countries – those of Central and West Africa, for example – reflect the fact that those countries are unattractive locations for productive capital. High wages in others, such as Singapore, reflect its excellent levels of education in the workforce, an uncorrupt rule of law and political stability.

Labour costs per capita for Osram's, the German-based company and the world's second largest producer of light bulbs, to manufacture light bulbs in China are a fiftieth of their costs in Germany; but it takes 38 times as many people to turn out the same number of light bulbs. Here we see per capita costs of cheap labour being largely cancelled out by lower skill and productivity levels.[6]

Further, wages rates in any economy are determined by its domestic labour market, not by wage rates in other countries. The taxi that I hail in Piccadilly is not in competition with taxis in Lahore. However, a growing range of skills command a price that is set globally. Many services can be exported to wherever the labour needed for them is cheapest – as has occurred when airlines have transferred ticketing and bookkeeping in India. But most wages are still set by domestic markets.

The decline in workers' bargaining power in the countries of the affluent north has not come from global free trade alone. To think that it could do so would be to exaggerate the impact of international trade and capital flows on national economies. Unemployment in the advanced countries is too significant to be attributed solely to trade with low-wage countries.

New technologies and the deskilling of parts of the population by inadequate education are central causes of long-term unemployment in advanced western societies. Growing income inequalities have been magnified by deregulation of the labour market and neo-liberal tax policies, but the root cause of falling wages and rising unemployment is the worldwide spread of new technology.

Newly industrializing economies and late industrial economies do not fall into simple, homogenous, mutually exclusive categories as far as wages are concerned. In some newly industrialized countries (NICs), such as South Korea, Taiwan and Singapore, wages are higher in many occupations than in some advanced countries, notably Britain and the United States. That is why South–North relocations by Asian multinationals to cheap-labour regions in the First World are nowadays not uncommon.

The Korean conglomerate Lucky Goldstar's decision in early 1997 to locate a factory in Newport, Wales, exported jobs from Korea to a hitherto First World European region that has low wages and low non-wage costs of labour. (It received a considerable subsidy from the British government to encourage it to do so.) A year before, Ronson moved its facilities for the production of cigarette lighters from Korea to Wales and saved nearly 20 per cent on its wage costs.[7]

These examples show that the impact of global *laissez-faire* on job security is no longer primarily on First World labour forces. As the mass demonstrations of workers in Seoul in January 1997 testified, the reduction of job security is worldwide.

First World countries are not homogenous as far as labour costs are concerned either. The wages that Siemens pays its German workers are high, but that is partly because, owing to much higher education and training levels in Germany, the productivity of Siemen's German workers is around twice that of its workers in the American plants.[8]

Yet the overall effect of unregulated global free trade is still to drive down the wages of workers – most particularly unskilled manufacturing workers – in advanced countries. If barriers to international trade are lowered, then – in what economists refer to as 'factor-price equalization' – the price of factors of production *including labour* will tend to converge. This is what economists mean when they talk of the prospect that 'your wages will be set in Peking'.[9]

New information technologies allow many goods, including an expanding range of services, to be produced in developing countries at a fraction of the labour costs they incur in more mature industrial societies. As the International Labour Organisation has put it succintly: 'Location decisions nowadays are very finely tuned to labour costs.'[10] This is an important truth. Ricardo's theory, in which capital was mobile only within its country of origin, and production was internationally practically immobile, is no longer relevant.

Our world differs from Ricardo's in another crucial respect. There are rapid rates of population growth in new industrializing countries. This serves to reinforce the downwards pressure of unregulated global free trade on wages in mature industrial economies. In most of the latter, population growth rates are low, and labour – at least skilled labour – is a scarce resource which commands a premium. In many newly industrializing countries where population is growing quickly, labour – including some kinds of skilled labour – is in practically inexhaustible supply.

When population growth is so uneven labour in NICs undercuts labour in mature industrial economies. When capital and production exercise unregulated mobility across the world they will tend to locate where labour is most abundant and least expensive. At present they can do this whether the labour they need is skilled or unskilled. As Michael Lind has put it:

> Within a generation, the burgeoning Third World population will contain not only billions of unskilled workers, but hundreds of millions of scientists, engineers, architects, and other professionals willing and able to do world-class work for a fraction of the payment their American counterparts expect. The free trade liberals hope that a high-wage, high-skill America need fear nothing from a low-wage, low-skill Third World. They have no answer, however, to the prospect – indeed, the probability – of ever-increasing *low-wage, high-skill* competition from abroad. In these circumstances, neither better worker training nor investment in US infrastructure will suffice . . . It is difficult to resist the conclusion that civilized social market capitalism and unrestricted global free trade are inherently incompatible.[11]

A survey in 1993 of 10,000 medium-sized German companies found that one-third of them were planning to transfer parts of their production to regions of the world, such as post-communist eastern Europe, where wages were lower and social and environmental regulation weaker. Many companies are outsourcing their computer programming needs to India, where programmers earn a fraction (around $3,000) of what they command in European countries or the United States. Many other examples could be quoted.[12]

The effects of a global market in driving down wages to the level they reach in cheap-labour, unregulated economies are enhanced by new information technologies. Many occupations are being decimated by new technologies. If bank tellers are a doomed profession, so are session musicians. In both cases their work can be synthesized or mimicked at low cost. New technologies would exert a downward pressure on incomes in many occupations even in the absence of a global free market. The substitution of technology for human labour creates dilemmas that no society (except, perhaps, Japan) has yet solved.[13]

Ricardo recognized that technological innovation could be job-destroying. He did not share the modern faith that new employment will always arise automatically from the side-effects of new technologies. As he noted, 'the discovery and use of machinery may be attended with a diminution of gross produce; and whenever that is the case, it will be injurious to the labouring class, as some of their number will be thrown out of employment, and population will become redundant . . . the opinion entertained by the labouring classes, that the employment of machinery is frequently detrimental to their interests, is not founded on prejudice and error but is conformable to the correct principles of political economy.'[14]

As has been noted, capital will migrate to the countries in which goods can be made for the world's consumers in rich countries at lowest labour costs. These will rarely be the countries in which such goods are consumed. As William Pfaff has commented, 'It is obviously no coincidence that Western trade unionism's bargaining power has suffered a dramatic and progressive decline since globalization began. Until the 1970s, investment in general had to confine itself to a national labour pool in order to manufacture for a national market. When it became not only technologically possible but economically advantageous to manufacture goods for rich-country consumers in poor and unregulated Asian, Latin American or African labour markets, labour in the advanced countries lost its bargaining power.'[16] Several academic studies tend to corroborate this observation.[17]

In countries of the First World it is the unprecedented combination of rapid technological change with global freedom in trade and capital movements, of labour market deregulation in advanced industrial societies with rapid population growth in developing countries, that has eclipsed the power of organized labour.

Global free markets and the passing of social democracy

Social democrats in Britain and other European countries who imagine that the social market economies with which they are familiar can be reconciled with a global free market have not understood the new circumstances in which advanced industrial societies find themselves.

Social market economies developed in a particular economic niche. They are bound to be transformed or destroyed by the industrialization of Asia and the entry into world markets of the post-communist countries.

The effect of competition from countries in which a regime of deregulation, low taxes and a shrinking welfare state has been imposed is to force downwards harmonization of policies on states which retain social market economies. Policies enforcing a deregulated labour market and cuts in welfare provision are adopted as defensive strategies in response to policies implemented in other countries. Tax competition among advanced states works to drain public finances and make a welfare state unaffordable. As a *Financial Times* editorial has noted: 'by eroding the revenue base, tax competition can become too much of a good thing . . . Bidding wars between countries can even undermine the collective revenue base. This increases the tax burden on less mobile industries and on labour, relative to capital.'[18]

Tax rivalry is only one mechanism through which competition among governments for mobile capital and industries works to drive down social provision and raise taxes on labour. The workings of the global bond markets reduce or remove from the world's social markets much of the freedom their governments had in the past to pursue counter-cyclical policies. They force them to return to a pre-Keynesian situation in which they have few effective levers of macroeconomic management. They are condemned to wait out cyclical downturns in economic activity – whatever their social and economic costs.

By penalizing governments which attempt to stimulate economic activity by borrowing or undertaking public works the markets force them back into a pre-Keynesian world in which governments responded to recessions by the disastrous deflationary expedient of expenditure cuts. Thus world bond markets mimic the workings of the Gold Standard. But they do so without replicating its semi-automatic character, which conferred a degree of stability on the economies it governed. They operate in a context of market uncertainties which makes speculative booms and busts (such as the global bond market crash of early 1994) inevitable. The mechanism of the Gold Standard has been replaced by the house rules of a casino.

Global capital markets do more than this. They make social democracy unviable. By social democracy I mean the combination of deficit-financed full employment, a comprehensive welfare state and egalitarian tax policies that existed in Britain until the late 1970s and which survived in Sweden until the early 1990s.

That social democratic regime presupposed a closed economy. Capital movements were limited by fixed or semi-fixed exchange rates. Many of the core policies of social democracy cannot be sustained in open economies. This applies to deficit-financed full employment and the welfare states of the post-war period. It applies equally to social democratic deals of equality. All social democratic theories of justice (such as John Rawls's egalitarian theory) presuppose a closed economy.[19]

It is only within a closed system of distribution that we can know if the principles of justice dictated by such theories are satisfied. More practically, it is only in a closed economy that egalitarian principles can be enforced. In open economies they will be rendered unworkable by the freedom of capital – including 'human capital' – to migrate.

Social democratic regimes presuppose that high levels of public provision could be funded unproblematically from general taxation. That proposition no longer holds. It is not even true of what economic theory understands to be real public goods. The logic of unfettered mobility of capital is that financing public goods becomes harder for all states. In the standard understanding of them, public goods are services enjoyed by all. They cannot be split up or partitioned, and they must be paid for out of taxation if they are not to be under-produced. In the technical literature of economic theory and public administration in which this standard view is found, public goods are such things as law and order, national defence and environmental conservation.

The classic solution to the problems of financing the provision of public goods is mutually agreed coercion. Everyone agrees that they will benefit if public goods are produced. They resolve the classical problem of the public goods trap – freeloaders who seek to enjoy public goods without paying their way – by requiring everyone to contribute through taxation. This classic solution breaks down when taxation is not enforceable on mobile capital and corporations. If sources of revenue – capital, enterprises and people – are free to migrate to low-tax regimes, mutually agreed coercion does not work as a means of paying for public goods. The kinds and levels of taxation levied in order to pay for public goods in any state cannot significantly exceed those found in states that are otherwise comparable.

Global mobility of capital and production in a world of open economies have made the central policies of European social democracy unworkable.[20] By so doing they have made today's mass unemployment a problem without a simple solution.

The monetarist theories that presently dominate the world's central banks and transnational financial institutions deny that any trade-off of price stability with full employment can be achieved. The intellectual credentials of such doctrines are not especially impressive. They appear to presuppose a view of economic life as tending to equilibrium of the sort that Keynes successfully criticized. In our time an equilibrium view of economic life has been anachronistically revived in the 'rational expectations' theories emanating from the University of Chicago. These are controversial theorizings which command no general consensus even among mainstream economists.[21]

Yet these dubious theories have inspired the structural adjustment programmes of the World Bank that, in countries as remote as Mexico and Nigeria, have imposed deep and enduring depressions of real economic activity in the pursuit of fiscal rectitude. Global bond markets simulate these structural adjustment programmes. They impose on the countries of the First World the deflationary disciplines of structural adjustment which have manifestly failed as emergency measures in developing countries.

Theories in which market equilibrium is achieved through the rational expectations of market participants are not shared by those who have made fortunes from their understanding of how markets work in practice. George Soros, commenting on the economic theory underlying the Maastricht agreements, in which a new European Central Bank overseeing a single European currency will be charged with the overriding objective of price stability, has noted: 'Underlying it all is an erroneous equilibrium theory of economics. John Maynard Keynes showed that full employment is not the natural outcome of a market equilibrium. To bring about full employment, an economy needs government policies specifically designed for the purpose . . . the invisible hand will not get us to a happy equilibrium.'[22]

Soros's conclusion applies with equal or greater force to the project of a single self-regulating global market as it does to the proposal for a single European currency controlled by a European Central Bank whose sole obligation is to maintain a stable price level.

By destabilizing any national government that attempts to break with these doctrines – such as that of François Mitterrand in the early 1980s – the world's bond and currency markets can act to make them self-fulfilling. They box in any state which tries to increase employment by a deficit-led expansion in economic activity. As Hirst and Thompson write:

The scale of short-term transactions in the international foreign exchange markets – one trillion dollars a day – dwarfs the flows of foreign trade and direct investment. It also means that the major central banks just do not have the reserves (singly or collectively) to defend a given exchange rate if the markets have made up their minds that it will move up or down. Traders and commentators undoubtedly have prejudices; they favour low inflation, 'sound money' public policies . . . These policies undoubtedly inhibit growth and they establish the short-term interest of major financial institutions as the supreme economic wisdom.[23]

During the 1980s, the largest sovereign nation-state, the United States, was able to deploy Keynesian-style expansionist policies when it engaged in a large arms build-up; but it is doubtful if anything similar could be attempted by the United States in present circumstances. President Clinton's experience early in his first administration, when bond markets inflicted high interest rates as a deterrent against potential fiscal laxity, taught him that even the world's 'borrower of last resort' is vulnerable to the judgement of the global market in government bonds.

The long-standing Swedish experiment in full employment, which by the early 1990s was already in serious difficulties, was brought to an end by the power of the global bond market. William Greider has described this paradigm case of the global markets in action:

Sweden felt the market's lash in the summer of 1994 when major international purchasers of its bonds went on strike, announcing that they would buy no more. Long-term interest rates soared into double figures, rising a full four percentage points that year, the highest borrowing cost demanded of any advanced industrial nation except Italy. Though Sweden had elected a conservative government determined to scale back its celebrated welfare state, the annual deficit was still above 10 per cent of GDP and the government's accumulated debt had grown explosively, from 44 per cent of GDP in 1990 to 95 per cent in 1995. To quell the bondholder's boycott, Sweden's central bank was compelled to tighten credit still further and the prime minister quickly announced plans for further spending cuts. Yet Sweden's economy – once the model of a stable, prosperous social democracy – was already deeply depressed, with unemployment around 16 per cent. The new measures would make things worse. At the next election, Swedish voters returned the socialists to power, though they would face the same dilemma.[24]

What happened in Sweden has implications for social market economies everywhere. Contrary to many conventional interpretations, the core of Swedish full employment was not the active labour policies pursued by successive Social Democratic governments. It was the willingness of these governments to use the state as the employer of last resort.[25] That was vetoed by the bond markets. The implication for other governments committed to maintaining social cohesion by avoiding mass unemployment is that they cannot do so by any policy which the bond markets judge to be fiscally imprudent.

Bond markets have knocked away the floor from under post-war full employment policies. No western government today has a credible successor to the policies which secured western societies against mass unemployment in the Keynesian era. The numbers of people excluded from access to work have been growing in most western societies for twenty years or more. This has occurred despite strong and nearly continuous economic growth in all advanced countries. The social democratic objective of full employment cannot now be achieved by social democratic policies.

To imagine that the social market economies of the past can renew themselves intact under the forces of downwards harmonization is the most dangerous of the many illusions associated with the global market. Instead, social market systems are being compelled progressively to dismantle themselves, so that they can compete on more equal terms with economies in which environmental, social and labour costs are lowest. The question social market economies face is not whether they can survive with their present institutions and policies – they cannot. It is whether the adjustments that are imperative will be made by a further wave of neo-liberal reforms or by policies which harness markets to the satisfaction of human needs.

The global free market versus European social markets

Germany is the test case for those who think that the social markets of the post-war era can survive in a global free market. The signs are not encouraging. The very conditions that made it highly successful in the decades after the Second World War are working against the German model today. The German post-war model had two cornerstones: a comprehensive welfare state and business corporations in which the interests of a range of stakeholders were represented in the governance of enterprises. Both of these cornerstones have been shaken by the competitive environment in which Germany has found itself after reunification.

Supporters of the Rhine model of German capitalism have not understood that the competitive niche in which the German social market thrived disappeared with the reunification of Europe, the industrialization of Asia and the new pressures of competitive deregulation. Michel Albert perceives clearly that the economic rivalry which dominates the world today is of capitalism against capitalism,[26] yet he fails to grasp its logic. He acknowledges that the internationalization of financial markets and the growth of world trade are implicated in the difficulties of the Rhine model; but he still expects 'the American hare' to be overtaken by 'the Rhine tortoise', even though he acknowledges the possibility that bad capitalisms will drive out good.[27]

The German social market economy differs fundamentally and radically from American free-market capitalism. It enfranchises stakeholders – employees, local communities, bankers, sometimes suppliers and customers – in corporate governance. Workers in large firms (over 800 employees) are assured of representation on supervisory boards along with representatives of shareholders and other stakeholders. The dispersal of power among a range of stakeholders in the German system is central in accounting for its low levels of economic inequality in comparison with Anglo-Saxon economies.

German capitalism accords a much lesser weight to share values than does any free-market economy. Equity markets and hostile takeovers are not central in it. A good many enterprises, including large and medium-sized firms, remain family-owned. Equally, the German labour market contrasts starkly with those of the United States and those fashioned on the American model (such as Britain). There is industry-wide collective bargaining over wages and a high degree of job security.

In Germany the slash-and-burn, hire-and-fire culture which permitted the American downsizings of the early 1990s is unheard of – or rejected. If German workers do lose their jobs they receive about two-thirds of their working incomes in unemployment benefit (as compared with around a third in Britain and less still in the US). In German social markets the treatment of labour as a marketable commodity is highly circumscribed. The chairman of Siemens, Germany's flagship electronics company, Heinrich von Pierer, is reported to have stated that 'The hire and fire principle does not exist here and I never want it to.'[28]

These features of the Germany economy arise from a long-standing cultural and political consensus about how markets must be shaped. They are designed to protect and foster social cohesion as well as promote economic efficiency. This economic consensus is central to the liberal democratic political culture that Germany has built since the Second World War. While there is no prospect of its being abandoned, it cannot renew itself without far-reaching reforms.

The economic philosophy which the German model embodies – the philosophy of Ordo-liberalism[29] – views market freedoms as legal and social artefacts, not fundamental human rights. It understands a market economy not as a state of natural liberty produced by deregulation, but as a subtle and complex institution, which needs recurrent reform if it is to be kept in good repair. In this economic philosophy market economies are not free-standing entities; they are extensions of core institutions such as the local community and the democratic state.

The German model we know today was inaugurated by Ludwig Erhard as an embodiment of Ordo-liberalism. The economic philosophy – sometimes called the Freiburg School – never entirely disappeared in Germany, despite the forced emigration of many of its exponents during the Nazi period. Erhard launched German economic liberalization in defiance of the planning-oriented economic policies of the Allied Occupation and of *laissez-faire* ideology. Germany's post-war economic liberalization probably owed little to Allied influences.[30]

A market economy of the kind envisioned in Ordo-liberal philosophy is embedded deeply in Germany's post-war culture. Why should a civilized and successful social institution be traded off for the endemic insecurity, social divisions and multiplying ghettos of the American free market? As David Goodhart has put it: 'The US model has produced a dynamic, vibrant country with an open door for many of the poorest of the earth. But given a free and informed choice where would most people rather be born if they did not know which class or ethnic group they would belong to – Detroit or Cologne?'[31]

However, the German model cannot be renewed in anything resembling its post-war form. This is only partly because of major policy errors made on the way to German reunification. The parity level at which the currencies of East and West Germany were merged was a basic mistake. West Germany's government and business class was unprepared for how much like other East European economies – much of it wasteful, polluted and technologically archaic – eastern Germany really was. A more realistic assessment of the East German rustbelt might have spared West German policy these mistakes.

Some of the costs of unification were unavoidable. West Germany could not avoid assuming the social security obligations of East Germany – it was a requirement of the German constitution. But it fuelled the slow-burning German fiscal crisis arising from its incompletely funded pensions system.

When all this has been taken into account, one fact remains clear. No other country, save perhaps Japan, could have sustained and managed the absorption of a bankrupt economy occasioned by the unification process. Certainly none of the Anglo-Saxon states could even have begun to have done so.

Some of the problems of the German economy are caused by the effort to comply with the highly deflationary fiscal conditions of the Maastricht Treaty. Chancellor Kohl's overriding concern with launching a single European currency led to policies in which demand in the economy has been choked off. If the single currency project founders, we may expect such policies to be abandoned.

The deeper reasons for the difficulties of the German social market today arise from the world in which a unified Europe must live. European unification has allowed hundreds of millions of workers to enter world markets. Their high education levels and low wages make them attractive to multinational corporations and international investors. This new competitive environment is bound to unravel the intertwining agreements about wages, conditions and job security that have held the German model together.

Though no German company has emulated American practice and relocated its plant wholesale in the post-communist East, German companies are steadily shifting production at the margin to the Czech Republic, Poland and elsewhere in eastern Europe. As the proportions of workers employed abroad by German companies approaches that of American, British and Dutch companies, these firms will find it harder to uphold the stakeholder relationships which have in the past shaped them.

At some point, social relationships among stakeholders will become more marginal in the life of German firms. The centripetal force of wage differentials in a unified Europe will unpick the knots of trust and convention that held together firms as social institutions in the post-war German social market. As stakeholder relationships become less central, so economic inequalities are likely to increase. A core feature of the post-war social market – its compression of inequalities of income and wealth – will be at risk.

The expansion of German firms abroad cannot avoid altering their role in German society. In 1997, Siemens expected to shed 6,000 jobs in Germany while expanding manufacturing overseas. By 1999 it will have more employees abroad than it has in Germany. This international expansion increases Siemens' need for foreign capital. As chairman Heinrich von Pierer, quoted earlier as an opponent of Anglo-Saxon hire-and-fire, has acknowledged 'We are in a global competition for loan and equity capital.'[32] Several other German corporations, such as Hoechst, the pharmaceuticals company, and Thyssen's, the steel group, have taken measures to increase profits and share prices quickly.

Global competition for equity capital works as a lever to raise the weighting given to share values in corporate policies. But it weakens the company's commitment to other stakeholders.

A social market begins to unravel when business relationships that have been long-term and based on trust become short-term, transactional and contractual. There are many signs that this unravelling is underway in Germany today. Large companies are more liable to focus on short-term cost reductions than on the maintenance of a long-term stable relationship in their treatment of their suppliers. Many companies are devising strategies to make labour costs more flexible downwards. The appointment of a cost-cutting executive from General Motors to manage the procurement division of Volkswagen in 1993 was a symbolic moment in the slow metamorphosis of the social market in Germany. Equally symptomatic is the fact that two of Germany's four post-war hostile takeovers have been mounted in the past six years.

None of this means that the German social market will assimilate the American model. The complex system of cross-holdings in Germany together with the institutions of co-determination will prevent this. These restraints on corporate policy will counterbalance the increasing power of shareholder interests. Capital markets will not acquire the power in the German economy that they have in American (and British) capitalism. German companies will not become hollowed-out virtual corporations whose chief functions are bill collection and profit distribution. But they are already on a path that is bound to transform the social market as it has been known for a whole generation in post-war Germany.

Nevertheless, the German social market is not about to collapse: it is too resourceful and it has too much political legitimacy for that. There are many adjustments it can make to the new competitive circumstances in which it finds itself. German companies are well-suited to a strategy of 'flexible specialization' in which traditional mass production methods are replaced by the versatile use of a broadly skilled workforce to produce a more diversified and customized range of goods.[33] The *Mittelstand* of small and medium-sized companies in Germany, often family-owned and sometimes over a century old, are strong and innovative. The research and development facilities of German firms remain exemplary.

It is a mistake to think that the only way German capitalism can move towards greater flexibility is by emulating American practice – in which flexibility goes hand in hand with job insecurity. The historic agreement in early 1997 between the IG Metall engineering union, one of Germany's largest trade unions, and the management of Osram, shows how the German model can respond to intensified global competition. Osram was considering transferring plans for a new production line from Germany to a site in Italy where labour costs are 40 per cent lower. According to a survey by DIHT, the organization bringing together Germany's chambers of industry and commerce, 28 per cent of West German manufacturers were planning similar moves over the next three years, with nearly two-thirds of them citing labour costs as the chief reason. The reality of sharpened world competition was plain to Osram's. Three-quarters of its employees work outside Germany and 90 per cent of its sales are to foreign customers. The company is constantly considering the location of its production. In these circumstances the trade union was willing to sign an agreement increasing flexibility over shifts that lengthened the working week. It is more than likely that this and other unions will agree to similar, more far-reaching deals in the near and mid-term future.[34]

Such deals show the German social market adapting to global market competition without abandoning the practices that distinguish it from the American free market. Yet none of the adjustments the German social market can make to exploit its comparative advantages will prevent the metamorphosis that is already underway. The logic of lower labour costs in post-communist Europe together with the mobility of German production means that whatever emerges from the current flux will differ as much from the post-war German model as it will from the free market.

There is no prospect of the German model becoming the norm for the economies of the European Union. In an enlarged, post-Cold-War EU containing some post-communist states as well as post-Thatcherite Britain the economic cultures and circumstances of the EU's members are too diverse. The social democratic project of extending Rhinish capitalism across the countries of the European Union is an anachronism.

The European Union cannot insulate itself from the pressures of competitive deregulation. A 'continental Keynesianism'[35] would aim to reinvent a social democratic regime that has ceased to be viable at the level of any nation-state at a transnational European level. Yet even a much more integrated Union equipped with a single currency and fiscal policy could not escape the consequences of competition with highly educated, low-wage workforces that European reunification and Asian industrialization have forced on it.

EU monetary and fiscal policies judged to be lax will evoke censure from global markets. Unregulated world currency markets with a chronic allergy to policies of job-creation through public borrowing will sell the European currency and provoke a crisis. If the EU pursues counter-cyclical policies perceived to be too expansionary, EU bonds will be dumped by world markets. The result will be higher interest rates and more unemployment.

Even an economy as large and varied as the EU's cannot hope to elude the constraints of global market competition enforced by foot-loose capital and companies. An economically integrated European Union could no more buck world markets than can the United States. Continental Keynesianism is a dead end.

Europe-wide social democracy has been removed from the agenda of history. But that does not mean that German capitalism is finished. On the contrary, whether or not the project of a single European currency succeeds, Germany will become again, as it was a hundred years ago, one of the world's great economic powers, turning eastwards to extend its economic influence.

In the coming century German capitalism will have many strengths. But they will be exercised fully only after a period of deep and traumatic reform.

The crisis of Europe's social market economies is profound. If they try to prop up the failing structures which they have inherited, they will still suffer many of the worst disorders of global capitalism. The evils of disordered capitalism cannot be escaped by policies which seek to renew the social market economies of the post-war era.

5   The United States and the Utopia of global capitalism

The United States is peculiarly ill-equipped for the world role it has assigned to itself. The doctrinaire optimism of American popular belief, eloquent at all official levels of American society, is an optimism which the nation developed and has been able to maintain since 1865 because of general prosperity and national isolation. The United States has, in these fortuitous conditions, become a society which today by a powerful optimistic alchemy transforms the prophetic pessimism of Judaism, and the injunctions of asceticism, humility, and self-sacrificing charity of Christianity, into the sentimental and vulgar consolations of a bourgeoisie . . . Such phenomena . . . are integrally related to an American international politics that assumes the possibility – indeed, the proximate possibility – of a fundamental reform of the institutions and behaviour of mankind at large. They are evidences of the continuing, and (as yet) invincible, isolation of American civilization from the major experiences of Western history and modern politics. They evidence the American national isolation from, or, more deeply, the American suppression of, the perception of human tragedy and desolation, or irrationality and perversity.

EDMUND STILLMAN AND WILLIAM PFAFF[1]

Global *laissez-faire* is an American project; but the United States has not always stood for a worldwide free market. For much of its history it nurtured a sense of its unique world mission by isolating itself from the world. Americans have long followed Thomas Jefferson in seeing themselves as 'the world's best hope'; but only lately has that hope been equated with the universal reach of free markets.

A global free market is the Enlightenment project of a universal civilization, sponsored by the world's last great Enlightenment regime.

The United States is alone in the late modern world in the militancy of its commitment to this Enlightenment project. At the same time, in the strength and depth of the fundamentalist movements it contains, America confounds Enlightenment hopes of modernity.

Nearly all contemporary states profess allegiance to some of the ideals of the European Enlightenment. Almost all are signatories to the UN Declaration of Human Rights. That declaration was a product of the Second World War, in which the Allies were ranged against a Nazi state which spurned the Enlightenment and all its works, while deploying modern technology in the service of racial slavery and a uniquely terrible genocide. The destruction of the Nazi regime by the Allies gave the Enlightenment faith in an emerging universal civilization another lease on life. The most significant outcome of the unravelling of the post-war global settlement is the rejection throughout much of the world of this Enlightenment ideal.

In China, Malaysia and Singapore, in Egypt, Algeria and Iran, in post-communist Russia and parts of the Balkans, in Turkey and India, the end of the Cold War has released powerful political movements which reject all westernizing ideologies. The future of this century's oldest westernizing regime, that of Attaturkist Turkey, is uncertain, as Islamist movements arise within it to challenge its secular, westward-leaning institutions.

European countries, particularly France, acknowledge an allegiance to Enlightenment values; but this is qualified by a sense of the abiding differences among cultures and by the recognition that the European supremacy which the Enlightenment took for granted is gone and will not return. Most European countries have been partly shaped by Enlightenment thinking, but all are now post-Enlightenment cultures.

Only in the United States is the Enlightenment project of a global civilization still a living political faith. During the Cold War this Enlightenment faith was embodied in American anti-communism. In the post-communist era it animates the American project of a universal free market.

The forty-odd years following the end of the Second World War were taken up by a global conflict between two Enlightenment ideologies – liberalism and Soviet Marxism. Both doctrines emanate from within the very heart of 'western civilization'. Both classical Marxism and Soviet communism were late flowerings of ancient western traditions. Rightly, their founders and followers saw themselves as heirs to a tradition that included the classical economic theories of Adam Smith and David Ricardo and the philosophies of Hegal and Aristotle. The conflict between Soviet communism and liberal democracy was not a clash between the West and the rest. It was a family quarrel among western ideologies.

The Soviet collapse was not a victory by 'the West' over one of its enemies. It was the ruin of this century's most ambitious westernizing regime. Its consequence has not been worldwide acceptance of western institutions and values, but instead the return of Russia to all the historic ambiguities of its relationship with Europe and the world.

The world that is emerging from the end of the Cold War cannot be seen clearly through the lens of any Enlightenment philosophy. A country whose policies are founded on Enlightenment hopes will find its expectations confounded again and again. It will be unprepared for the return of history in the post-Enlightenment world.

The central problem the United States faces today is that its institutions and policies are predicated on an early modern ideology that has little purchase on late modern conditions. It is a problem that may prove to be insoluble.

Resurgent religions, ancient ethnic enmities and territorial rivalries, the use of new technologies for purposes of war rather than wealth-creation do not accord well with Enlightenment expectations of secularization and the propagation of peace through trade. They betoken a reversion to the classical sources of political and military conflict between and within states.

According to the ideologies of the Enlightenment, liberal as well as Marxist, such conflicts are not endemic to the human condition. They are developmental phases in human progress.

Neo-conservatives who maintain that democratic capitalist states are the only legitimate form of government, and that such governments will never go to war against one another, are as much captivated by the illusion that the historic sources of human conflict can be transcended as the most vulgar Marxist. They thereby repudiate the traditional practice of diplomacy, which aimed to contain and moderate the sources of destructive conflict without imagining that they could be eradicated.

The re-emergence of ethnicity, territory and religion as deciding forces in war and politics makes a mockery of any diplomacy which rests on Enlightenment ideas of *homo economicus* and a universal civilization. Those who hold to the conviction that worldwide modernity will banish these forces have obviously not asked themselves why economic liberalization and religious fundamentalism so often go together.

Like that of the former Soviet Union, American foreign policy has been based on Enlightenment expectations more than on any understanding of national interest. The Cold War was a conflict between opposed variants of the same Enlightenment project. In the late modern, post-Enlightenment world in which the United States must live, a foreign policy that takes its bearings from such universalist ideas will have little leverage on events.

As Henry Kissinger has observed tersely, 'A clear definition of the national interest needs to be an equally essential guide to American policy.'[2] Insofar as the foreign policies of the United States remain guided by hopes of the evanescence of the historic sources of conflict it will be rudderless in the world that is coming about in the wake of the Enlightenment.

America today is not treading a path which all other societies will follow. It is detaching itself from other 'western' cultures in the extremity of its experiment in free-market social engineering and in the intensity of the fundamentalist movements which that experiment is evoking.

As in other countries, fundamentalist movements are a response by American society to the derelictions wrought on it by a radically modernist economic system.

The neo-conservative ascendancy in America

Since the 1980s there has been no serious challenge to the economic philosophy of the free market in the United States. It was then that a free-market orthodoxy established its ascendancy over American public culture. It became entrenched by the events of 1989, when the Berlin Wall came down and the Soviet regime entered the final phase of its collapse.

The Soviet collapse granted a new lease of life to the faltering American conviction that the United States embodies the modern age as no other country does. 'Declinism' – the perception that American power and prosperity are waning – was snuffed out. The world appeared to be converging on American values and institutions. Since then, modernity, the free market and the universal reach of American institutions have become virtually synonymous in the American public mind.

Today's project of a single global market is America's universal mission co-opted by its neo-conservative ascendancy. Market utopianism has succeeded in appropriating the American faith that it is a unique country, the model for a universal civilization which all societies are fated to emulate.

Earlier this century, the American messianic tradition had a noble and generous expression in the Rooseveltian liberalism that helped defeat Nazism in Europe. Today the free market has displaced this American liberal tradition. It has gone far towards establishing itself as the unofficial American civil religion.

The ascendancy of the free market in recent American discourse is a remarkable phenomenon. It has made liberalism illegitimate in American public culture. To be perceived as a liberal is a political liability. Liberal opinion in the United States today is the voice of a besieged minority; American liberals have been reduced to marginality by a conservative strategy in which liberalism has been represented as an entrenched orthodoxy.

Yet liberalism is dominant in the United States only in the sense that genuine conservative philosophy no longer exists. The elegant apologies for imperfection in Santayana and Lippmann, Mencken and Voegelin are scarcely historical memories at a time when conservatives have become ranting evangelists for global capitalism. Today, American conservatism is a crankish and sectarian species of Enlightenment ideology – nineteenth-century libertarianism.

The Right's strategy in achieving an ascendancy over American opinion in the 1980s was not complicated. It sought to identify American institutions with the free market. The history of the United States hardly warrants such a bold equation. Like England, the United States espoused an early version of *laissez-faire* in its domestic economic life during the nineteenth century. Unlike its English exemplar, the free market in America was hedged around with protectionism and, until the end of the Civil War, with slavery.

American government has never observed a rule of non-interference in economic life. The foundations of American prosperity were laid behind the walls of high tariffs. Federal and state government were active in building railways and highways. The West was opened with an arsenal of government subsidies. Outside the economic sphere, American government was more invasive of personal liberty in the pursuit of virtue than that of any other modern western country. No other modern western state, for example, has attempted the enforcement of Prohibition. To represent the United States as a country with a history of minimum government requires considerable imagination.

Yet the unrestrained capitalism of the United States prior to the First World War sought to demonstrate its legitimacy by invoking a *laissez-faire* economic philosophy and a minimalist doctrine of government. Such notions were often deployed to attack the trust-busting progressive reformers of a later generation and to defend as the natural result of unfettered competition the many monopolies established in the nineteenth century. A golden age of American *laissez-faire* is an historical myth; but its use as one of the supports of the American free market today has many historical precedents.

In the American myth founding the Constitution embodies principles that are timeless and universally authoritative. In this mythology the United States is not a particular regime that has arisen in definite circumstances and will at some time pass away, it is an embodiment of universal truths whose future is assured by history.

In the Right-wing thinking that has been ascendant in the United States over the past two decades,[3] the universal principles of the Founders, the American claim to exemplary modernity and the institutions of the free market, have been assimilated into one another. As a result, the spread of the free market has been represented as the cutting edge of modernity and identified with the extension of American values.

If the authority of American institutions is universal and the free market is at the heart of them the reach of the American free market must be global. Free markets are not seen as merely one local way of organizing a market economy, with their own mixture of advantages and blemishes. They are understood as a dictate of human freedom everywhere.

In this Right-wing rendering of 'the American Creed' a surreal inversion of history has been quietly accomplished. The dogma that free markets are the most effective means of wealth creation touches the world's actually existing capitalisms at virtually no point. In the world's most successful emerging economies modernization has not meant adopting American-style free markets. It has meant continuous state intervention on a large scale.

For the most successful newly industrializing countries – Singapore, Malaysia, Taiwan, Japan and now China – adopting free markets would amount to replicating a phase of development at which the United States arrived in early modernity. For these Asian countries to adopt free markets would be a retreat from the late modern world. In fact none of them has sought to emulate the American free market, and none ever will.

The free market ideology which America is presently propagating is not – except, in a perverse and paradoxical way, in the United States itself – a vehicle of modernization. It is a relic of the seventeenth-century Enlightenment. It belongs to John Locke's world, not ours. Its assertion of universal human rights rooted in the dictates of a Christian deity, its insistence that American folkways are a deliverance of natural law and its regime of limited government and private property – these Atlantic pieties mask the plural world in which the United States must live.

Nor does this archaic worldview match the creative hybridity of American life. Like much in contemporary American discourse, free-market thinking embodies a cultural inheritance that is at odds with the strongest and most innovative forces in the world today.

It would be a mistake to accept American free-market economic philosophy at face value and interpret its effect as turning back the clock in the United States. In practice, engineering the free market in late twentieth-century America is far from an exercise in nostalgia. It is a *tour de force* of high modernity. Freeing up markets is not a conservative project, it is a programme for an economic and cultural counter-revolution. In the United States, as elsewhere, fundamentalism is not a return to tradition. It is an exacerbation of modernity.

Remoulding American society to suit the imperatives of free markets has involved the use of corporate power and federal government to bring about levels of economic inequality unknown since the 1920s and far in excess of those found in any other advanced industrial society today. It has encompassed an experiment in mass incarceration, accompanied by an elite retreat into walled proprietary communities that has left the United States far more divided than Latin American countries such as Argentina and Chile. It has deployed welfare policies to protect family values that market forces have already destroyed. It has gone in tandem with a nativist crusade against 'relativism' and 'multiculturalism' – ill-defined enemies that for practical purposes can be identified with life as it is lived by most Americans today.

This is not a programme for cultural or institutional continuity in the United States. As its more candid publicists have admitted, it is a game plan for a cultural civil war. In practice it has meant a rupture of the liberal capitalism that produced America's post-war economic supremacy.

The upshot of America's lurch to the Right is, as yet, uncertain. In the United States, as elsewhere, free markets evoke powerful social and political counter-movements. The chronic economic risk that they impose on the majority of the population is fertile ground for populist politicians. In the politics of insecurity the advantage does not ordinarily lie with politicians who espouse an agenda of further deregulation and shrinkage of government.

The fate of a Rightist demagogue such as Newt Gingrich in passing swiftly from political centrality to mocked marginality supports former Reaganite David Stockman's judgement that 'The abortive Reagan revolution proved that the American electorate wants a moderate social democracy to shield it from capitalism's rougher edges.'[4]

When Reaganite activists claimed to have set in motion a revolution in the United States they were, as it has turned out, not exaggerating. The Right in America can no longer be identified with a politics of institutional continuity and social cohesion. Its policies are not those of trimmers but of radicals. Its goals demand large-scale social engineering, not reverence for the inheritances of history. Its rhetoric does not invoke prudence or imperfectibility. It is a ranting eulogy of technology, a demonization of government and a militant assertion that all social evils are problems soluble by market forces.

In the 1980s, in the United States, Britain and some other countries, a defunct philosophy was revived in order to give a rationale to the large ruptures in policy and society that the goals of the Right then dictated. It is an index of the shift in discourse that the objectives and strategies of the Right dictated that this was not a conservative but instead a paleo-liberal creed.

Ronald Reagan was not himself any kind of liberal. He may not even have intended the economic counter-revolution that in fact occurred. The political economy of Reaganism was not notably free-market-oriented. It was a species of military-led, protectionist

Keynesianism. Large budget deficits were incurred in order to finance tax cuts and military expenditures. Much of American industry received enhanced protection by subsidies and tariffs. Reaganite fiscal and trade policies had little, if anything, to do with the regime of balanced budgets and free trade that New Right governments had attempted to introduce in Britain and New Zealand. Except for its tax and deregulation policies, what happened as a consequence of Reagan's presidency may be more significant than what he did during it.

The chief indirect effect of Reagan's presidency was to condone economic inequality in the United States, and produce a business culture in which the social costs of enterprise could be ignored with a good conscience. As Godfrey Hodgson has written: 'The stagnation of American incomes, and the growth in inequality, were essentially the consequences of the actions of corporate management, both directly in industrial corporations and indirectly as a result of intellectual fashions embraced in the financial sector. Political deregulation freed managers' elbows. A political climate encouraged them to take less account of non-economic considerations. Corporate business imposed greater inequality. Conservative doctrine rationalized it.'[5]

The freedoms of corporate executives in a deregulated economy – to hire and fire, to downsize and delayer, to award themselves share options and munificent bonuses – were not seen as special privileges granted within a peculiar variant of capitalism. They were the exercise of inalienable human rights. American capitalism was freedom in action. The structure of the American free market coincided with the imperatives of human rights. Who dares condemn the burgeoning inequalities and social breakdown that free markets engender, when free markets are no more than the right to individual freedom in the economic realm?

The philosophical foundations of these rights are flimsy and jerry-built. There is no credible theory in which the particular freedoms of deregulated capitalism have the standing of universal rights. The most plausible conceptions of rights are not founded on seventeenth-century ideas of property but on modern notions of autonomy. Even these are not universally applicable; they capture the experience only of those cultures and individuals for whom the exercise of personal choice is more important than social cohesion, the control of economic risk or any other collective good.

In truth, rights are never the bottom line in moral or political theory – or practice. They are conclusions, end-results of long chains of reasoning from commonly accepted premises. Rights have little authority or content in the absence of a common ethical life. They are conventions that are durable only when they express a moral consensus. When ethical disagreement is deep and wide an appeal to rights cannot resolve it. Indeed, it may make such conflict dangerously unmanageable.

Looking to rights to arbitrate deep conflicts – rather than seeking to moderate them through the compromises of politics – is a recipe for a low-intensity civil war. The American conflict over abortion has been aggravated by a legalist culture of non-negotiable rights until it has blown up into such a war. It is a conflict that cannot now be arbitrated or resolved. The culture of unconditional rights can only speed the United States towards ungovernability.

The claims of contemporary theories of rights are inordinate; but they are well designed to effect a closure of political discourse.[6] In the United States, as it has been reshaped by the neo-conservative ascendancy, the authority of rights has been used to shield the workings of the free market from public scrutiny and political challenge. An ideology of rights has been used to confer legitimacy on a novel successor to American liberal capitalism.

In fashioning a public culture in which the imperatives of the free market, the interests of corporate America and the demands of human freedom could no longer be distinguished, the Reagan presidency set the agenda not only for George Bush but also for Bill Clinton.

A line was drawn under the liberal era in American government when in August 1996 President Clinton signed the Welfare Reform Act. By divesting the federal government of most of its responsibilities for welfare provision Clinton reversed Roosevelt's most crucial reform. In the political climate that the neo-conservative ascendancy has created Clinton may have had no choice but to do what he did – to stave off the worst excesses of the Right-wing Republican platform by implementing those parts of it which have electoral support.

Freud believed that civilization demanded a trade-off in which people exchanged self-realization for security. He understood politics as the rational administration of the repression necessarily entailed by this exchange. This Enlightenment view is ill-matched to the political practice of late twentieth-century America. There are many Americans who are ready to trade off security for the pursuit of happiness; but they are often reluctant to admit the exchange they are making.

One of the tasks of a political leader is to conceal the choices his society has already made. In Clinton's case it has been to generate the illusion that a society in which individual choice is the only undisputed value can meet the human need for stability. Clinton has done this by colluding with the American public in maintaining the self-deception that a law-and-order policy can be a surrogate for the social institutions that free markets have destroyed. By acting as a political shaman through whom the contradictions of his culture can be articulated without being perceived or resolved, Bill Clinton may prove to be the prototype for the statecraft of the post-modern period.

Like other Enlightenment ideologies, market utopianism inspires an hubristic disregard of history in its followers. They never tire of telling us that ideas have consequences. They have not noticed that these consequences are rarely those expected or hoped for; and never only those. Among the consequences of engineering the American free market in the 1980s have been a new economic insecurity in the American middle classes.

The new American economic insecurity

To think of late twentieth-century American as a culture of contentment is anachronistic. America today is not a society in which an affluent majority looks on with complacent disdain at an underclass mired hopelessly in poverty and exclusion. It is a society in which anxiety pervades the majority. For most Americans, the ledge of security on which they live has not been so narrow since the 1930s.

It is notable that these anxieties are not a side-effect of economic stagnation. Quite the contrary. During the past fifteen years the American economy has been in nearly continuous expansion. Productivity and national wealth have grown steadily. The restructuring of American industry has enabled it to reclaim markets once thought lost forever to Japan. As in mid-Victorian England, freeing up markets in late twentieth-century America has engineered a spectacular – and unrepeatable – economic boom.

At the same time, the incomes of most Americans have stagnated.

Even for those whose incomes have risen personal economic risk has increased perceptibly. Most Americans dread a mid-life economic dislocation from which – they suspect – they may never recover. Few think now in terms of a lifelong vocation. Many expect, not without reason, that their incomes may fall in future. These are not circumstances which nurture a culture of contentment.

According to J. K. Galbraith, writing in 1993, 'What is new in the so-called capitalist economies – and this is a vital point – is that the controlling contentment and resulting belief is now that of the many, not just of the few. It operates under the compelling cover of democracy, albeit a democracy not of all citizens but of those who, in defence of their social and economic advantage, actually go to the polls. The result is government that is accommodated not to reality or common need but to the beliefs of the contented, who are now the majority of those who vote.'[7] This may be an accurate portrayal of the United States during the Reagan presidency. It does not describe it in the late 1990s.

America is no longer a bourgeois society. It has become a divided society, in which an anxious majority is wedged between an underclass that has no hope and an overclass that denies any civic obligations. In the United States today the political economy of the free market and the moral economy of bourgeois civilization have diverged – in all likelihood permanently.

The *embourgeoisement* that was the subject of innumerable unremarkable sociology textbooks has been reversed. That theory predicted the long-term integration of working people into the middle classes. It was supported by trends in most advanced western countries for a generation after the Second World War. Sociologists, economists and practising politicians in all parties have viewed *embourgeoisement* as an unstoppable long-term trend. They are unprepared for its reversal.

The middle classes are rediscovering the condition of assetless economic insecurity that afflicted the nineteenth-century proletariat. To be sure, though they have been stagnant over the past twenty years, the incomes of the middle-class Americans remain much higher than those of working people then or now. Even so, in their ever greater dependency on increasingly uncertain jobs, the American middle classes resemble the classic proletariat of nineteenth-century Europe. They are experiencing economic difficulties similar to those which confront workers who have lost the protective support of welfare provisions and labour unions.

Another endemic risk is family breakdown. The increases in economic risk that go with the mutation of capitalism in late twentieth-century America have occurred in a society in which families are more fragile and more comprehensively fractured than in almost any other country. In 1987 the average duration of American marriages was seven years.[8]

How many American households eat together as families? How many children live in the same neighbourhoods or cities as their parents? If an American becomes unemployed, can he or she find support from an extended family, as can Spaniards and Italians in European countries? American families are more fractured than those of any European country, including Russia, where the extended family has survived over seventy years of communism.

One reason for the weakness of families in the United States is the extraordinarily high levels of mobility that are required of workers. Deregulated labour markets impose an imperative of travel across the map of the USA which is far in excess of that which exists in any European country. In the UK – a more unsettled society than most in Europe – workers are twenty-five times less likely than American workers to move to a different region of the country.[9] Especially when economic necessity dictates that families have two incomes, as it has done in the United States over the past twenty years, the imperatives of the labour market may, and often do, pull partners in directions that are difficult to reconcile. But this is only one way in which the workings of an economy that has been re-engineered as a free market conflict with traditional institutions. The enforced lack of commitment to a place also works against stable neighbourhoods.

Yet, despite the much greater demands a deregulated labour market makes on its workers and its psychological and social costs for families and neighbourhoods, the better employment record often claimed for it is easily exaggerated. One survey suggests that around 10 per cent of the workforce (about 13.5 million people) is underemployed. This figure includes 4.5 million part-time workers who wish to be full-time and workers who have unsuccessfully sought employment in the past twelve months. The US Bureau of Labor statistics estimates that 12.2 million workers are employed as a contingent labour force of contract workers.[10]

As one of the UK's most distinguished economists has noted: 'Open unemployment is, of course, lower in the US. But once we allow for all forms of non-employment, there is little difference between Europe and the US: between 1988 and 1994, 11 per cent of men aged 25–55 were not in work in France, compared with 13 per cent in the UK, 14 per cent in the US and 15 per cent in Germany.'[11]

Further, US employment has grown as fast as it has partly because US productivity has been low – around half that of most European countries. Given this discrepancy in productivity it is hardly surprising that the US has been able to generate around twice as many jobs per unit of output than the countries of continental Europe.

Lastly, all estimates of America's employment record must take into account America's incarceration rates: over a million people who would be seeking work if American penal policies resembled those of any other western country are behind bars in the US. It appears not to have occurred to those who wish to export the American labour market throughout the world to radically different cultures such as Britain or Germany to ask whether America's sky-high levels of market-driven labour mobility might account for the fact that, whereas in Britain fewer than one in a thousand people are incarcerated, that figure in America is approaching one in a hundred. Once this larger context is taken into consideration the American superiority in job-creation looks slight, perhaps even illusory.

The new insecurity of the American majority has developed against this background. Luttwak has commented:

As entire industries rise and fall much faster than before, as firms expand, shrink, merge, separate, 'downsize' and restructure at an unprecedented pace, their employees at all but the highest levels must go to work one day without knowing whether they will have their job the next. That is true of virtually the entire employed middleclass, professionals included. Lacking the formal safeguards of European employment protection laws or prolonged post-employment benefits, lacking the functioning families on which most of the rest of humanity still relies to survive hard times, lacking the substantial liquid savings of their middleclass counterparts in all other developed countries, most working Americans must rely wholly on their jobs for economic security – and must therefore now live in conditions of chronic acute insecurity.'[12]

Through its effects on the family the American free market weakens one of the social institutions through which a liberal capitalist civilization renews itself. By its impact on the distribution of incomes it imperils the social condition of equality that observers from de Tocqueville onwards have seen as one of America's central achievements.

Rising inequality and the American majority

Declining incomes in America affect the working majority, especially the majority of poor people who are in work. The United States is the only advanced society in which productivity has been steadily rising over the past two decades while the incomes of the majority – eight out of ten – have stagnated or fallen. Such a growth in economic inequality is historically unprecedented. It has happened in no other advanced democracy, not even in the two English-speaking countries, Britain and New Zealand, in which free market policies were imposed most systematically in the 1980s. Nor did it occur during the era of the nineteenth-century free market in England or the United States.

The average weekly earnings of the 80 per cent of rank-and-file working Americans, adjusted for inflation, fell by 18 per cent between 1973 and 1995, from $315 a week to $258 per week. At the same time, between 19798 and 1989 the real annual pay of American corporate chief executives (CEOs) increased by 19 per cent, or two-thirds in post-tax terms.[13] Luttwak notes that, according to some of the best available assessments, the net worth of the richest 1 per cent of American families, which accounted for 31 per cent of the nation's total private wealth in 1983, amounted to over 36 per cent of the nation's wealth in 1989.[14]

In his seminal study of the effects of Reaganism on American inequality, Kevin Phillips writes:

In 1987, to plot the rearrangement of effective overall tax rates, the economists at the Congressional Budget Office took all federal taxes – individual income, Social Security, corporate income and excise – and calculated the change in their combined impact on different income strata after 1977. Families below the top decile, disproportionately burdened by Social Security and excise increases and rewarded less by any income tax reductions, wound up paying higher effective rates. The richest families, meanwhile, paid lower rates, largely because of the sharp reduction applicable to nonsalary income (capital gains, interest, dividends and rents).

Phillips concludes: 'These shifts go a long way to explain both the surge in consumption and the rising inequality of income. America's richest 5 per cent (and richest 1 per cent, in particular) were the tax policies' new beneficiaries.'[15]

Godfrey Hodgson has summarized the evidence and its implications concisely and powerfully:

Between 1973 and 1993 . . . the income of the bottom 60 per cent of Americans fell by 3.2 per cent, from 34.9 to 31.7. Three per cent, 3.5 per cent, sound like small numbers. But 3 per cent of the United States national income is not a trivial amount. We are talking about something like $200 billion that used to go to the worst-off three-fifths of the population, and now goes to the best-off fifth . . . Over the whole period since the late 1970s, the United States economy has grown substantially in real terms. Over the same period, the income of the average American has hardly grown; only in the late 1980s did it climb back to its 1973 level.[16]

The stagnant incomes of the majority in America's 'winner-take-all' capitalism[17] are not the inevitable by-product of technological innovation. Comparisons with no less technologically developed economies suggest strongly that they are the result of public policies. According to well-researched estimates, in 1990 American CEOs earned roughly 150 times the average worker's salary, while in Japan the figure was 16 and in Germany 21.[18]

These inequalities are the result of American policies, not of pressures which all advanced societies confront. Tax cuts have been direct in their impact; but fiscal measures have also affected income and wealth distribution. As Michael Lind has noted: 'Unlike any other democracy in the First World, the United States since Reagan has treated massive borrowing, rather than taxation, as a more or less permanent method of financing government expenditures in peacetime.'[19] This policy of heavy borrowing further tilted the balance in favour of those who possess financial assets and against ordinary wage-earners.

Such policies have left the United States standing out alone with a distribution of income and wealth that resembles the Philippines or Brazil more than it does any of the world's other major economies. Even in post-communist Russia levels of inequality may be lower.[20]

The distinguished American banker and financial commentator, Felix Rohatyn, has summarized the process the US is undergoing: 'What is occurring is a huge transfer of wealth from lower skilled, middle class American workers to the owners of capital assets and to a new technological aristocracy with a large element of compensation tied to stock values.'[21] In America today the wage-earner takes second place to the coupon-clipper. Did the American voters who elected and then re-elected Ronald Reagan understand that the result of his tax and fiscal policies would be a Latin American-style *rentier* regime in the United States?

The United States today is not the paradigm 'post-historical' society of which Francis Fukuyama speaks. It is entering a new and intractable period in its history, in which old enmities among races and classes will be expressed in ways we cannot foresee.

America's great incarceration

American crime rates have always been higher than in most European countries. What is new is the recourse in the United States to a policy of mass imprisonment as a surrogate for the controls of communities which unregulated market forces have weakened or destroyed. At the same time, affluent Americans are withdrawing in ever larger numbers from cohabitation with their fellow citizens into gated proprietary communities. Some 28 million American – over 10 per cent of the population – now live in privately guarded buildings or housing developments.[22]

At the end of 1994, just over 5 million Americans were under some form of legal restraint. According to Department of Justice figures, around a million and a half of them were in jail – state, federal or local. That means one in 193 adult Americans is a prisoner, or 373 out of every 100,000 Americans. That compares with 103 per 100,000 when Ronald Reagan became President in 1980. Three and a half million Americans were on probation or parole.[23]

The US incarceration rate at the end of 1994 was four times that of Canada, five times that of Britain, and fourteen times that of Japan.

Only post-communist Russia had a larger proportion of its citizens behind bars.[24] In California, around 150,000 people are in jail. The Californian jail population is now eight times the level it reached in the early 1970s. It exceeds that of Britain and Germany combined.[25]

By the start of 1997 around one in fifty adult American males was behind bars and about one in twenty was on parole or probation. This is ten times the rate in European countries.[26]

The rate of incarceration varies considerably across the American population. In 1995 around 7 per cent of America's Black population spent some time in jail.[27] Blacks are approximately seven times likelier than Whites to be imprisoned. One in seven Black men has been imprisoned at some point in his life. In 1992 over 40 per cent of all Black males between eighteen and thirty-five years of age living in the District of Columbia were in prison, on probation, on parole awaiting trial, or on the run.[28]

Such figures suggest that race and class inequalities are now intertwined in the United States in ways that resemble some Latin American countries.[29] They support Michael Lind's characterization of Brazilianization in America: 'The chief danger confronting the twenty-first century United States is not Balkanization but what might be called Brazilianization. By Brazilianization I mean not the separation of cultures by race, but the separation of races by class.'[30]

The extraordinarily high rate at which the United States imprisons Black males has consequences that have gone unnoticed by America's ranters for family values. One of the chief causes of single-parenthood in the inner cities is the absence of fathers who have been incarcerated. How can the family be revived in America's inner cities when a large part of the male population is in jail for much of its life?

In part, no doubt, America's puritan 'war on drugs' is to blame. Around 400,000 of the burgeoning prison population in the US are drug violators, many of them Black. At the same time, drug use in the US is more endemic and less controlled than in any developed country. The connections between mass incarceration, family breakdown, the drug war and racial enmity in the US are many and deep-rooted. It may well be too late for them to be disentangled.[31]

The confluence of ethnic and economic divisions and antagonisms in the United States is not found in any other First World country. The free market has produced a mutation in American capitalism, as a consequence of which it is coming to resemble the oligarchical regimes

of some Latin American countries more than the liberal capitalist civilization of Europe or the United States itself in earlier phases of its
history.

America's incarceration rates run parallel with its rates of violent
crime. Take its figures for homicide and gun-related crimes. As of
1993, the male homicide rate was 12.4 per 100,000, compared with 1.6
for the European Union and less than one (0.9) for Japan.[32] In 1994,
0.98 out of 100,000 in Japan were murder victims compared with 9.3
Americans, while for rape the figures were 1.5 in Japan and 42.8 in the
US. With regard to robbery, there were 1.75 cases per 100,000 in
Japan, and 255.8 in the United States.[33]

For all crimes of violence apart from homicide American levels are
considerably higher than those of post-communist Russia. In 1993, for
every 100,000 people there were 264 robberies (as against 124 in
Russia), 442 assaults (compared with 27 in Russia) and 43 rapes (by
comparison with 9.7 in Russia).[34] However, in an ominous development, levels of property crime in Britain have recently surpassed those
in the US, though the US remains far ahead of all other advanced
western countries in its levels of lethal violence.

Murders of children are especially common in the United States.
Nearly three-quarters of all murders of children in the industrialized
world occur in the US. The US has by far the highest rates of child-
hood suicide, homicide and firearms-related deaths of any of the
world's twenty-six richest countries.[35]

Part of the explanation lies in America's incorrigible gun culture.
Part comes from the fact that the economic redundancy of the family
has left more children unsupervised than in other countries. In 1987
infant mortality in East Harlem and Washington DC was roughly the
same as that in Malaysia, Yugoslavia and the former Soviet Union.[36]
A baby born in Shanghai in 1995 was less likely to die in its first year
of life, more likely to learn how to read, and could expect to live two
years longer (seventy-six years) than an infant born in New York.[37]

High rates of crime and incarceration in the US go in tandem with
equally exceptional levels of litigation and numbers of lawyers.
America has at least one-third of the world's practising lawyers. In
1991 there were around 700,000 lawyers in the United States, with a
figure of around 850,000 being projected for the turn of the century.
At present there are over 300 lawyers per 100,000 Americans, as compared with 12 per 100,000 in Japan, just over a hundred per 100,000 in

Britain and just under a hundred per 100,000 in Germany.[38] Tort liability payments accounted for about 2.5 per cent of American GNP in 1987, and for about eight times less (0.3) in Japan.[39]

These figures on incarceration, violent crime and litigation portray a society in which the law has become almost the only functioning social institution and prisons among the few remaining means of social control.

The private, gated communities whose high walls and electronic security devices protect their inmates from the dangers of the society they have deserted are a mirror image of America's prisons. They stand as a symbol of the hollowing-out of other social institutions – the family, the neighbourhood, even the business corporation – that in the past supported a functioning society. The combination of high-tech prisons, walled-off proprietary communities and virtual corporations may come to be recognized as an emblem of early twenty-first-century America.

In late twentieth-century America, the free market has become the engine of a perverse modernity. The prophet of today's America is not Jefferson or Madison. Still less is it Burke. It is Jeremy Bentham, the nineteenth-century British Enlightenment thinker who dreamed of a hyper-modern society that had been reconstructed on the model of an ideal prison.

Why history hasn't ended

Today, as in the past, American thought is pervaded by a sense of the novelty of the American condition. Yet, with only a few exceptions, it fails to grasp what is really new in the circumstances of the United States today.

America persists in identifying modernity throughout the world in relation to itself – at a time when in East Asia modernization is advancing swiftly by repudiating or ignoring the American model. It sees itself as the paradigm of 'western civilization' at just the moment when its resemblances to other 'western' societies are weaker than they have ever been.

The most influential of recent contributions to thinking about America's place in the late modern world do not track the contours of the world in which the United States must now navigate. This is true of

Francis Fukuyama's vision of the end of history and Samuel Huntington's thesis of the class of civilizations. Both are incorrigibly Americocentric, purveying a view of the world that is unrecognizable to the majority of Asians and Europeans. Fukuyama's claim that 'democratic capitalism' constitutes the 'final form of human government' and its global reach 'the triumph of the Western idea'[40] was confounded by a turn of events that many of his critics in Europe and Asia had anticipated. After the conflict between Enlightenment ideologies was over the world returned to the classical terrain of history.[41]

Fukuyama was able to argue that history had ended because he had modelled large-scale historical conflicts on twentieth-century rivalries between ideologies. But this is an unthinking generalization from a brief historical period. At most, political ideology has been a major source of social and military conflict between 1789 and 1989. This was the epoch, extending from the French Revolution to the Soviet collapse, in which wars were fought – or at least justified – by invoking the rival political religions that sprang from the European Enlightenment. In any more extended or fine-grained historical perspective, however, few wars have ever been occasioned chiefly by ideological antagonisms.

Throughout nearly all of human history, wars have arisen from territorial and dynastic conflicts, from religious and ethnic enmities, and from the divergent economic interests pursued by sovereign states. This was the case even in the Age of Enlightenment between 1789 and 1989. Conflicts between Turks and Armenians in the nineteenth century, between Catholics and Protestants in Ireland in the 1920s and over the past thirty years, between Greeks and Turks in Cyprus in the 1960s, along with many others throughout the world, were in no sense ideological. They were struggles over territory and religion, ethnicity and economic advantage.

It was only in the forty-odd years of the Cold War – and then only intermittently and partially – that ideological differences were major sources of conflict among states. When the Cold War ended so did the role of ideology as an occasion of war. But that meant only that much older sources of war and conflict returned with undiminished force. As had always been true before the Cold War, so in its aftermath, wars were fought for reasons of territory, ethnicity and religion.

To think that history would end because a conflict between ephemeral Enlightenment ideologies had come to a close exhibits a parochialism that is hard to credit. It is a telling mark of the condition of intellectual and political life towards the end of the century that such absurd speculations could ever have seemed credible.

Fukuyama conflated modernization with westernization. Consider the historic event that, more than any other, evoked his hubristic triumphalism. The Soviet collapse was the rejection of a *western* project – the Marxian project of economic modernization through central economic planning. It did not signify Russian acceptance of another western modernist ideology – the neo-liberal creed of privatization and free markets.

Nor has the Chinese market reform been motivated by any impulse to copy western models or absorb western values. It has always been an indigenously Chinese development owing little, if anything, to western advice or example. Indeed, market reform in China has necessitated a retreat from the westernizing Marxian model of economic and political development that was applied in the Maoist period. In China, as in many other parts of the world, modernizing the economy has not gone with westernization of society or government. It has been accompanied by a blossoming of indigenous capitalism and repudiation of western influence.

Fukuyama's interpretation of recent world history is plausible only if one believes that the world is insensibly approximating the American condition; and that the United States is the exemplary 'post-historical' society in which the traditional sources of conflict are withering away. In Europe and Asia such claims are commonly received with incredulous contempt.

For observers outside the United States, as indeed for many Americans, it is obvious that the historical sources of social and political conflict – racial, ethnic and religious divisions, for example – are present in abundance in late twentieth-century America.

'The clash of civilizations' versus the evanescence of 'the West'

Samuel Huntington's thesis of the clash of civilizations[42] recognizes that modernization and westernization are today not converging but diverging trends.

For Huntington, it is the fault lines between civilizations and not the divergent interests of states that will shape the conflicts of the post-Cold War world. As he puts it: 'The rivalry of superpowers is replaced by the clash of civilizations. In this new world the most pervasive, important and dangerous conflicts will not be between social classes, rich and poor, or other economically defined groups, but between peoples belonging to different cultural entities . . . And the most dangerous cultural conflicts are those along the fault lines of civilizations.'[43] The end of the Cold War, Huntington rightly holds, means the end of secular ideologies as a major source of international conflict. His inference from this fact is that in future 'civilizational conflicts' will be the major source of war.

Huntington's thesis that clashes of civilizations are the chief source of wars has many incidental difficulties. The 'civilizations' that make up the world today are not easily identified. It is hard to know where Latin America figures in his account; the Jews are consigned, after some hesitation, to an appendix of 'the West'; contemporary Greece is categorized as not belonging to 'western civilization'; the ancient, far-flung and long literate civilization of Tibet is written off – because, perhaps, it has no future in contemporary China. It is difficult to find principled justifications for these judgements.

There are several other examples of categorizations which are arbitrary or anomalous. Huntington's taxonomy of civilizations is not entirely confident. He appears to believe that there are in the world today between six and nine civilizations: Sinic (Chinese), Japanese, Hindu, Islamic, Western, Latin American, Buddhist, Orthodox and African.

Huntington has doubts about whether some of these cultures merit the honorific title of civilization. The criteria that must be met for membership of that exclusive club are unclear. For the most part the criterion he tacitly invokes reflects his American obsession with multiculturalism: a people or a culture is a civilization if it is politically active as an American minority. Otherwise it is ignored.

Even if his taxonomy were accepted, Huntington's claim that wars in our time are conflicts between 'civilizational groups' does not square with the evidence. The 'human waves' of footsoldiers who perished in the Iraq–Iran war died in a conflict that occurred within a single 'civilization'. The genocide of Tutsis by Hutus was 'intra-civilizational', as was that in Pol Pot's Cambodia. Huntington might reply that these were local conflicts, whereas the civilizational clashes he is describing are global.

Yet the First World War is well described as a European civil war. The Korean War and the Vietnam War were not civilizational conflicts; they were strategic engagements between states all of which justified their claims by invoking 'western' ideologies. In the Second World War, 'western countries' such as Britain and the US were allied with an 'Orthodox' country, the USSR, against another 'western' state, Nazi Germany. Such examples are easily found.

Now, as in the past, wars are commonly waged between peoples of different nationalities or ethnicities, not between members of different 'civilizations'. Whether wars are waged by sovereign states or by irregular militias, the logic of military competition often compels alliances that bring together different 'civilizations'. In the conflict between Armenia and Azerbaijan, Iran has thrown in its lot with Christian Armenia, not with Islamic Azerbaijan. The Byzantine kaleidoscope of shifting alliances in the Balkans and Central Asia offers no support to Huntington's grand simplifications.

As Robert Kaplan has shrewdly commented: 'Huntington's hypothesized war between Islam and Orthodox Christianity is not borne out by the alliance network in the Caucasus. But that is only because he has misidentified which civilizational war is occurring there. Azeri Turks, perhaps the world's most secular Shi'ite Muslims, see their cultural identity not in terms of religion but in terms of their Turkic race. The Armenians, likewise, fight the Azeris not because the latter are Moslems, but because they are Turks, related to the same Turks who massacred Armenians in 1915.'[44]

Huntington's taxonomy of civilizations not only fails to correspond with cultural realities, it also fails to map onto most actual wars. Even so, this is not the chief objection to his account. The division of humanity into clashing civilizations has radical shortcomings that a more historically nuanced application of it could not have avoided. A division of peoples and cultures into competing civilizations belongs with the Enlightenment interpretation of history that Huntington is attacking.

The idea of 'civilization' presupposes that all 'civilized' societies are tokens of a single type. They are all embodiments of a single scheme of values whose opposite is 'barbarism'. This was the view of the main thinkers of the Enlightenment in all its different expressions:

French (Condorcet, Diderot, Voltaire), German (Kant, Marx), Scottish (Hume, Smith, Ferguson), English (Bentham, John Stuart Mill) and American (Thomas Jefferson, Benjamin Franklin). It was this idea that the chief critics of the Enlightenment, above all J. G. Herder, sought to replace with the concept of an irreducible diversity of human cultures.

Herder and other thinkers of the Counter-Enlightenment[45] used the notion of a fundamental diversity of cultures to attack the vehicle through which the idea of a universal civilization was at that time being propagated – French cultural imperialism. It is a criticism of Enlightenment universalism that is no less salient today, when the United States has succeeded to the role that France and England once occupied.

The late twentieth-century reality – America versus the rest

Huntington attacks the Enlightenment conception of universal values. It was this simple-minded view that underpinned the Enlightenment dualism of civilization and barbarism. It suggested that all civilized people have the same basic values and want the same things.

We need not endorse 'relativism' in order to reject this delusion. Contrary to relativists,[46] there are evils and goods that are universally human. Security from violent death, or from starvation, are not 'goods' that are culturally variable. Moreover, there are ethical and aesthetic standards that enable us to identify high achievement across cultures. Homer's *Iliad* is a greater cultural achievement than the screenplay of *Silence of the Lambs*, even as the Zen temple at Ryoanji is superior to a drive-in church. But the reality of universal goods and bads does not mean that one political and economic system – 'democratic capitalism', say – is the best for all humankind. Universal human values can be embodied in a variety of regimes.

It is common sense that some societies do better than others in economic, educational and cultural terms. Yet there is nothing to suggest that 'western' cultures are always at the top of the league. American neo-conservatives who rail against the contemporary belief that all cultures are equal do so in the innocent belief that theirs is the best.

Huntington is little less Americocentric. He criticizes the universalism that is the tacit foundation of nearly all American thinking; but he remains firmly within the dualist, sometimes Manichean tradition that has long informed American foreign policy. His argument follows the Enlightenment's bipolar classification of cultures into civilized and barbaric. It divides the world into two, 'the West and the rest'. 'The West' is one; 'the rest' are many.

Western civilization is not universal but, according to Huntington, it is unique. It has a single identity that persists over long periods of time and spans many countries. This unique 'western' identity is, he says, at risk today. He tells us that 'the principal responsibility of western leaders . . . is to preserve, protect and renew the unique qualities of Western civilization. Because it is the most powerful Western country, that responsibility falls overwhelmingly on the United States of America.'[47] The US should do this, he advises, by nurturing the 'Atlantic civilization' that unites the societies of North America and western Europe through such devices as a Transatlantic Free Trade Area (TAFTA).

If this is not done the future he foresees is bleak. 'The peoples of the West,' he warns darkly 'must hang together, or most assuredly they will hang separately.'[48]

Yet today the very idea of 'western civilization' is questionable. 'The West' may have had reality when it meant western Christendom – though the wars of the Reformation were among the worst in history. It had some cultural purchase when both America and Europe could be regarded as descendants of a common Enlightenment project, but these historic affinities are waning fast. In present circumstances, discourse about 'the West' is a symptom of intellectual lag. It harks back to the strategic solidarity between western Europe and the United States that was forged during the Second World War and the Cold War.

In the aftermath of the Cold War, however, the relationship between the United States and Europe has more in common with that between the Wars, when America was seen to be – and saw itself as – *sui generis*. The grandiose American-led project of NATO enlargement echoes the Wilsonian reconstruction of Europe after the First World War. There is now no 'western civilization' of which the United States could be leader. The uniqueness to which Huntington refers is not that of 'the West'; it is that of the United States.

Consider one of the components of western civilization to which Huntington refers: religion. Now, whereas most European countries are post-Christian, the United States remains a country of wide-spread, intense and often fundamentalist religiosity. It is not only that church-going and avowed religious belief remain far higher than in any other western country, it is that very many Americans retain religious beliefs and practices that have become marginal practically everywhere else. Just under 70 per cent of Americans believe in the devil, compared with a third of the British, a fifth of the French and an eighth of the Swedes. Around a quarter of Americans are born-again Christians for whom diabolical possession is not a metaphor but literal reality.

Robert Mapplethorpe – the gifted photographer whose sado-masochistic studies caused something of a stir in the United States in the early 1990s – exhorted his photographic subjects to 'do it for Satan'. In any European country, Mapplethorpe's incantation would have raised questions about his psychological balance. In the United States it evoked a real cultural presence.

In the depth and extent of its religiosity the United States stands alone among advanced countries. Every one of the fifty state governments in the United States has agreed to accept federal funding to advance the absurd project of promoting sexual abstinence among American teenagers. In July 1997 the Christian Coalition sponsored in Congress a constitutional amendment that could make the teaching of creationism in American schools mandatory.[49] To refer to the United States as a secular society is preposterous. America's secular traditions are weaker than Turkey's.

As Lipset has pointed out, this difference between the United States and every other advanced country is widening, not narrowing: 'The strength of American religion shows no sign of weakening. Polls by Gallup and others . . . indicate that Americans are the most church-going in Protestantism and the most fundamentalist in Christendom . . . In 1991, 68 per cent of the adult population belonged to a church and 42 per cent attended services weekly, much higher ratios than in any other industrialized nation.'[50]

America's exceptional religiosity has been noted by many observers since de Tocqueville. Its persistence and increasing strength today suggest that the standard social-scientific model which we inherit from the social thinkers of the European Enlightenment, in which modernization develops in tandem with secularization, is radically flawed. The United States does not fit the model of a modern society that has been inherited from the Enlightenment. Yet it is more pervaded by Enlightenment superstitions and illusions than any other late modern culture.

The 'American Creed' makes the connection between America and modernity essential, not accidental. Today that creed has been high-jacked by the neo-conservative ascendancy. The resistance of the world to being made over as a universal free market endangers not only the conservative hegemony in the US but also the American worldview which it has appropriated. The discovery that America's path is a singularity that in no sense plots the course of universal history in the modern world will be a catalyst for large cultural changes. Its effect must be to strip the United States of its self-image as the paradigm of modernity.

It is partly the inveterate universalism of American culture that accounts for the sectarian intensity of its debates about 'multiculturalism'. In the longer and larger history of the species, multicultural societies are the common condition of humankind. All the world's empires – such as the Roman, Chinese, Ottoman, Romanov, British and Hapsburg empires – encompassed a copious diversity of cultures. Each had a dominant culture, and at times some had universalist goals; but none of them ever consistently attempted to convert their subjects to a single way of life or set of beliefs.

When an American Right-wing foundation gave a large sum of money to an Ivy League university to spend on courses on 'western civilization' it was distressed to find, some years later, that it had not been spent. The reason was that university faculty members could not agree on what constituted 'western civilization'. It seems to have occurred to neither party that their difficulty could be resolved by spending the money on feminism or multiculturalism. For, like many other late modern social movements, these are – in their most radical and sectarian manifestations – peculiarly American phenomena. If such radical social movements do not belong to 'American civilization', nothing does.

A characteristic American blind-spot in Huntington's account is his claim that universalism is immoral because it leads to imperialism. Yet empires may be, and often have been, multicultural; and imperialism may not be always immoral. It is only in the United States that these premises of Huntington's command unquestioned assent.

A more cogent objection to universalism is that it is incompatible with the mentality that is needed to sustain an imperial role in the world. Long-standing empires – the Ottomans, the Hapsburgs, the Romans – endured by legislating for cultural diversity. They did not attempt to make the world over in their own image, or not frame their policies in the faith that the world secretly reveres them. Yet neither Fukuyama's post-historical world order nor Huntington's western bloc is conceivable without a worldwide American imperial role.

In fact nothing is more alien to the American mind today than an imperial mentality. The American intervention in Bosnia was prompted by the belief that intractable political and military conflict can be resolved by the imposition of a cleverly contrived constitution. It expressed *the Dayton illusion*: that a short-lived American intervention can extend to other regimes and cultures American values and procedures – a legalist culture of rights and a model of negotiation between states and communities that derives from the practice of corporate law – whose authority is strictly local.

America's business and political classes are proceeding on the premise that they can project American values to the last corner of the earth – without incurring the casualties, or the expense, that usually go with empires. It is a curious presumption, which makes sense only if America's elites imagine that the United States has somehow exempted itself from the burdens that every imperial power throughout history has had to endure.

America as an emerging post-western nation

Huntington asserts that a major obstacle to the reassertion of American leadership of 'western civilization' is the refusal by a significant part of the American population to accept a 'western' identity. He tells the reader: 'The American multiculturalists . . . wish to create a country of many civilizations, which is to say a country not belonging to a civilization and lacking a cultural core. History shows that no country so constituted can long endure as a coherent society. A multicivilizational United States will not be the United States; it will be the United Nations.'[51]

Like political correctness, the excesses of multiculturalism are soft targets. The advance of ethnic exclusivism in late twentieth-century America – in the Black separatist movement led by Louis Farrakhan, for example – is an obstacle to the renewal of any kind of liberal civil society. At the same time it is an impediment to a coherent sense of national identity. If American multiculturalism means such projects of ethnic separatism, the fate of the United States will be to oscillate between an Enlightenment illusion of universality and the ugly realities of Balkanization.

Huntington ignores many past and present states that have been successfully multicultural for long periods. In the world today, the United Kingdom and Spain are reasonably coherent multinational states, while Australia, New Zealand, Singapore and Malaysia are stable multicultural societies. By no means all stable modern polities are monocultural. Nor are all modern states bound to become multicultural. Japan will remain a monocultural state in any foreseeable future.

The 'clash of civilizations' passes over large cultural shifts that are underway in the United States itself. It is no longer realistic to think of the US as an unequivocally 'western' society. There is much that points to its becoming, in a generation or so, one of the world's emerging post-western countries. Demographic trends suggest that in a generation or so there will be a near-majority of Asian, Black and Hispanic Americans. By the year 2050, according to the US Census Office, Hispanic Americans will outnumber the combined total of Blacks, Asian Americans and American Indians, and non-Hispanic Whites will have declined from 73.1 per cent of the population in 1996 to 52.8 per cent.[52]

As a consequence of these demographic changes the United States will differ sharply from other countries in the Americas, such as Chile and Argentina, that remain unambiguously European in their ethnic mix and cultural traditions. Why should we expect a population in which Americans of European descent are approaching a minority to accept European cultural and political traditions? Indeed, why should anyone think it desirable?

A population that is no longer predominantly European will produce political elites whose cultural affinities are no longer with the countries of Europe. This is a development that is already evident in the shifts within the American political classes that occurred with the passing of the Bush Presidency. The old, East Coast elites whose worldview was shaped by the Second World War and the Cold War and whose cultural allegiances were Atlanticist have become already politically marginal.

This does not mean that the loyalties of the new elites are Hispanic or Asian. On the whole they are becoming more indigenously American; but the American identity they embody is no longer a construct of an early modern European ideology. It is that of an emerging post-western nation.

Australia and New Zealand are perhaps the clearest exemplars of the transformation of former European colonies into post-western multicultural states. They are more successful multicultural societies than the United States, partly because they are not burdened by the illusion of a universal mission.

Is the American free market reformable?

America today is not the regime of democratic equality that de Tocqueville described and praised. Nor is it the society of expanding opportunities which the post-war New Deal embodied. It is a country riven by class conflicts, fundamentalist movements and low-intensity race wars. Political solutions to these ills presuppose reform of the free market. It is doubtful whether such reform is a real political possibility in America today.

In a political climate in which the ideals and policies of the New Deal have been delegitimated by the conservative ascendancy, issues of economic justice can arise only on the farther fringes of political life. Ross Perot, Ralph Nader and Pat Buchanan all traded on popular distrust of political elites. Each sought to mobilize voters' anxieties about the new economic inequalities in the United States to the benefit of his campaign.

It may be a portent for the future that only in the 1996 campaign of Pat Buchanan did issues of economic justice make a significant impact on mainstream American political life. Buchanan fused issues of economic fairness with a fundamentalist culture-war and nativist hostility to the rest of the world. Despite the populist appeal of such a combination he was swiftly marginalized – the likely fate of any similar campaign in future.

It remains doubtful whether manifest discontent among voters can evoke much of a response in the American political mainstream. Through lax regulation of campaign contributions, money has greater leverage in the United States than in any other western polity. What reason is there to suppose that such a political system can respond effectively to the discontents of an anxious majority? Yet a polity in which popular discontent is expressed chiefly in movements on the fringes of political life is not a functioning democracy.

The neo-conservative ascendancy has identified the free market with America's claim to be the exemplary modern nation. It has appropriated America's self-image as the model for a universal civilization in the service of a global free market. For a public nurtured on such illusions the coming years will be traumatic.

In the world's most successful economies the free market is an emblem of atavism, not a symbol of the future. The countries of East Asia are hugely different from one another, in their political institutions, economic systems and cultural traditions. What they have in common is a rejection of the quasi-religious attachment to free markets evinced in American policy and a repudiation of the enlightenment ideal of a universal civilization which the global free market embodies.

Servility to the dogmas of the free market cannot engender modernization as the twentieth century draws to a close. In the contest between the American free market and the guided capitalisms of East Asia it is the free market that belongs to the past.

The perception that countries which subscribe to none of the tenets of 'the American Creed' are surpassing the United States is too painful to enter into public consciousness. To accept that countries can achieve modernity without revering the folkways of individualism, bowing to the cult of human rights or sharing the Enlightenment superstition of progress towards a world civilization, is to admit that America's civil religion has been falsified.

For most Americans such a perception is intolerable. Instead, evidence of the superior economic growth, savings rates, educational standards and family stability of countries that have repudiated the American model will be repressed, denied and resisted indefatigably. To admit this evidence would be to confront the social costs of the American free market. The free market works to weaken social cohesion. Its productivity is prodigious; but so are its human costs. At present the costs of the free market are taboo subjects in American discourse; they are voiced only by a handful of sceptical liberals. If the fact that free markets and social stability are at odds could be admitted, the conflict between them would not thereby disappear, but it could perhaps be moderated.

The central dilemma of public policy today is how to reconcile the imperatives of deregulated markets with enduring human needs. By removing this question from the political agenda the neo-conservative ascendancy has denied America the chance of showing how the free market might be made more humanly tolerable. The 'American economic model' is not, in fact, entirely homogeneous. On the West Coast, some businesses may have succeeded in combining a high degree of flexibility with sensitivity to the human needs of their employees and of society. So long as the possibility that free markets can conflict with vital human needs is denied, this 'Californian model' cannot be properly assessed, still less emulated, in the rest of the United States.[53]

In the most likely scenario for the coming decades, the United States will preserve its self-image as a universal model by turning further inwards. It will filter out from its perceptions any that might disturb its confidence that the world is moving its way.

Yet America will not retreat into isolationism and protectionism. Too many corporate interests would be harmed by such a retreat. The increasing recourse to 'plantation production', in which manufacturing is sited in cheap-labour zones abroad, has produced a situation in which a fifth of all imports to the US originate from foreign subsidiaries of American multinational firms.[54] American capital will veto wholesale trade protection. In the coming years American isolation will not be economic or military; it will be cognitive and cultural.

The contemporary American faith that it is a universal nation implies that all humans are born American, and become anything else by accident – or error. According to this faith American values are, or will soon be, shared by all humankind. Of course such messianic fancies are commonplace. In the nineteenth century the claim to be a universal nation was made by France, Russia and England. Now, even more than in the past, it is a perilous conceit.

The United States has built the illusions and superstitions of the Enlightenment into its view of itself. In other times this might matter less. Today it threatens to render intractable the most difficult task of the age – that of contriving terms of peaceful and productive coexistence among peoples and regimes that will always be different.

6 Anarcho-capitalism in post-communist Russia

> The Bolsheviks . . . represent an alien philosophy of life, which cannot be forced upon the people without a change of instinct, habit, and tradition so profound as to dry up the vital springs of action, producing listlessness and despair among the ignorant victims of militant enlightenment.
>
> BERTRAND RUSSELL[1]

> With few exceptions Russian writers really despise the pettiness of the West. Even those who have admired Europe most have done so because they failed most completely to understand her. They do not want to understand her. That is why they have always taken over European ideas in such fantastic forms.
>
> L. SHESTOV[2]

Russia has been the site of two experiments in western utopianism during this century. The first was Bolshevism. In its earliest and most radical phase – War Communism – it produced deindustrialization and famine. It led to Stalin's 'revolution from above', in which the collectivization of agriculture destroyed peasant farming in Russia. The second was shock therapy. Implemented briefly in the aftermath of the Soviet collapse, shock therapy aimed to construct a free market in post-communist Russia. It produced instead a species of mafia-dominated anarcho-capitalism.

Both Utopian experiments had enormous human costs. Both were failed modernizations guided by western theories or models that had little relevance to Russia's history and circumstances.

Between 1918 and 1921 the Bolsheviks attempted to transform Russia into a communist economy. The War Communism which the Bolsheviks tried to impose on Russia during those years embodied an authentic Marxian vision. It aimed to abolish capitalism, in which private property, market exchange and the institution of money are central, and construct an economy that was collectively owned and rationally planned.

War Communism was consistent with some Russian traits, such as the hostility to commercial self-enrichment and the sense of the country's messianic role that have always been a feature of Russian Orthodox Christianity. Yet it was not a simple expression of Russian traditions. It waged war on the *mir*, the peasant community, and all the traditions of Russian peasant life; but in this it embodied a brutal modernization from above that had antecedents in the despotic westernization imposed by Peter the Great.

War Communism was inevitably conditioned by the paradoxes of Russian history; but its roots were in the European Enlightenment to which classical Marxism belonged.[3] Like the Great Leap Forward in China, War Communism was a western Utopia. It was not an expedient forced on the Bolsheviks by the exigencies of war but a Marxian embodiment of the Enlightenment project of a universal civilization.

In the aftermath of the Soviet collapse in 1991 another westernizing project was undertaken in Russia. Through policies of shock therapy implemented by Yegor Gaidar, the post-communist government of Boris Yeltsin attempted to follow the advice of transnational organizations and western advisers and transplant an American-style market economy in Russia.

Predictably, and indeed inevitably, the attempt failed. A new species of Russian capitalism emerged, different from any in the West and from those that have developed in other post-communist countries. Russia's future lies with this indigenous capitalism, not with the model that Gaidar, as the last of a long line of Russian westernizers, tried in 1992–3 vainly to impose on the country.

The policies of Yeltsin's government since the abandonment of shock therapy suggest that he and his advisers have recognized that modernization on the model of any western market economy is not feasible in Russia. Nor, perhaps, is it desirable.

In Russia today economic development and state-building are inseparable. They must go together if the bandit capitalism of the immediate post-communist period is to be outgrown. A modern state with effective institutions of enforcement is a precondition of sustainable modernization.

The modernity that Russia has yet to achieve cannot simply be that of a European nation. Inevitably, it will be that of a country having both European and Asian interests and traditions. Neither the economic nor the political institutions of any other country can be transplanted to the unique circumstances of post-communist Russia. Loose talk about Russia as a transitional state does not answer the only question that matters: transition to what?

The anarchic capitalism which replaced Soviet central planning is surely a developmental phase, not an endpoint in Russian economic development. But it is not evolving in the direction of any western economy. It is developing into a hybrid species of capitalism which increasingly resembles that of pre-revolutionary Russia. This is not the free market of recent western textbooks, but a capitalism in which extensive state intervention coexists with large areas of unregulated entrepreneurial activity.

If Russia does develop in this way it will be resuming an indigenous modernization, begun in the last decades of Tsarism, from which it was deflected by the First World War and seventy years of Soviet rule.

Soviet War Communism and post-communist shock therapy

As was true of the Soviet Union throughout its seventy-odd-year history, War Communism was an attempt to modernize Russia on a western model. Richard Pipes has written that 'War Communism as a whole was not a "temporary measure" but an ambitious, and as it turned out, premature attempt to introduce full-blown communism.'[4]

Like all utopias, War Communism required an unprecedented alteration in human nature before it could be established. As Figes has put it: 'the ultimate aim of the Communist system was the transformation of human nature. It was an aim shared by the other so-called totalitarian regimes of the inter-war period. This, after all, was an age of Utopian optimism in the potential of science to change human life . . . The Bolshevik programme was based on the ideals of the Enlightenment – it stemmed from Kant as much as from Marx – which makes Western liberals, even in this age of post-modernism, sympathize with it.'[5]

Lenin recognized that War Communism was a Utopia. The Bolsheviks, he observed, were engineers of souls. In his Utopian blueprint *State and Revolution* he envisaged a communist society in which there was no army and no police force and all remaining state functions could be performed by anyone. In the short run it might be necessary to retain some of the practices of capitalism. In the longer run, a rational economy would be moneyless, propertyless, stateless and yet centrally planned.

Lenin thought these were attainable goals. In this he followed Marx and was endorsed by Trotsky. Through his advocacy of the 'militarization of labour', Trotsky was one of the chief architects of War Communism. Equally, Stalin returned to a version of War Communism after the Bolsheviks' brief experiment with markets in the New Economic Policy. The core of the Soviet system was always the certainty that human beings must be reshaped to fit the needs of a new, 'rational' economy. The thought that the economy exists to serve the needs of human beings was dismissed.

From the first, Soviet Communism emulated the techniques of efficient management of the most advanced capitalist societies. Lenin sought to implement 'Taylorism' – the American engineer F. W. Taylor's theories of 'scientific management'.[6] Taylorism used piecework and time-and-motion studies in an effort to remould the psychology of the worker – a vision satirized in the Russian writer Zamyatin's anti-Utopian novel *We*.[7]

Bolshevik doctrine required human beings to function as resources of the economy. It deployed 'managerial science' in an effort to engineer far-reaching alterations in human psychology. The similarities of Bolshevik social engineering with the doctrine and practice of free marketeers the world over today are instructive.

In Russia – as in Cambodia, Romania, China and the early years of Castro's Cuba – the attempt to construct an economic system from which market exchange had been removed was a path to disaster. By destroying prices it left no means whereby anyone – whether state planning boards or managers of enterprises – could assess relative costs and scarcities. Worse, it removed any incentive to workers to direct their efforts where they were most needed. In turn, that made a recourse to coercion unavoidable.

As Figes has put it, 'Without the stimulus of the market, which they still rejected on ideological grounds, the Bolsheviks had no means to influence the workers apart from the threat of force . . . This was the basis of the militarization of heavy industry: strategic factories would be placed under martial law, with military discipline on the shop-floor and persistent absentees shot for desertion on the "industrial front".[8]

The rejection of market exchange as the central organizing practice of a modern economy leads inexorably to heavy reliance on state coercion. The human costs of that Utopia have included millions of deaths and broken lives beyond counting. Its economic benefits have proved slight, speculative or illusory. Those who suffered or died because of the Soviet project did so for nothing.

Pipes summarizes the course of Soviet War Communism: 'In its mature form, which it attained only in the winter of 1920–1, War Communism involved a number of sweeping measures designed to place the entire economy of Russia – its labour force as well as its productive capacity and distribution mechanism – under the exclusive management of the state.' These measures included far-reaching nationalization, the liquidation of private commerce, the elimination of money as a unit of exchange and accounting, the imposition of a single comprehensive economic plan, and the introduction of compulsory labour.[9]

War Communism failed in all its objectives. According to Marxian theory, communist economic organization would be far more productive than capitalism had ever been. Yet the actual result of the radical measures implemented during the period of War Communism was a massive drop in industrial production.

'The narrowly economic objective of Soviet industrial policies under War Communism was, of course, to raise productivity. Statistical evidence, however, demonstrates that the effect of these policies was precisely the contrary . . . under War Communism, the Russian "Proletariat" fell by one-half, industrial output by three quarters, and industrial productivity by 70 per cent.' Pipes concludes that 'Utopian programs, which Lenin had approved, had all but destroyed Russian industry and decimated Russia's working classes'.[10]

The upshot of War Communism was a long step backwards. Russia – which before the First World War had been one of the world's fastest growing economies – was deindustrialized. Agriculture too was heavily set back. War Communism contributed to the famine of 1921–2 through its policies of requisitioning grain from peasants. Even when in 1921 Lenin relaxed the policy of requisitioning he clung to the Utopian project of abolishing market exchange in agricultural products: 'In abandoning grain requisitioning, Lenin clung compulsively to the hope that he could avoid granting freedom of trade, that he would not have to allow the market to sully the purity of communist relations . . . Utopianism died hard. But reality proved stronger.'[11] By the time Lenin altered the policy of requisitioning the threat of famine was already clear. According to Soviet sources the famine claimed over 5 million lives.[12]

War Communism was abandoned. In 1921 the Bolsheviks were compelled to appeal for international aid, as a result of which 'at one stage, the American Relief Administration and other foreign aid organizations were feeding over 10 million mouths'.[13] There was a workers' rebellion in Kronstadt, and the New Economic policy was introduced. Lasting until around 1926–7, it restored market exchange, particularly in agricultural products. As Becker comments, NEP was introduced by Lenin 'to create a breathing space for the Party, replacing grain requisitioning with taxes and reopening food markets as part of a massive retreat from the moneyless and propertyless Utopia he had tried to create after 1918'.[14]

The great famines which Russia suffered later (such as the famine of 1932–3) came not from the attempt to socialize industry but from the collectivization of agriculture. Like War Communism, the Soviet collectivization of farming was a direct application of Marxian doctrine. Both Marx himself and Georgi Plekhanov, the first great Russian Marxist thinker, believed the future of agriculture demanded the industrialization of farming and the eradication of peasant traditions.

Marx saw the future of agriculture as a development of nineteenth-century industry in which peasant small-holdings would be replaced by gigantic factory farms. In part this was because Marx took the nineteenth-century capitalist factory as his model of the rational organization of production; but it also followed from his belief that society could not be socialist until most of its members were industrial proletarians.

The Marxian dogma that farming must be industrialized was the core of the Bolshevik project of modernizing Russia. The effect of collectivization and 'dekulakization' (the elimination of the richer peasantry) was that traditions of peasant farming in Russia were virtually destroyed. Some of the skills of farming survived in the small private plots on which the survival of ordinary people, in the period of post-communist shock therapy as in that of Soviet collectivization, often depended. Yet the price of the Bolshevik policy of forcing Russia to accept a modernization modelled on nineteenth-century European industrial development was to weaken permanently its capacity to feed itself.

According to Conquest's estimates, between 1930 and 1937, 11 million peasants died in the Soviet Union and a further 3.5 million perished in the Gulag.[15] Ellman has calculated that between 7 and 8 million people died of starvation in the USSR in 1933.[16] The outcome was the same, though on an even larger scale, when Mao used Soviet agricultural collectivization as his model for modernizing China.

In the last decade of Tsarism another road to modernization had been taken. In a law enacted on 9 November 1906, the reformist Prime Minister, P. A. Stolypin, had freed peasants from obligations to their communes and entitled them to apply for a share in them, which was to be held as private property. As a result, between 1906 and 1916, just under a quarter of the peasant households of European Russia filed petitions to assume private ownership of their allotments.

There is considerable controversy about the effects of Stolypin's reforms. Whether they could have prevented revolution in Russia if Stolypin had not been assassinated in 1911, and the First World War had not deflected Tsarist Russia from further reforms, cannot be certain. Yet it is clear that, unlike War Communism and agricultural collectivization, Stolypin's reforms promoted a modernization that fitted with many of Russia's distinctive needs and circumstances.

Both War Communism and collectivization expressed the same Marxian project, which was to construct an economy in which market exchange had been eliminated. Notwithstanding episodes such as the New Economic Policy in the 1920s and Gorbachev's *perestroika*, and despite the black markets that were endemic within it throughout its history, that project animated the Soviet Union for as long as it existed.[17]

From the start of the Soviet regime until its close it was embarked upon a doomed project of modernizing Russia on a western, Marxian model. This is not to deny that there was sometimes support among Russians for the project. Indeed such support may have been strongest during the worst, Stalinist times. It is perverse to argue, as Alexander Zinoviev has done, that Stalinism was an exercise of popular power; but it is true of some of the worst atrocities of Stalinism, as of the Chinese Cultural Revolution, that they could not have occurred with the active collaboration of ordinary people.[18]

Yet the *raison d'être* of the Soviet state throughout its existence was a modernization whose origins and objectives were unambiguously 'western'. In the first biography of Lenin to make use of the archives that have become available since the Soviet collapse, Volkongonov comments that 'War Communism . . . was the basis and essence of Lenin's Policy, and only its total collapse forced him to grab the lifebelt of NEP. War Communism . . . did not completely die, but survived in various forms even until the end of the 1980s.'[19] The Bolshevik project which the Soviet system embodied throughout its history was that of imposing a western modernity on Russia, but without capitalism.

The effect of this project was to derail the indigenous modernization begun in late Tsarism. One of the principal Soviet bequests to Russia's post-communist government was an agricultural economy in ruins. Because Russia is now an urban society its dwindling rural population lives in isolation as well as poverty. Between 1991 and 1995 its numbers fell from 38.5 million to 35 million, as those who could escaped to the cities. Harvests have shrunk, with the 1996 harvest just over that in 1995 – itself the worst for thirty years.[20]

Soviet grain production never matched that achieved in late Tsarist times, but maintaining Soviet production has proved an unattainable goal for post-communist Russia. Ill-conceived land privatization schemes have only added to the hardships of rural workers for whom peasant capitalism is not even a memory. If collectivization created a rural proletariat in Russia, 'forced decollectivization' has produced a rural underclass.

The thinking that inspired market reform in Russia differs from Leninism in the economic system that it aimed to install. But its consequences in human suffering and economic devastation have been in some ways strikingly alike.

Like the Utopia envisaged by Lenin, the global free market aims to bring into being a state of affairs that has never hitherto existed in human society – and which goes far beyond the mid-Victorian English free market and the liberal international economic order that existed until 1914. In a global free market the movements of goods, services and capital are unfettered by political controls imposed by any sovereign state, and markets have been detached from their original societies and cultures. This is a Utopia divorced from history, hostile to vital human needs, and finally as self-destroying as any that has been attempted in our century.

Global *laissez-faire* does not require totalitarian regimes. It does not extend the state so as to incorporate all other institutions but reduces it to its most narrowly repressive functions. Many of the functions of social control are devolved to markets, which mould public opinion and shape consumer preferences.

The global free market is a post-totalitarian Utopia. It requires the exercise of force chiefly at the peripheries of its power, and in the early stages of its construction.

Both the Soviet system and the free market are experiments in economic rationalism. Free marketeers tell us that the unprecedented productivity of a rational economic system will remove the causes of social conflict and war. Soviet Marxists used to assure us that socialist planning would make scarcity a thing of the past. Both tell us that rising productivity will of itself solve most social problems, both exalt economic growth over all other goals and values.

Like the Bolsheviks, the shock troops of the free market are resolutely hostile to any tradition that stands in the way of what they view as economic progress. If their goals demand the sacrifice of a few cultures on the way, it is a price which free marketeers do not shrink from paying.

Global *laissez-faire* and the communist project that animated the former Soviet Union have many of the same enemies. They are hostile to national and cultural differences in economic life and to the inheritances of tradition and history. They resent the backwardness of peasants and village life. They are intolerant of the unruly individualism of the bourgeoisie and the refractoriness of working people.

The chief victims of the global free market, as of War Communism and the Soviet system, are peasants and – to a lesser but still notable extent – urban industrial workers and the professional middle classes.

Shock therapy: another western Utopia

To be used as a testing ground for western utopias seems to be Russia's fate in the twentieth century. Soviet communism was such a Utopia, but so were Gorbachev's reforms and the policies of shock therapy which followed the Soviet collapse.[21]

The Soviet system which Gorbachev sought to renew was not reformable. It lacked political legitimacy in Russia and in the 'near abroad' of the Soviet nationalities. Outside its enormous military sector, the Soviet economy worked only insofar as it sheltered black and grey markets. The Brezhnev 'era of stagnation' was, for some people in some regions of the Soviet Union, an era of boom, since it institutionalized corruption and so enabled market exchange to flourish.

Gorbachev's reform programme began as an anti-corruption campaign. Its main aim was an 'acceleration' (*uskoriniye*) of the economy. Among its first results was an economic slowdown, followed by collapse. The Soviet system of central planning could not function without the markets it condemned as criminal.

The policies of shock therapy that were imposed in the wake of the Soviet regime were, in part, simply a recognition that the former economic system had comprehensively collapsed. But they were also an attempt to rebuild Russia on the model of yet another western Utopia. They were policies that had achieved some of their objectives in other countries, though they proved to be unworkable in Russia.

By the time shock therapy was applied in late 1991 a gradual transition from central planning was impossible. The old Soviet economy had already largely disintegrated. Gorbachev's policies of structural reform of the economy (*perestroika*) and political liberalization (*glasnost*) had produced chaos. Not only the central planning institutions but much of the apparatus of the Soviet state had fallen apart. The machinery for a programme of gradual reform was lacking. A phased dismantling of the old institutions and policies was not among the options of Russia's first post-communist government.

Boris Yeltsin's principal inheritance from Mikhail Gorbachev was the impossibility of gradualism. The chief constituency for Gorbachev's reforms was always among opinion-formers in western countries; in the former Soviet Union *perestroika* evoked ridicule and contempt.

So manifestly unrealizable were Gorbachev's reforms that by the summer of 1989 it was clear to a western observer that the Soviet Union had reached a pre-revolutionary condition: 'what we are witnessing in the Soviet Union is not the middle of a reform, but the beginnings of a revolution, whose course no one can foretell.'[22]

Gorbachev's policies had revealed a system whose legitimacy was so slight that even those who most benefited from it, the communist nomenklatura, were unwilling to resort to repression to defend it. Uniquely, a vast empire with a terrible history of repression ceased to exist without significant violence on the part of either the rulers or the ruled. When the coup launched against Gorbachev on 19–21 August 1991 proved abortive it was evident that the new, post-Soviet era was irreversible.[23]

The appointment in November 1991 of Yegor Gaidar to oversee Russia's transition to a market economy showed that Yeltsin understood that reform in a series of orderly sequences was no longer – if it ever had been – a possibility. Some kind of shock therapy – swift, radical and far-reaching measures rather than piecemeal, incremental reforms – was unavoidable.

Yet the models on which Russian shock therapy was based – the successful control of inflation in some Latin American countries and the emulation of that success in post-communist Poland – had little application in Russia. The longevity of the communist regime in Russia and the enormous size of its military-industrial complex, accounting for around a third of GDP,[24] were unique. More generally, the weakness in Russia of anything resembling the civil institutions that had made Poland the first post-communist country, together with the absence of traditions of legitimate private business, meant that the preconditions of successful shock therapy were lacking. Shock therapy presupposes a strong society and a robust, if repressed, economy. It cannot create them, and where it is applied in their absence its results are predictably perverse.

With the effective abandonment of shock therapy in 1993–4 it was clear that Yeltsin had perceived that Russia's circumstances, together with its longer history, made the transplantation of any western economic model impossible.

The costs and failure of shock therapy cannot be denied. Even so, that did not mean that there was a workable alternative policy of economic reform in late 1991. It was reasonable to argue that piecemeal change was impossible in the catastrophic conditions of 1991–2, but it was unreasonable to expect policies that had been applied with some measure of success in Bolivia or Poland would have similar results in the circumstances that prevailed in Russia.[25]

Many of the human costs incurred by these policies could not have been avoided. They were imposed on Yeltsin's government as an historical fate – the legacies of the Soviet system and Gorbachev's failed programme of reform. But part of the tragedy of shock therapy arose from the fact that it was an attempt to import into Russia an economic system modelled on the theories of Adam Smith.

In an almost inevitable irony this Smithian theory of economic modernization had much in common with the Marxian theories on which Soviet institutions had been based. As Jonathan Steele has commented, 'Karl Marx's theory of historical inevitability has been taken up by a new breed of social engineers, ensconced in the International Monetary Fund, the US State Department, Western European governments and the editorial offices of most major western newspapers.'[26]

A constant feature of all these doctrines is their economic rationalism. Commenting on the Marxian materialist theory of history that underpinned the Bolshevik project in Russia, Bertrand Russell wrote in 1920:

> To desire one's own economic advancement is comparatively reasonable; to Marx, who inherited eighteenth-century rationalist psychology from the British orthodox economists, self-enrichment seemed the natural aim of man's political actions. But modern psychology has dived much deeper into the ocean of insanity upon which the little barque of human reason insecurely floats. The intellectual optimism of a bygone age is no longer possible to the modern student of human nature. Yet it lingers in Marxism making Marxians rigid and Procrustean in their treatment of the life of instinct. Of this rigidity the materialistic conception of history is a prominent instance.[27]

Russell was himself optimistic. The rationalistic view of political life in which economic self-interest is central did not disappear with Soviet Marxism. It returned to Russia, seventy years later, with neo-liberal economics. Another species of rationalism animated the short-lived Russian experiment in economic modernization by shock therapy.

A quasi-Marxian belief in the political supremacy of economic self-interest, crudely interpreted to mean rising income and expanded consumer choice, was the intellectual basis of policies of shock therapy in Russia. Like the historical materialist theory that informed Bolshevik political practice, the neo-liberal theories on which shock therapy was based neglected both enduring human needs and Russia's particular circumstances and traditions.

Gaidar framed his policies under the influence of economists like Jeffrey Sachs, who see American capitalism as the model for market economies everywhere. 'Global capitalism is surely the most promising institutional arrangement for worldwide prosperity the world has ever seen'.[28] Sachs believes that world prosperity will be promoted if the institutions of the American free market are made universal. He sees no reason why Russia should be an exception to this proposition.[29]

In truth, neither the circumstances of Russia in the early 1990s, nor its longer history, permitted the reconstruction of the economy on any such western model. Only an extraordinary blindness to history permitted western advisers such as Sachs to imagine that the question of Russia's European or Asiatic identity, unresolved since Peter the Great, could be settled by a few years of market reform.

The core of Gaidar's programme was freeing prices. On 2 January 1992, price controls were lifted on 90 per cent of traded goods. By the next day queues had vanished from the shops – and prices had risen by 250 per cent. Wages rose by only about 50 per cent, so that for a time enterprises became much more profitable. When prices were freed much of the economy was dominated by monopolies, so those fortunate enough to control them received a windfall gain while most people were worse off.

Skidelsky writes of Gaidar's price liberalization that 'in that first year Russians suffered terribly, their living standards dropping by as much as 50 per cent. They kept going only by taking to their plots of land and growing their own food.'[30]

The second component in Gaidar's programme of shock therapy, privatization, involved many inequities that gave the post-communist renewal of Russian capitalism an inauspicious start. Launched in July 1992 by Anatoly Chubais, a Leningrad economist who in November 1991 had become head of the Russian Federation's Committee on State Property, Gaidar's government had privatized three-quarters of Russia's medium-sized and large-scale industrial enterprises by the end of 1994, with over half of Russian GDP being generated in the private sector.[31]

The subsequent history of Russian privatization bears out Sherr's warning in mid-1992 that 'The . . . risk is that the West . . . will promote bogus forms of privatization, which could benefit few and alienate many. The result could be, not for the first time in Russian history, a rejection of Western values and influence.'[32]

As with price liberalization, the gains from privatization were unevenly spread. Workers and managers were allowed to purchase blocks of shares on special terms, as a result of which enterprise insiders (managers and workers) were majority stakeholders in 70 per cent of all enterprises. Vouchers issued to the public to give them the right to buy a share were bought up by insiders. In many cases managers were able to enrich themselves from the property of the former Soviet state.

As in most other post-communist countries, Russian privatization benefited the one and a half million or so particularly privileged party members more than it did any other section of the population. The drift of assets from formerly state-owned enterprises towards a rich minority is likely to continue for some time, as workers sell their shares to raise the cash they need to meet the necessities of daily life.

Nevertheless, in late 1994, the average Russian privatized company still had over 40 per cent of its shares owned by its workers and over 10 per cent by the state. This pluralist pattern of ownership seems likely to persist. Russian capitalism will not evolve towards the Anglo-Saxon model of shareholder ownership; it will be a pluralist system containing many owner-managed firms, as in Germany.

The third element in Gaidar's shock therapy policies was stabilization of the state's finances. In line with the orthodoxy propagated by the IMF he aimed for a balanced budget in which money was not printed simply to finance government activities. Accordingly military procurement was reduced by about two-thirds and industrial subsidies were drastically lowered. There was a severe monetary squeeze. As a result, by early 1996, the inflation rate had fallen to around 40 per cent. In narrow anti-inflation terms the policy was a success.

Russia never had a 'stabilization policy' – a sudden, one-off price rise followed by relative price stability – of the kind that slashed inflation in Poland. That has led some proponents of shock therapy to argue that it was not really applied to Russia.[33] But their argument is at best inconclusive, since the same political conditions that ruled out gradualism also precluded a one-off monetary shock. Currency changes in Russia are popularly associated with Stalin's regime. A programme of economic reform that began with a change of currency would be not merely unpopular but massively and dangerously illegitimate.

The political results of shock therapy were not favourable to its supporters. In the parliamentary elections of December 1993 Gaidar's Russian Choice party achieved only 13 pert cent of the vote, whereas Vladimir Zhirinovsky's misnamed, anti-Semitic and xenophobic

Liberal Democrat Party achieved 24 per cent. Shock therapy, which had been the only available economic strategy, ceased to be politically viable. Its social costs had become insupportable.

Social costs of Russian shock therapy

Poverty and crime were far from unknown in the Soviet Union throughout its history. Yet shock therapy further impoverished the Russian majority and criminalized the economy to an unprecedented degree.

The collapse of economic activity and the disintegration of state services have caused living standards to drop for the majority, and have cast a part of the population into utter destitution. About a half of the middle and professional classes has been ruined. Birth rates and life expectancy have fallen more steeply than in any other modern peacetime country. At the same time, the enfeeblement of the state has exposed all Russians to exploitation by organized crime.

In his survey of the effects of market reform Peter Truscott comments: 'The Russian Federation's economic reforms had a devastating effect on the majority of the Russian people.'[34] Between December 1991 and December 1996 consumer prices increased 1,700 times. As a result 80 per cent of the Russian population have no savings of any kind.[35] Low-income earners account for around a third of the population (between 44 and 50 million people), but they are at risk of falling into the category of the destitute – the 15–20 per cent of the population (22 to 30 million people) that cannot afford medicines or new clothes. Around 5–10 per cent of the population (7 to 15 million people) suffer from severe deprivation and malnutrition.

In all, around 45 million people have fallen into poverty since the transition to a market economy began in Russia in 1991.[36] At the same time, 'New Russians' who profited from market reforms – between 3–5 per cent of the population, around 4.4 to 7.2 million people – had an average monthly income of between $500 and $100,000 in 1995.[37]

Victor Ilyushin, who was appointed by Boris Yeltsin as a first deputy prime minister after the 1996 presidential election, has stated that one quarter of Russian citizens live below the official subsistence level of $70 a month, while real incomes for the population have fallen by 40 per cent. Economic inequality has risen dramatically. Layard and Parker claim that 'The new rich are better-heeled than the nomenklatura ever were . . . But even so, inequality still falls short of that in the United States; it is close to the level in Britain.'[38] Far more people live in near-absolute poverty in post-communist Russia, however, than in Britain or the United States.

Unemployment has risen to levels that can only be imprecisely estimated. A report of the International Labour Organisation estimates unemployment at 9.5 per cent in July 1996, but notes that this is likely to be considerably less than the real figure. Very meagre benefits discourage workers from registering as unemployed. Many enterprises keep workers on their books to avoid tax and redundancy payments, but do not pay them wages. Moreover, in 1994, nearly 5 million people worked part-time and between a fifth and a third of those who had jobs were on forced leave from them.[39]

The ILO report suggests that more than a third of the population belongs to what it calls the 'suppressed unemployed', and refers to official Russian joblessness figures as an 'administrative artefact' which conceals the true unemployment level 'in the most cruel way possible'.[40]

Rising unemployment has followed an historic collapse in economic activity. Since 1989 Russia's recorded economy has halved in size – a bigger fall than in America during the Great Depression. In mid-1997 Russian GDP was still shrinking, bringing the contraction of economic activity since 1991 to nearly 40 per cent.[41]

The Russian state has ceased to pay many of its employees and dependants. As the Centre for Strategic and International Studies in Washington has recorded: 'The government has not been paying its employees, the armed services, doctors, teachers and scientists . . . The salaries, wages and transfer payments of 65–67 million citizens were in arrears at the end of 1996 . . . For the 36 million pensioners . . . pensions were not being paid on time.'[42]

One problem in measuring real Russian jobless levels comes from rising numbers of premature deaths. The number of people of working age who died from alcohol-related causes more than tripled between 1990 and 1995.[43] The number of suicides among men of working age rose 53 per cent between 1989 and 1993.[44] Another cause of early death in post-Soviet Russia is crime. In 1994 30,000 murders were reported in Russia, three times the per capita rate in the US and twenty times the British and European rate.[45]

Russians are twenty times likelier to die of accidental poisoning than Americans.[46] Part of the explanation lies in one of the legacies of the Soviet period – a level of pollution unmatched anywhere in the world apart from China. Murray Feshbach and Alfred Friendly note in their seminal book *Ecocide in the USSR* that pollution was partly responsible for infant mortality rising in the Soviet Union to levels found in Third World countries and American cities: 'After bringing the death rate of children in their first year of life down from 80.7 per thousand in 1950 to 22.9 in 1971, the USSR – alone among industrialized nations – saw infant mortality, as officially calculated, rise again to 25.4 per thousand in 1987, roughly the same level as Malaysia, Yugoslavia, East Harlem and Washington DC.' Feshbach and Friendly concluded: 'Although the ties between environmental abuse and illness remain inevitably more presumptive than proven, there is little question about the extent of pollution itself. Few industrialized areas of the Soviet Union are environmentally risk-free, and some form of severe ecological condition obtains in 16 per cent of the country's land area, where one fifth of the population lives.'[47]

The environmental pollution that Feshbach and Friendly document was a legacy of the Bolshevik attitude to nature.[48] In this, as in most other respects, the Bolsheviks were faithful followers of Marx. They regarded nature as at best a resource to be exploited for human purposes, at worst a foe to be conquered. The western Promethean attitude to the natural world informed Soviet policies throughout the life of the regime. It was also one of the causes of its collapse.

The slow response of the Soviet leadership to the Chernobyl disaster was a trigger for the first popular political movements to span the USSR. These environmental movements mobilized broad coalitions around opposition to vast projects of dam-building in Siberia. Together with nationalist movements in the Soviet 'near abroad', it was these mass ecological movements, far more than intellectual dissent, that were the real internal catalysts for the Soviet collapse.

Russia's pollution is apocalyptic in its scale and human consequences. In the birthplace of Genghis Khan – Baley, in the Chita region of the Russian Far East – more than 95 per cent of children are mentally deficient, rates of stillbirths are five times higher than the Russian average, rates of child mortality 2.5 times higher and of Downs syndrome four times higher. Births of children with six fingers and six toes, with hare lips, wolves' mouths, back deformities, huge heads and missing limbs are common. In Baley radioactive sand from uranium mines which provided material for the Soviet Union's first atomic bomb was used to build homes, hospitals, schools and nurseries. In 1997 that inheritance was compounded by the post-Soviet disintegration of public services. Staff at the local hospital had not been paid for ten months and the hospital's director could not afford to heat it in winter.[49]

The Russian population itself is shrinking fast. In 1985 fifty-year-old males could expect to die earlier than men who reached the same age in 1939.[50] In one year, 1993, male life expectancy fell from sixty-two to fifty-nine, which is the same as that in India and Egypt.[51] By 1995 life expectancy in Russia was lower than in China.[52]

Since 1985 the birth rate has almost halved. Russia's population is currently declining by about one million a year, with the death rate outrunning the birth rate by 1.6 times.[53] It is likely to fall by about a fifth over the next thirty years, from 147 million to 123 million – an unparalleled demographic collapse.

The life expectancy of a Russian male aged sixteen a century ago was higher than his counterpart today. Despite two world wars, a civil war, famine and millions of deaths in the purges and the Gulag, a sixteen-year-old male had a 2 per cent higher chance of reaching sixty then than he does today.[54]

The life expectancy of Russians has continued to fall throughout the period of market reform. As *The Economist* has commented: 'After five years of economic reform, life expectancy has dropped from 74 years in 1992 to 72 for women, and from 62 years to 58 for men. That places Russia roughly on a par with Kenya.'[55]

Public services have been one of the major casualties of Russian economic reform. Health funding amounted to 3.4 per cent of state expenditure in the Soviet period. It now amounts to 1.8 per cent. Russians who cannot pay do not receive treatment. Truscott observes that 'With an average monthly wage in March 1996 of 740,000 roubles ($153), the price quoted for a heart bypass operation in a state hospital the same year was 28–35 million roubles, far beyond the reach of the average Russian.'[56]

Partly as a consequence, tuberculosis, hepatitis and syphilis have increased greatly. AIDS is spreading rapidly through a pandemic of intravenous drug use, though its present incidence cannot be measured because of failing public services. The number of diptheria cases recorded has risen from 800 to 1991 to 40,000 in 1994.[57]

Stephen Cohen's summary of the human costs of market reform in Russia seems fair: 'For the great majority of families, Russia has not been in transition but in an endless collapse of everything essential for a decent existence – from real wages, welfare provisions and health care to birthrates and life expectancy; from industrial and agricultural production to higher education, science and traditional culture; from safety in the streets to prosecution of organized crime and thieving bureaucrats; from the still enormous military forces to the safeguarding of nuclear devices and materials.'[58]

The hopes harboured for Russian shock therapy by its western advocates and Russian supporters were illusions. Adam Smith's system of natural liberty presupposes an effective state, including a rule of law. Without that background market exchange cannot be relied upon to be beneficial. Instead it just becomes another system of exploitation.

In Russia, Gaidar's shock therapy was implemented by a government whose state was in ruins. The rule of law did not exist. It had not existed in Russia since 1917. Much of the Russian population was wary of market exchange and feared it would lead to exploitation. These popular prejudices expressed ancient Russian suspicions of commerce, strengthened by the experience of Soviet black markets. They were further strengthened by the anarcho-capitalism that was born of shock therapy from the ruined Soviet state.

Anarcho-capitalism in post-communist Russia

In less than a decade Russia has moved from a functioning totalitarian regime to near anarchy. The fall of the Soviet state was not, as many observers appear to have thought, a triumph of western privatization policy. It was a world-historical event whose consequences will take generations, perhaps centuries, to work themselves out.

The species of capitalism that is emerging in Russia today is deeply marked by its Soviet antecedents. The criminalized markets that flourished in the recesses and interstices of the Soviet state thrive now in its ruins.

Russian anarcho-capitalism is an economic system marked by an enfeebled, corrupt and, in some regions and contexts, virtually non-existent state; a weak or absent rule of law, including the lack of a law of property; and the pervasive presence throughout economic life of organized crime. Though these are features found in some measure in all post-communist countries, anarcho-capitalism of this highly developed kind is rare. It flourishes where, as in Russia, the state was itself criminalized and autonomous civil institutions destroyed in the communist period.

This economic system is not a transitional phase in an evolution towards a western-style market economy. But that does not mean that it is not developing. Over time, perhaps spanning more than a generation, Russia's post-communist anarcho-capitalism is likely to evolve into something akin to the highly successful state-led Russian capitalism that generated the rapid economic development of Russia in the last decades of the Tsarist regime.

As in Japan, late nineteenth-century capitalism was driven in Russia by a developmental state. During the half-century before the First World War Tsarist Russia was a fast-developing state which resembled Prussia and Japan in the rates of growth and scale of the modernization it achieved.

Contrary to conventional wisdom Russia is far from having been a stagnant, Asiatic despotism from time immemorial. It abolished serfdom in 1861, a year before slavery was abolished in the United States by Abraham Lincoln. By twentieth-century standards late Tsarist Russia was not especially repressive. In 1895, the Okhrana, the Tsarist secret police, had only 161 full-time employees, supported by a Corp of Gendarmes of less than 10,000 men, while by 1921 the Bolshevik secret police, the Cheka, accounted for over a quarter of a million men, not counting Red Army, NKVD and militiamen.[59]

As Layard and Parker write, in the late nineteenth century 'Russia entered a period of racing economic growth comparable to that of early nineteenth-century Britain, 1870s America, or China today. In 1880–1917 Russia laid more miles of railway track than any country in the world at that time; its industrial production grew at an annual rate of 5.7 per cent over the whole period, accelerating in the four years before World War 1 to 8 per cent.'[60] Late Tsarism was an era not of stagnation but of swiftly advancing modernization.

Nevertheless, this was not a golden age. Late Tsarism was flawed by policies of Russification, anti-Semitism and a deadweight of bureaucracy. It was burdened not only by the inheritances of serfdom but, more profoundly, by the absence in Russia of anything resembling the independent nobility that went with European feudalism. Russia had lacked such a class since the centralizing rule of Ivan IV ('the Terrible') and Peter the Great. Unlike Japan, Russia's modern inheritance was not so much feudal as absolutist. Unlike China, modernization in Russia has always had to confront the legacy of serfdom.

Yet in comparison with other developing states, and with what came afterwards, late Tsarism was a success story. How stable its development would have been in the absence of the First World War is uncertain. But there can be little doubt that the conventional history of late Tsarism underestimates the modernization that it achieved.

The state-led capitalism of large, often oligopolistic firms, functioning in tandem with a wild, frontier capitalism in Siberia and elsewhere, that emerged in the last decades of the nineteenth century seems set to be the model for Russia's economic development in the twenty-first century.

That development will not occur steadily. It will encompass many struggles between town and country, between regions and conflicting economic interests, conducted against the background of a Russian state that will remain weaker in most respects than its Tsarist predecessor.

The Russian capitalism that is being born today has inevitably been deformed by the circumstance of its inception. Russian market reforms took place against a background in which not only the economy but also the Soviet state had foundered. Yet the Soviet inheritance has conditioned profoundly the early stages of post-Soviet economic development. Conceived obscurely in the dark places of the Soviet state, Russian capitalism today could not have come to birth without its manifold links with crime.

A symbiosis of the state with organized crime has a long history in Russia. It has always been at the heart of Soviet institutions. The Soviet state was lawless: it contained nothing akin to an independent judiciary; the legal code permitted the state practically unlimited discretionary power. For ordinary citizens to keep within the bounds of law was an impossibility – if only because the law itself could mean anything that the authorities decided. Economic life functioned in a climate of continuous disregard of regulations.

In the Soviet Union corruption was not a problem; it was a solution in an otherwise unworkable economic system.[61] Inevitably, any kind of enterprise acquired criminal associations in ordinary people's perceptions. Often, such associations were real. As Alain Besancon noted in 1976:

> alongside the Soviet non-economy is a real economy that corresponds to the standard definition of an economy: a rational management of scarcity, expressed in accounting terms. But this economy is not official; it exists outside the law and cannot use public measuring devices. So it is clandestine, illegal and primitive, resembling sometimes the vast Arab trade at the time of the Arabian Nights, sometimes the trade of the Chinese compradors, and sometimes the deals concluded by the American mafia and the activities of the Cosa Nostra in New York and Chicago. As such, it generates a considerable part of national wealth, and permits the official system of production to function.[62]

The Soviet state itself operated as a mafia organization. During the Brezhnev era the links between the mafias and the nomenklatura, which had existed for decades, were strengthened. The criminalization of the economy and government in Russia precedes the Soviet collapse by a long way: it was reinforced by Gorbachev's economic reforms, which led to shortages that only increased further the role of criminal organizations in the informal economy. Those who imagine that organized crime did not exist in the Soviet period show only that they have failed to understand the Soviet state or the economy it created.[63]

The fall of the Soviet Union was itself an occasion for crime on a grand scale: 'In its final eighteen months the Soviet Union became a paradise for the bold and the unscrupulous; its entire product and resources, its stores of wealth, were prised loose and torn from hand to hand. Another gigantic redistribution of spoils took place. Here was the asset-stripping of a nation.'[64]

In the Soviet system entrepreneurship and criminality were fused. When it disintegrated criminal gangs and government bureaucrats were in a position that enabled them to profit greatly from market reforms. Unavoidably the mafia has acted as the midwife of post-communist Russian capitalism.

What imploded in 1989–91 was not a despotism or a tyranny of the classical kinds identified in the conventional typologies of political science. It was a totalitarian regime in which nearly all assets were state property. No doubt these assets had long been used to benefit a small privileged élite – the nomenklatura. In the near-anarchy in which the Russian government tried to implement its reforms the nomenklatura, often in conjunction with criminal gangs, were able to expropriate state assets and make them their personal property.

As Stephen Handelman has written, 'The principal pools of capital available for domestic investment following the Soviet collapse (other than foreign loans) were the coffers of the Communist party and the *obshchaki*, the treasure chests of the Thieves World. The capital was channelled into commercial enterprises, banks, luxury shops and hotels. It not only spurred the equivalent of Russia's first consumer boom but also merged bureaucrats and gangsters into a uniquely Russian form of crime boss – the comrade criminal.'[65]

In post-communist Russia organized crime is ubiquitous. About three-quarters of privatized firms and commercial banks are compelled to pay between 10–20 per cent of their turnover to mafia organizations. Though all such estimates must be speculative – since, like the former Soviet economy, much of the Russian economy is black – the income of the mafia may amount to about 40 per cent of Russian GDP, and around 40 per cent of new businesses may have acquired their starting capital from mafia-controlled sources.[66] In the first half of 1995 kidnapping and armed assault increased by 100 per cent and 600 per cent respectively. Contract killings are commonplace. Since 1992 eighty-five bankers have been attacked and forty-seven murdered. There are believed to be around 150 mafia organizations, which – according to the Russian Ministry of Internal affairs – control between 35,000 and 40,000 enterprises and around 400 banks.

Russia's mafias are not ethnically homogenous, nor do they usually act in concert. A significant part of the recent explosion of violent crime probably reflects turf wars among rival mafia clans. Yet most mafia organizations share a common origin in the criminal activities of the former Soviet state. At the very end of the Soviet state, late in December 1991, around thirty heads of Russia's criminal organizations met in Moscow to discuss how to protect themselves from new gangs coming from the Caucasus – Georgia, Chechnya, and Armenia. They also discussed how to corrupt the officials of the new regime they perceived on the horizon.[67] Some of the biggest beneficiaries of Russian organized crime are not the criminals themselves but the state officials paid off by them.

As Handelman has put it, 'Those making billions were, for the most part, those who made millions in the Soviet era – neither by arranging black-market sales of state goods or from the byzantine system of bribery. The old state, in effect, had criminalized the new.'[68]

The corruption and lawlessness of the crumbling state institutions bequeathed to its first post-communist government was one reason why shock therapy could not have the limited effectiveness in Russia that it had elsewhere. Another was the militarization of the Soviet economy. In no other country where shock therapy has been applied was military production so central to economic life. To suppose that the prescriptions of Smithian economic liberalism were workable in such circumstances was folly.

When the Soviet state fell apart it left in its wake the world's largest military-industrial complex (MIC). It began to fall apart at once, and its decomposition was quickened by shock therapy. The decomposing Soviet MIC proved a fertile ground for Russia's scavenging criminals gangs. As Handelman records,

> Six months after the USSR disintegrated, defense orders had dropped by more than 40 per cent, and 350,000 workers had lost their jobs. A year later, there were so many idle plants that an estimated one million workers received pay for doing nothing . . . In the city of Yekaterinburg, where about a quarter of the labour force, or some five hundred thousand people, worked for military industries, local gangs were some of the most important clients for the grenades and rocket-launchers that once went to the state. The mob lords and black marketeers also provided the muscle and international contacts necessary to market strategic raw materials, weapons, and metals abroad.[69]

The Soviet MIC was one of the first casualties of market reform. In 1992 the World Bank estimated that it employed over 5 million people (around 7.5 per cent of the workforce). According to a recent Russian estimate, former MIC employees together with their families total over 30 million people – around an eighth of the population.[70]

Under Gaidar's policies of shock therapy defence procurement was reduced by about 70 per cent. By 1993 the total output of Russia's defence industry had halved. For the most part this did not reflect conversion of military production to civilian uses but rather a sheer decline in the MIC's economic activity. Arbats has written: 'In 1992, the MIC's 1,100 plants were found to have lower average wages than any other branch of industry, owing to stringent government cutbacks (68 per cent) in appropriations for purchases of military technology and arms . . . Funding for conversion is nil, many MIC factories have shut down entirely, and there's no money for wages or pensions.'[71]

The Russian government tried to slow the decline of the defence industry by promoting arms sales. As a result, by the summer of 1996, according to the US Congressional Research Service, Russia was the world's largest arms exporter to the developing world, with China as its largest customer.[72] Russia's defence spending has fallen to something close to the norm for western democratic countries. Nevertheless the role of the MIC in the Russian economy and state is, and will remain, considerably greater.

Furthermore, much of what remains of the Russian MIC is no longer under the full control of the government. It is now a complex composed of many autonomous, semi-privatized structures. As Sherr has put it. 'Leading arms of the (Russian) state have become semi-commercialized entities, operating with mixed agendas.'[73]

The partial break-up of Russia's MIC, which was the backbone of the former Soviet Union, has led many observers to fear that the Russian state will fall apart entirely. Some fear another 'Time Of Troubles' (1598–1613) – a period, perhaps protracted, of full-scale anarchy or civil war. They point to the war in Chechnya as an index of the difficulty Russian military forces have in repressing even small insurrections, and forecast a progressive fragmentation of the Russian Federation.

The speculative investor Jim Rogers has forecast: 'I predict further unravelling. Before it is over, I expect to see 50 countries, 100 countries . . . Authority in the former Soviet Union has devolved into the rule of the warlord, that political leader who always surfaces with the breakdown of central power . . . When an empire becomes unstable and lawless, a period ensues in which warlord fights warlord. Today, Soviet warlords include gangs, the Mafia, dictators, liberators, and communists . . . Very likely, the Russian people will welcome whichever demagogue makes the most lavish promises.'[74]

That is a hyperbolic scenario, but with some element of truth. Unlike China, Russia faces a Hobbesian problem of order. The Russian Federation is a construction left over from empire, not a modern nation-state. Aside from the attempted breakaway in Chechnya, however, there are no militarily significant secessionist movements within the Russian Federation. A wholesale break-up of the Russian Federation requires a degree of militancy which few of its peoples presently exhibit. Nothing in the past few years suggests a widespread taste for military adventure among Russians or most of the Russian Federation's non-Russian peoples.

A more likely development is that fear of another 'Time of Troubles' – the period of anarchy and civil war in the late sixteenth century whose historic memory lives on in Russian song and folk-lore – will act as a catalyst for a strengthening of the Russian state. The criminalization of Russian capitalism today will trigger demands that the regime of extensive presidential authority that Yeltsin inaugurated be further extended.

It is hard to exaggerate the weakness of the Russian state today. Yet the institutions of the state in Russia, particularly those concerned with law and order, will in time be renovated. Russian traditions of strong executive authority require effective institutions of government. Yeltsin's programme of military reform, aiming to replace the conscript forces of the former Soviet Union with a modern army of professional soldiers, is a sign that institution-building has begun.

The renovation of the Russian state need not be a move towards authoritarian dictatorship. Other democratic states, such as France under de Gaulle, have contained institutions allowing strong executive authority. The growth of such institutions in Russia could be a step towards constructing a modern state that could exercise a strategic role in the development of Russian capitalism akin to that in late Tsarism.

The reconstruction of the Russian Federation as a modern nation-state is nevertheless a daunting task. It requires bold experimentation in the devolution of power through federal institutions together with the growth of a Russian sense of nationhood that is not based on ethnic exclusion. It will not meet the need for personal security unless it includes a reliable, independent judicial system. In a country whose traditions have always been imperial and authoritarian these will not develop quickly.

Without an effective modern state Russia's natural environment cannot be protected from further exploitation and degradation – this time in the service not of the hubristic economic plans of the Soviet period but of short-term commercial profit, much of it going into mafia coffers. Without such a state Russia's ruined public services cannot be repaired and the institutions of the market will not be popularly legitimate.

Aside from Bolshevism no political ideology has ever been so unfitted to Russian modernization than that which promotes free markets through minimum government. In Russia today, a modern market economy will be born as a creature of strong government.

If the current drift of Yeltsin's policies is a guide to post-Yeltsin politics, the Russian state has resumed a strategic role in the development of Russian capitalism. Such an outcome reinforces a basic truth – that neither the Bolshevik forced march to industrialization nor the shock therapy that have been imposed on Russia this century enabled Russia to achieve a genuine modernity.

There are clear risks in any Russian strategy of state-building. It could entrench rather than weaken the power of the mafias. If it was associated with narrow ethnic nationalism it could revive painful historical memories in Russia's non-Russian peoples and neighbours and could easily become xenophobic. Without an independent judiciary law enforcement could become merely another exercise in repression. A strong Russian state could well degenerate into a traditional tyranny.

Yet there is no real alternative to state-building in Russia. Colluding in a drift to anarchy cedes the political territory of strong government to an atavistic coalition of ex-communists and neo-fascists. Such a coalition of reactionaries is no more capable of generating sustainable modernization than the romantic westernizers who tried to implement shock therapy. Yeltsin's policies signal that he understands a more eclectic, selective approach is needed if Russia is to have a modernization that fits a country which straddles Europe and Asia.

Eurasian Russia

In some countries the passing of Soviet power has been followed by a swift return to European institutions and traditions. In the Czech Republic, in Hungary, in the Baltic states and in Slovenia, being in the

Soviet bloc meant being forcibly wrenched out of a European mode of life. For these countries the post-communist period has been a rediscovery of 'normal times'. Such times have been variously identified – sometimes with the democratic republics of the interwar years, sometimes with the Habsburg Empire – but their European provenance is beyond doubt.

This transition to 'western' institutions and values has occurred not because westernization and modernization are universally one and the same, but because the traditions of these particular countries have always been those of European peoples. For them history has not ended with the fall of communism. It has been resumed after a half-century's interruption.

In some post-communist countries the issue is more complicated, however. For Poland 'Europe' – which means in practice the institutions of the European Union – is a solution to age-old difficulties. It promises to resolve historical dilemmas arising from the country's position – geographic and geostrategic – between Germany and Russia. Whether 'Europe' will live up to these hopes is another matter. What is clear is that Europe's present role is to answer persistent questions of security and national identity that in Poland's history have been a source of tragedy.[75]

In yet other post-communist countries the passing of the communist period has given another lease on life of European traditions that had never been dominant but which had long striven to become so. In Romania the fall of the communist regime, which occurred not with the toppling of Ceausescu but several years later, in the elections of 1996, has renewed a struggle between those who see it as a backward European country and those who see in its traditions of Orthodox Christianity a reason why Romania can never be merely another European state. Yet these cultural and political divisions have not impacted on Romanian national policy, which has continued to seek a closer relationship with the European Union and with NATO. Only in Serbia have 'anti-western' political forces been dominant throughout the post-communist period.

In Russia the deep gulf between the generation that was formed by the Soviet experience and the new Russians who grew to maturity in the years of the Soviet débâcle ensures that there will be no turning back. Only the old dream of a better yesterday. There is little prospect of an anti-western tilt of the kind advocated by some contemporary

Slavophiles (among whom Solzhenitzyn may be counted). If, as is likely, Russia ceases to imitate western countries, it need not thereby become anti-western in its foreign policies.

The abandonment of shock therapy still marked a decisive retreat for Russia's westernizers. The parliamentary and presidential elections that were held between 1993 and 1996 showed that, while a proportion of the Russian population favours economic reform on a western model, it is a minority.

The disastrous showing of Mikhail Gorbachev in the presidential elections, in which he achieved less than 1 per cent of the vote, had many causes; but among them a rejection of the unambiguously western conception of Russia's future that he embodied must be central. The Russian majority will not in any foreseeable future support economic modernization on narrowly western lines. As a result, the project of modernizing Russia on any western model has been derailed.

In his presidential election manifesto, Yeltsin referred to 'Russia – a Eurasian state, which with its resources and unique geo-political situation is going to become one of the largest centres of economic development and political influence.'[76] This key statement reveals the pivotal role in post-communist Russian thinking of 'Eurasian' theories.

For the Eurasians, Russia's unique history and circumstances – its geography, its diversity of peoples, its history as a centre of Orthodox Christianity and its record of failed attempts to westernize – make a final, unequivocal choice between Asia and Europe, between the 'East' of Orthodox Christianity and the 'West' of the Reformation, the Renaissance and the Enlightenment, an impossibility.

The Eurasian movement dates back to the 1920s. At that time émigré thinkers produced a manifesto, *Exodus to the East: Forebodings and Accomplishments: A Profession of Faith by the Eurasians*.[77] As Layard and Parker summarize the Eurasian view, it is that Russia is '"a geopolitical civilisation" on its own'.[78] Nekrich and Heller say of the Eurasians that for them 'Russia was not only the West but the East, not only Europe but Asia as well. In fact it was not Europe at all but Eurasia.'[79] As in the 1920s, Eurasians today are influenced by nineteenth-century Russian thinkers such as Konstantin Leontiev.[80]

Truscott quotes Ruslan Khasbulatov, the Speaker of the Russian Parliament, as stating in 1992 that 'While (Peter the Great) imposed elements of western culture in Russia . . . the spiritual and cultural fabric of the Russian people remained untouched. As a result, we have Russia, which is neither Europe nor Asia but a very special, very peculiar part of the world.' Assessing the role of Eurasian thinking in shaping Russian policy, Truscott concludes:

> the West has assumed that Russia, emerging from the Soviet period, will develop a political and economic system based on Europe and the United States. While this may have been tried at the beginning of Yeltsin's era, it is not the case today. The Duma elections of 1993 and 1995, and the presidential election of 1996, show unequivocally that this will not happen. The Western model of democracy and a market economy has been decisively rejected by the Russian people . . . The result has been . . . a new approach to relations with the West. Russia will adopt a more selective approach, absorbing certain Western ideas and values (including technological and commercial skills) while evolving a peculiarly Russian model of democracy and market-orientated economy.[81]

A Eurasian policy squares with many of the circumstances of post-Soviet Russia – its geography and ethnic diversity, its strategic environment and its natural assets. Layard and Parker summarize the strategic reasoning that dictates a Eurasian policy for Russia:

> Over the four decades of the Cold War, they (the Eurasians) argued, the world was divided between capitalist West and communist East. As that division disappears, it will be replaced by a division between rich North and poor South. Russia straddles the divide. Geographically northern, Russia, the Eurasians said, is more like part of the South economically. Even if reform goes well, they claimed, thirty years will go by before Russia can join the club of rich countries. Even then, Russia's interests will still differ from those of other northern states. Russia is up against the poor South in a way that no other northern country is. In particular, it has long borders with the poor South – the Transcaucasus, the states of central Asia, and China. And it has to be especially careful about its relations with Islamic nations, because seven of its neighbours are Muslim and Russia itself contains 18 million Muslims. As it was, by 1995 Russia was embroiled in three wars involving non-Russian nations – in Tajikstan, Chechnya, and

Bosnia . . . For its own security, therefore, Russia cannot afford to ignore its neighbours to the south and southeast.[82]

In strategic terms the Russian case for a Eurasian policy is difficult to rebut. Unlike any European country, Russia is a Pacific power. Its defence and commercial relationships with China are more important, in a long-term perspective, than its relations with any 'western' state.

Yet the strength of Eurasian thinking in post-communist Russia does not reflect only these strategic realities. It expresses the deeper truth that Russia has never succeeded in identifying itself unequivocally with either Europe or Asia. Eurasian strategy embodies this enduring Russian ambivalence.

The resources of Russian capitalism

The indigenous capitalism that looks set to emerge in Russia confronts formidable obstacles; but it has some powerful compensating advantages too. The Russian Federation produces over 10 per cent of the world's oil output, 30 per cent of the world's gas, and 10–15 per cent of the world's non-ferrous metal ores. Russia's natural resources are vast.[83]

In some ways Russia's human resources are no less extraordinary. Russians remain one of the best-educated peoples in the world, with levels of literacy and numeracy well in excess of those in the United States and many European countries. A 1996 report comparing children in St Petersburg and Sunderland found high levels of educational motivation in Petersburg. Russian children 'tended to perceive education as an end in itself . . . To be literate and cultured has traditionally been greatly valued by the society . . . they wanted to be an educated person.' Despite Russia's emerging identity as an Eurasian state, Russians retain a better knowledge and understanding of the history and cultural canon of Europe than most unambiguously 'European' peoples.

By contrast with Russians, British children value education chiefly as a means to the acquisition of job qualifications. Despite this pragmatic approach, the choice of subjects for study by British children seems guided more by an aversion to intellectual difficulty than by their perceived usefulness.[84]

Like that of Japan and Singapore, Russia's schooling reflects the traditions and values of nineteenth-century bourgeois Europe. Though educational levels in the countryside are sometimes very low, Russia generally remains a country in which education is valued for its own sake. This gives it an advantage over western countries which genuflect to the 'knowledge economy' but whose schools must function in a proletarianized culture in which education has primarily utilitarian value.

By comparison with most western societies Russia is a country whose cultural vitality is unexhausted. Its present combination of punk post-modernism and resurgent tradition, of wild capitalism with popular revulsion against commerce, may appear unstable to western eyes. But, though such contradictions may be the source of future political conflicts, they are not inevitably destructive. As in pre-revolutionary times they can be a source of cultural – and economic – creativity.

The connective tissues of social life have renewed themselves in Russia to a surprising degree. The extended family, which has all but ceased to exist in the Anglo-Saxon capitalist world, has survived Soviet communism in Russia.[85] Its survival partly accounts for the ability of Russians to cope with the hardships of market reform. As Layard and Parker observe: 'Two institutions have been crucial to survival: the extended family and the private plot of land. The extended family . . . is a strong element in the system of social security. Adult children almost always help their parents in old age, and people also help their siblings if they are in trouble.'[86] It is the comparative weakness of 'individualism' in Russia that has allowed mutual aid in the extended family to persist to a degree unknown in many western, and particularly Anglo-Saxon, societies.

The Russian middle classes, which grew slowly during the Soviet period, have been weakened by the chaos and deprivation following shock therapy. Yet, paradoxically, one of the legacies of the Soviet period is a bourgeois tradition of resourcefulness and acquisition of skills that has equipped young middle-class people to adapt to the new conditions and, in many cases, to earn far more than their parents. These Russians retain the capacity to function, sometimes even to thrive, in desperate circumstances. In this they are well-equipped for the anarchy of global markets.

In terms of natural and human resources, then, Russia remains one of the best-endowed countries in the world. But it is also one of the worst governed. A renovation of the institutions of the Russian state is a crucial precondition of today's post-communist anarcho-capitalism developing into an indigenous Russian capitalism akin to that which flourished under late Tsarism. Without the institutions of a modern state the umbilical cord that connects Russian capitalism with the former Soviet Union and the mafia cannot be severed. Until it has a strong, effective state, Russia will not have a genuine market economy but rather a kind of criminal syndicalism. Until Russia has solved its Hobbesian problem it cannot be a modern state.

The western philosophy that was imported during the short period of shock therapy was not designed to address the distinctive circumstances and needs of Russia today. That neo-liberal creed differed from Leninism chiefly not about the ends of policy, but in regard to means – and not always then. In the years 1989–93 both these western-oriented strategies of modernization reached the end of the road and the search for an indigenous modernization was taken up again.

In taking up again a path of development that was broken off by the First World War, communism and, briefly, by shock therapy, post-Soviet Russia is not setting itself in opposition to 'the West'. It is recognizing the reality that modernizing Russia by trying to emulate the West has failed. A non-western, Eurasia Russia need not be an anti-western Russia.

How Russia interacts with western Europe and the United States depends chiefly on the governments of those countries, which in current circumstances hold the initiative on most economic and security issues. Triumphalist policies on the part of western powers can only make the emergence of a modern Russian state more difficult. If there is a risk that Russia may become a Weimar state, it is enhanced by western policies which treat it as one.

In fact there is nothing in the emergence of a Eurasian Russia that need threaten the vital interests of any western state. If conflicts do arise as Russia develops a market economy that reflects its history and present needs they will occur because Russian capitalism cannot be fitted into the Procrustean framework of a global free market.

7 Occidental twilight and the rise of Asia's capitalisms

for America to be displaced, not in the world but only in the Western Pacific, by an Asian people long despised as decadent, feeble, corrupt and inept is emotionally very difficult to accept. The sense of cultural supremacy of the Americans will make this adjustment very difficult to accept.

Americans believe their ideas are universal – the supremacy of the individual and free, unfettered expression. But they are not – never were.

LEE KUAN YEW[1]

The total failure of Marxism . . . and the dramatic break-up of the Soviet Union are only the precursors to the collapse of western liberalism, the main current of modernity. Far from being the alternative to Marxism and the reigning ideology at the end of history, liberalism will be the next domino to fall.

TAKESHI UMEHARA[2]

Any attempt to impose one's own will or values upon others or to unify the world under a certain model of 'civilization' will definitely fail . . . No one economic system is good for all countries. Each must follow its own path, as China has.

QIAO SHI, CHINESE POLITBURO[3]

In January 1850 Lord Palmerston, the British Foreign Secretary, ordered the British navy to blockage Piraeus and seize Greek ships. He did so to compel the Greek government to meet the demands of Don Pacifico, a Portuguese national from Gibraltar who was also a British subject. Don Pacifico claimed that over £30,000 was owed to him in compensation for damage done to his house and property during a riot in Athens in 1848. Don Pacifico's claims were dubious; but, in a speech in the House of Commons in June 1850, Palmerston defended his action by quoting from the New Testament the phrase *civis romanus sum* (I am a citizen of Rome). Palmerston's interpretation of this phrase captured the *pax Britannica* at its apogee: 'So also,' declared Palmerston 'a British subject, in whatever land he may be, shall feel confident that the watchful eye and the strong arm of England will protect him against injustice and wrong.'[4]

Nearly a century and a half later the axis of the world tilted. In Singapore in 1994, an American student, Michael Fay, was sentenced to six strokes of the cane for writing graffiti in a public place. After strong American diplomatic representations, including a personal intervention by President Clinton, the punishment was reduced to four strokes: it was not rescinded.

In responding to American intervention in this way Singapore artic- ulated a fundamental shift in the distribution of power in the world. At the mid-Victorian height of the *pax Britannica* Lord Palmerston was able to claim the authority to act unilaterally in the defence of the interests of British subjects in any part of the world – regardless of the national jurisdiction under which they might find themselves. At the peak of America's post-Cold War power a small Asian city-state was able to defy it.

Singapore rejected the universality of western values. It spurned America's intervention and the doctrines of human rights that the United States was propagating throughout East Asia. It affirmed its own values against the liberal model of human rights and the eco- nomic culture of market individualism that the United States sought to implant throughout the world. It pointed to its achievements as a post-liberal city-state – stable, cohesive, highly educated and fast-grow- ing – as proof that its model of modernization and development was superior to anything 'the West' had to offer.[5]

The liberal international economic order of the pre-1914 world depended on the ability and willingness of Britain to use naval power anywhere in the world. No such willingness exists on the part of the United States today. America's lead in military technology makes it the world's most truly global power. But its population is unwilling to bear the financial and human costs of being an imperial regime.

There is another profound difference between the *belle époque* and our late modern *fin de siècle*. Before 1914 the identification of mod- ernization with westernization was questioned by almost no one. Even twentieth-century anti-colonial movements – in India, China and most of the world that was subject to European imperial control – rarely doubted that freeing their countries from western power entailed modernizing them on a western model.

In much of the developing world Marxism functioned as an ideology of westernizing revolutions. In Turkey, one of history's most gifted political modernists, Kemal Attaturk, founded this century's most enduring westernizing regime on the principle that becoming a modern state demanded a thorough rupture with the country's indigenous cultural traditions.

Until the end of the Cold War modernization and westernization were equated nearly everywhere. The one exception was Japan.

Indigenous modernization: the paradigm case of Japan

When, in 1853, Commodore Perry forced Japan open to trade for the first time since the country was closed to the outside world in 1641 he did more than disturb a way of life that had been unchanged for over two hundred years. He ended an experiment that may be unique in human history. During the Edo period Japan had renounced the technology of early modern warfare and reverted from the gun to the sword.[6] Japan's ruling elite did what western theories of scientific progress say is an impossibility – they reversed technological evolution.

The arrival of Commodore Perry's black ships made it clear to Japan's subtle and watchful elite that the sealed and peaceful way of life they had enjoyed for over two hundred years had no future. They knew what might be in store for them from western powers by observing the fate of China in the Opium Wars. In his letter to the shogun Commodore Perry threatened that if the country did not open itself to trade it would be visited by 'large ships of war', perhaps in the spring.[7] Perry's black ships ended Japan's experiment in isolation and low technology – an experiment that had 'proved . . . that a no-growth economy is perfectly compatible with prosperity and civilized life'.[8] At the same time it set Japan on an ambitious course of modernization, as a result of which it would enter the twentieth century with a fleet that destroyed the Russian Imperial Navy at Tsushima in 1903.

The great merchant house of Mitsui has endured from the closed Edo period through the era of modernization, the Meiji Restoration

(1868–1912) and the Allied Occupation after the Second World War, to become one of the great Japanese institutions of the present day. Its longevity marks a fundamental truth about industrialization in Japan – it did not entail, as in some countries of continental Europe, a decisive break with a feudal social order.

Japan's corporations developed as grafts on institutions inherited from its medieval age. The modern industrial economy that Japan began to develop in the last decades of the nineteenth century embodied a social order that was in its most vital parts unbroken. Spearheaded by its warrior class, the *samurai*, Japan's modernization was possible because the feudal order that was its departure-point had *not* broken down.

The Marxian model of the bonds of technology working through and breaking apart old social structures has little application in the Japanese case. Nor does the liberal story of society evolving through the growth of knowledge and innovation in ideas. No narrative of modernization that is modelled on western histories captures the Japanese experience.[9]

The theories of neo-classical economics have only a limited value in illuminating economic life in Japan today. Japanese companies compete against one another for markets as ruthlessly as anywhere else; but Japanese capitalism differs profoundly from the Anglo-Saxon market individualism on which most of the great social theorists based their model of capitalism, and from that advanced by the Washington consensus.

In their dealings with their employees and the rest of society Japanese market institutions rely on networks of trust rather than upon a culture of contract. They are far less dislocated from the structure of their surrounding communities than American corporations. Their relations with the institutions of the state are close and continuous. The ethical life which Japanese capitalism expresses is not individualist and shows no sign of becoming so.

These deep and abiding differences between the capitalism of Japan and that of England and America mark a fundamental truth. Both the supporters and the critics of capitalism have fastened on individualism as one of its central features. But the connections between capitalism and individualism are neither necessary nor universal: they are historical accidents. The early theorists of capitalism – Adam Smith, Adam Ferguson, Karl Marx, Max Weber and John Stuart Mill – mistook them for universal laws because the evidence on which they based their theories was for the most part limited to a few western countries.

A beginning can be made in understanding Japan only if it is accepted that by the end of the nineteenth century it had already modernized. It had long been highly literate, urban life was expanding rapidly, new technologies had been absorbed and a centralized state was in place. Japan had acquired these marks of modernity without westernizing its social structures or its cultural traditions. The catalyst for modernization in Japan was the trauma of contact with threatening western power; but Japan's modernization was nevertheless indigenous.

Enlightenment philosophies of history tell us that countries modernize by replicating western societies. Those philosophies and the theories of modernity they supported had already been falsified by Japan by the start of the twentieth century.

It is true that Japanese modernization involved many eclectic borrowings from western countries. The calendar was changed, a banking system developed, education expanded, a system of commercial law created and a modern army and navy built up. All these innovations involved some emulation of western practices, particularly Prussian (in reforming Japan's legal system, schooling and army) and British (in developing the Japanese navy). Japanese officers attended western academies and Japanese engineers travelled to western countries to study ship-building techniques.

Yet none of these adaptations had the result of altering Japan's social structures or cultural traditions. Nor were they meant to do so. Japan's industrialization was promoted with the aim of preserving national independence. Japanese westernizers did not prevail in the recurrent debate on the meaning of modernization.

Implicitly, and in more recent times explicitly, Japan's policy-makers rejected the view that modernization means convergence on the same western institutions and values. As Waswo notes, they made clear their 'rejection of the so-called convergence hypothesis, which states that there is a universal logic to industrialism and that the social relationships found in the first nations to industrialize (individualism, a free labour market, and so on) must inevitably develop elsewhere.'[10]

A version of the convergence hypothesis is, of course, one of the foundations of the Washington consensus. Yet in Japan, more than in any other country, the Washington consensus on economic development is overturned by the evidence of history.

From the first, Japanese industrialization was drive forward by a developmental state. As it had in many other countries, such as Tsarist Russia, rapid industrialization occurred in Japan under the aegis of strong, centralized, interventionist governmental power. As Paul Kennedy has put it 'Japan had to be modernized not because individual entrepreneurs wished it, but because the "state" needed it . . . The state encouraged the creation of a railway network, telegraphs, and shipping lines; it worked in conjunction with emerging Japanese entrepreneurs to develop heavy industry, iron, steel, and shipbuilding, as well as to modernize textile production. Government subsidies were employed to benefit exporters, to encourage shipping, to get a new industry set up. Behind all this lay the impressive political commitment to realize the national slogan *fukoku kyohei* (rich country with strong army).'[11]

Economic and industrial development has been animated and concerted by the institutions of the state at every point in Japanese history. But the sharp distinction between state and society that has developed in European countries since the early modern period has few resonances in the history of Japan. The importance of *wa* – harmony – as a value in Japanese life militates against the top-down relations of hierarchy that have long been associated with state institutions in Europe. As Sayle has observed, 'The Japanese government does not stand apart from or over the community; it is rather the place where *wa* deals are negotiated.'[12] In this Japan differs strongly not only from European countries but also from China and Korea.

The centralized state constructed in Japan during the Meiji period resembled closely the classical nation-states of nineteenth-century Europe. In many ways Japan remains a nineteenth-century nation-state. It is a developmental state, to be sure, not the minimum state of the Washington consensus. But neither is it a welfare state of the sort that was established in western Europe and the United States after the Second World War. As Peter Drucker has noted, 'Viewed through the glasses of traditional political theory, that is, of the political theory of the eighteenth and nineteenth centuries, Japan is clearly a "statist" country. But it is statist in the way in which Germany or France in 1880 or 1890 were statist compared with Britain or the United States.'[13] In its post-war evolution, however, Japan diverged from all western societies.

Japanese capitalism developed from the traditional enterprises of the feudal period.[14] Industry has always been organized in closely knit networks of large firms. In the Meiji period they were the *zaibatsu*, powerful, family-controlled holding groups. The pre-war *zaibatsu* survived the attempt made during the Occupation to impose American-style anti-trust legislation on them to become the *kigyo shugan*, or intermarket groups, of the present day. After the Occupation, the great firms, (Mitsui, Mitsubishi, Sumitomo and others) reassembled themselves, though with much less family control than before, helping to constitute the network of enterprise groups that governs the Japanese economy today. It has been well said that in Japan '*zaibatsu* and other affiliations link industrial, commercial and financial firms in a thick and complex skein of relations matched in no other country'.[15] These large enterprise groups coexist with a vast diversity of small firms in Japan; but they set the framework within which these other enterprises work.

The interconnections of the Japanese economy that embed it in the life of society have been a target of attack of American negotiators and transnational organizations for decades. Pilloried as bulwarks of protection, their role in nurturing social cohesion has gone uncomprehended – or else it has been rejected. The function of small corner shops in maintaining cities as viable social institutions does not appear in the Washington consensus. The possibility that corner shops may do better in safeguarding social cohesion than mass imprisonment is considered outlandish – if it is considered at all.

As a perceptive British observer has commented:

The US Justice Department reports that, at its last count, 1, 100 Americans were in prison. That is nearly one in 200 of the entire population, men, women and children . . . why do we look to America for economic and social models, from deregulation and institutional investor power to workfare schemes, if they produce this kind of society? . . . [It] is, however, the blueprint for virtually all international institutions . . . The OECD (in its annual report on Japan) urged yet more deregulation . . . ending protection for small shops . . . The OECD crows contentedly that one in 15 of Japan's stores has closed in the past three years. Small shops are disappearing faster than ever before. Modest efficiency gains are being gained at the cost of a big social upheaval.[16]

The demands made on Japan by the Washington consensus go further than dismantling its small shops. They include lowering savings rates, abandoning its full employment culture and embracing market individualism. Together they amount to the demand that Japan cease to be Japanese.

Japan's most unforgivable sin against the Washington consensus is its full employment culture. It has an unemployment rate of around 3–4 per cent, as compared with an average in OECD countries of about 8 per cent; it has a higher proportion of the population employed than the OECD average for all categories of workers, including the young; it had the lowest unemployment rate of any OECD country in 1993, even including part-time workers.

By no means all Japanese employees enjoy lifetime employment, which is uncommon outside the large firms. Yet 43 per cent of employees in Japan had worked for the same employer for more than a decade in 1991, compared with 33.5 per cent in a range of OECD countries. Job security has been preserved in Japan more than in any other country.

Japan has sustained its full employment culture through the worst recession it has ever suffered – the cataclysmic drop in economic activity following the collapse of the 'bubble economy' in 1989 – and despite a steady fall in manufacturing employment for the last thirty years. What would happen to the level of employment in the United States if, as in Japan, the stock market crashed by around 70 per cent?

As Martin Wolf has justly commented: 'If an economy is judged by its ability to distribute gains from economic activity widely, while shielding those least able to bear the costs of recession, Japan's was as remarkable in its years of trial as in those of glory.'[17]

The survival of the core feature of the Japanese economy in the post-war period – the unwritten social contract that assures job security to much of its population – is now under threat from the global free market. Developed after the Second World War, partly in response to economic pressures such as skill shortages, but partly as a strategy for industrial and social peace, the Japanese social contract guaranteeing full employment has prevented the growth of a proletariat and, in more recent times, of an underclass. By comparison with most western countries, Japan is an egalitarian society in which nearly everyone is middle class.

If Japan's policy-makers yield to the demands of the Washington consensus, Japan will join all those western societies in which mass unemployment, epidemic crime and the collapse of social cohesion are problems without solutions.

Japan's social contract for job security may not survive in its present form. The guarantee of lifetime employment in one firm is no longer credible. Competition with other East Asian economies makes some loosening up in the labour market unavoidable. The question is whether Japan can preserve its *culture* of full employment while moving away from the post-war guarantee of lifetime job security with a single firm.

Japan is a highly mature industrial society. In this it resembles the late modern economies of western Europe more than it does the newly industrializing economies that surround it in East Asia. It has succeeded in accelerating industrial development which spanned well over two centuries in Britain into a period of about a century and a quarter. Between 1890 and 1913 the urban population doubled but the numbers who worked on the land remained about the same. In 1914, over three-fifths of the Japanese population was still employed in agriculture, forestry and fishing.[18]

Yet during these years, alone among the world's non-Occidental countries, Japan embarked on an ambitious programme of industrialization that, despite the catastrophe of the Pacific War, has made it the technology-intensive economy it is today.

There is a great deal in the Japanese model that cannot be exported. Japan's unique degree of cultural continuity and homogeneity guarantees that. But Japan's circumstance as a highly mature industrial society may afford it an opportunity to achieve in the late modern era something as unique as its renunciation of technology in the Edo period.

Japan, since the pricking of the bubble economy, has been a no-growth economy. In a condition of debt deflation, it has found itself in the classic dilemma diagnosed by Keynes when he spoke of governments who attempt to revive demand by lowering interest rates as 'pushing on a string'. In Japan in the late 1990s, as in the United States during the Great Depression, even interest rates of 0.5 per cent have not stimulated borrowing. Economic growth is becalmed. Has Japan arrived first at a condition of satiation, long feared but not yet reached in western countries, in which further economic growth at the rate achieved during most of the post-war period has become unsustainable?

One Japanese economist has reminded his readers of J. S. Mill's observation that 'a stationary condition of capital and production need not be a stationary state of human improvement'.[19] Can Japan achieve something akin to the 'stationary-state economy' advocated by John Stuart Mill, in which technological progress is used to enhance the quality of life rather than merely to expand the quantity of production?[20]

Elsewhere in the world the vision of a no-growth economy has proved a chimera. Perhaps in Japan's uniquely mature industrial society the collapse of economic growth could be an opportunity to reconsider the desirability of restarting it. But that would involve defying the central imperative of the Washington consensus, which dictates that social betterment is impossible without unending economic growth.

China's failed modernization: Mao's Soviet model

Mao Zedong's celebrated statement that 'The Soviet Union's today is China's tomorrow'[21] encapsulates the central thrust of the failed modernization imposed on China by the Maoist regime. Despite the numerous occasions on which the two states came into conflict, the Soviet Union always remained the exemplar of a modern society in Maoist China. The disasters of the Maoist period cannot be fully understood unless the role of Marxism as a westernizing project in China is grasped.

The Soviet example was the inspiration for Mao's disastrous Great Leap Forward (1958–60) which triggered an artificial famine in which around 30 million people perished. Mao followed his Soviet mentors in believing that if China's economy was to be modernized its farming would have to be industrialized. As in the Soviet case, the model for farming in China under Mao was not the peasant smallholding but the nineteenth-century capitalist factory.

Again, Mao followed the Soviet example in adopting a Promethean stance to the environment – an attitude hitherto uncommon, or unknown, in China. In the Maoist period ruthless uses of technology and a doctrinal Marxian denial that China could ever suffer from a Malthusian problem of population left the country with overstretched natural resources and environmental devastation worse even than the Soviet Union's.

None of these features of Mao's regime can be traced to Chinese traditions. As recently as the late nineteenth century many Chinese believed that railways disrupted the natural harmonies of nature. In deference to these sentiments, the first railway built in China, near Shanghai, was purchased by the government and torn up.[22] The vast dams and absurd campaigns against pests undertaken under Mao were applications of some of the Enlightenment project of subjugating nature, transmitted to China from classical Marxism via the Soviet example.

Yet again, Maoist totalitarianism had no precedent in China's history. As Simon Leys has argued, 'inasmuch as it is totalitarian, Maoism presents features that are foreign to Chinese political traditions (however despotic some of these traditions might have been), while it appears remarkably similar to otherwise foreign models, such as Stalinism and Nazism.'[23] To argue that Mao's totalitarian regime was a development of traditional Chinese despotism does not square with the incomparably more coercive and invasive role of the state under Mao.

Leys is right to note that Chinese political practice has often been despotic. Law has long been highly developed in China; but the institution of a judiciary independent in its workings from the executive power of the state is almost unknown. Moreover, in the writings of the legalist school there was something akin to a political philosophy of unlimited despotism. Yet never in Chinese history has there been a regime as invasive as Mao's. As Leys has put it: 'In the mid-sixteenth century, Chinese officialdom consisted of some ten to fifteen thousand civil servants for a total population of about one hundred and fifty million. This tiny group of cadres was exclusively concentrated in the cities, while most of the population was living in the villages . . . The great majority of Chinese could spend an entire lifetime *without ever having come into contact with one single representative of imperial authority.*'[24]

Government in classical China was never as invasive as most modern states, and never approached remotely the degree of control which the Maoist regime achieved. As Mehnert has written, 'Not even in the days of the First Emperor in the third century BC, and certainly never since that time, have the Chinese people known a government as severe and totalitarian as that of the Communist State.'[25]

The decay of the core of China's traditional culture, the family and clan, began in the nineteenth century. The collapse of the Qing dynasty in 1912 was the end of a long process of decomposition. The mandarins believed it was possible to adopt new technologies from the West while leaving the Chinese state and Chinese society untouched. At the very end of the Qing era, an attempt was made to appropriate western technologies, especially railways, and around the turn of the century the army was reorganized. Various institutional reforms were considered, particularly in the relations of central with local government, but not much was achieved, and in 1912 the political institutions of Qing China fell apart.

A republic was declared; but modernization had not really begun. The war with Japan and the conflict between the Guomindang Nationalists and the communists further desolated traditional Chinese society without implanting modern institutions.

Mao's regime marked a watershed in China's history. It represented the unqualified triumph of a strategy of modernization through the emulation of a western, Soviet model. It launched a succession of assaults on what remained of traditional life in China. Nevertheless, the core of Chinese society has remained sufficiently intact through the vast upheavals of the Maoist regime to make the economic culture of the Chinese mainland in post-Mao times a recognizable variation on the capitalism long practised by the Chinese overseas.

Until the market reforms introduced by Deng Xiaoping, China had not begun to modernize on the basis of Chinese traditions. Even though, in Taiwan and in the family businesses found throughout the Chinese diaspora, there was a model for Chinese capitalism. Classical China had been autarchic, sealed off from the rest of the world, intellectually and economically, for many centuries. The very idea of an economy as a separate sphere of social life, subject to its own laws, was lacking: the traditional word for economy, *ching chi*, means literally the administration of a surplus.[26] The western idea of market exchange as a realm separate from personal and family life is foreign to Chinese traditions.

When autarchy broke down, as it did in the second half of the nineteenth century, it was because China was subjected to an enforced opening to trade with western powers. Unequal treaties between China and western governments established 'treaty ports', which functioned not only as channels for trade but, from 1895 onwards, as centres for foreign industries. As in Japan, and practically everywhere else apart from England, China's industrialization was state-led. But the state which guided China's first faltering steps towards industrialization was defenceless before the western powers.

In China, as in Japan, humiliation at the hands of western states generated intellectual movements demanding modernization. But in China, in contrast to Japan, modernization nearly always meant westernization. China's modernizers differed only as to how far westernization should be taken, and what should be its guiding philosophy. Some favoured the liberal progressive ideas of John Stuart Mill and John Dewey, others – somewhat later – the revolutionary thought of Marx and his Soviet disciples. Few Chinese ever doubted that becoming modern meant adopting western values.

China's modernizers did not embody the interests of any definite economic group. In Japan modernization was pushed ahead by the *samurai*, the warrior class, who were in danger of losing their social position because of changes in the economy. No such group existed to advance modernization in China.

China was different from Japan in yet another way. It had not been a feudal country for millennia. As Mehnert has summarized his crucial point, 'In China there has been virtually no peasant serfdom for over two thousand years . . . Even in the thirties of this century, when the situation had sharply deteriorated as compared with earlier times, the Chinese peasant class consisted, according to the reliable research of J. L. Buck, of fifty-four per cent property-owners only, seventeen per cent tenant-farmers only, and the remaining twenty-nine per cent of peasants who farmed their own as well as leased land.'[27]

The absence of a feudalism in China, together with the fact that the Maoist regime failed to destroy peasant traditions, is one of the most fundamental reasons why Deng's economic reforms have largely worked, while those of Gorbachev did not. This was not a fault of Gorbachev's; it was an historical inheritance about which he could do nothing.

The fundamental differences between traditional China and feudalism in Europe, Russia and Japan were disregarded by Chinese revolutionary intellectuals who from the 1920s onwards imbibed Marxian theories in Moscow. As Becker has written in his invaluable study of the origins of China's greatest famine, 'The origins of Mao's great famine lie as much in Russian as in Chinese history'.[28] He elucidates this decisive point:

The theories that the Chinese Communists learned in Moscow and from advisers such as Borodin and Otto Braun were based on an analysis of feudalism which existed in Europe and Russia in the last century. When the future leaders of China, men such as Deng Xiaoping or Liu Shaoqui, studied at the 'University of the Toilers of the East', their textbooks referred to the liberation of the serfs, the overthrow of the landed aristocracy and the break-up of vast feudal estates in Germany, France or Russia. China was quite different, as both eighteenth-century Jesuit missionaries and scholars such as R. H. Tawney, writing in the 1920s, pointed out. There was no landed aristocracy, no dominant clan of Junkers or squires, no feudal land law, no great estates worked by corvee labour. And, unlike in Europe, there were no commons, pastures, or forests in public hands. Ministry of Agriculture statistics produced in 1918 showed that in China there was a higher percentage of peasant proprietors in the farming population than in Germany, Japan or the United States.[29]

The Marxian theories adopted by China's intellectual élite had little application to Chinese circumstances or history. Yet they formed the basis of the model of modernization that Mao Zedong imposed on China. It was the implementation of a western, Soviet-style modernization in the Great Leap Forward that caused the worse famine in China's long history.

Opposed by some within the Chinese Communist party as 'false, dangerous and Utopian agrarian socialism', Mao established agricultural collectives in emulation of Stalin: 'For Krushchev, then in charge of agriculture was implementing Stalin's plans to create still larger collectives – giant farms, as big as provinces, that were organized around agro-cities.'[30]

The result was disaster. In China in 1957, before the Great Leap Forward, the median age of death was 17.6 years; in 1963 it was 9.7. Half of those dying in China in 1963 were under ten years old.[31]

Mao's modernization failed for many reasons, but central among them was the fact that the Soviet project which it emulated was incompatible with the needs of a modern economy. The economy that the Communists inherited from the Nationalist, Guomindang regime contained many large state enterprises. It was not until the mid-1950s that they attempted to collectivize it. There was no economic justification for collectivization. It was done because the Soviet economy, the model of a modern economy in Mao's China, was collectivized.

The Great Leap Forward was not just an attempt to industrialize Chinese agriculture and collectivize industry on a Soviet model. It was also a systematic attack on traditional Chinese practices and beliefs. Peasant traditional beliefs had been under siege since the communist victory in 1949, but it was in the Great Leap Forward, and then the Cultural Revolution, that they were finally almost destroyed: 'Everything connected with traditional beliefs was smashed up in the Great Leap Forward.'[32]

The attack on traditional China was resumed in the Great Proletarian Cultural Revolution of 1966–76. The 'four olds' – old customs, old habits, old culture and old thinking, as embodied in books, money, documents and antique art treasures – were assaulted in one of history's greatest convulsions. Leys has written: 'the "Cultural Revolution" was a civil war that was prevented from running its full course. It is currently estimated by the Chinese themselves that nearly a hundred million people were to some extent directly involved in the violence of the "Cultural Revolution" – either as active participants or as victims.'[33]

The Cultural Revolution set back China's economy and education for a generation. It uprooted much of Chinese traditional culture that had somehow survived the Great Leap Forward. It left deep psychological and social scars. To a greater extent even than in Russia during the Stalinist period the Cultural Revolution weakened the bonds of social solidarity in China. Severely damaged, possibly only the family emerged as a living social institution.

The destruction of Chinese traditions in the Great Leap Forward and the Cultural Revolution went in tandem with the degradation of China's natural environment. In a characteristically hubristic Maoist programme designed to eradicate all pests, war was declared on China's sparrows. The sparrows were exterminated, resulting in a plague of the insects the sparrows had controlled, and consequent damage to crops.

The Soviet 'war on nature' was emulated in other, even more destructive policies. Dams were constructed throughout China, most of them collapsing soon after, but some surviving into the 1970s.

When the dams in Henan province broke down, the worst damburst in history ensued, killing nearly a quarter of a million people.[34]

Mao's legacy to his successors was a level of environmental degradation graver in its consequences than Russia's because it coincided with a problem of overpopulation. The scale of environmental damage inflicted by Mao's regime is chronicled in Vaclav Smil's pioneering study, *The Bad Earth: Environmental Degradation in China*.[35]

China's Malthusian problem is recognized by the government in its one-child policy, which represents one of the most fundamental departures from Maoism. Yet, even with this programme in place, China's population will grow by about a quarter – around 300 million people – over the next twenty years. A part of this increase results from population growth during the Maoist period, when large families were encouraged.

Apart from Bangladesh and Egypt, China has less arable land than any other developing country. About a tenth of China's territory, containing nearly two-thirds of the population and producing almost three-quarters of all its output, is below the flood level of major rivers. Population growth impacts directly on the use of scarce arable land in China – making it even scarcer. As Smil has noted, 'During the past 40 years, China has lost about a third of its cropland to soil erosion, desertification, energy projects (hydro stations, coal mining) and to industrial and housing construction . . . Even if these losses were to be made up by reclamation of new land (such opportunities are increasingly scarce), population growth alone would reduce per capita farmland availability by more than ten per cent during the 1990s, and by 15 per cent by the year 2025.'[36]

By the early decades of the coming century China is likely to be the world's single largest contributor to global warming. By 2010 China could become the leading producer of the gas which produces the greenhouse effect. Aside from its effects on the rest of the world, such a development could increase China's vulnerability to both droughts and floods.[37]

The economic implications of these environmental limits are sobering: 'The size of China's population and the stresses it puts on the environment prevent any simplistic contemplation of China ever emulating Japan or duplicating fully the achievements of smaller, so-called Dragons of the region . . . The Chinese can never import 98 per cent of their fossil fuels as the Japanese do, or 75 per cent of their food and feed grains as South Koreans do: the world market simply does not have so much fuel and food.'[38] These limits will be stringent under any policies. They are as severe as they are today, partly as a consequence of Mao's Marxian denial that China could ever have a Malthusian problem.

Mao's legacy to his successors was environmental devastation, a country decreasingly able to feed itself, and a desolated society. As Roderick MacFarquhar has tersely observed of Mao, 'He sought Utopia, but China almost ended up in a state of nature.'[39] Until Deng's reforms, sustainable modernization on the basis of China's indigenous capitalism had not yet begun.

Chinese capitalism

As in other economic cultures, Chinese capitalism comes embedded in the networks and values of the larger society. Some features of capitalism in mainland China today derive from the recent political history of the country; but its central and enduring characteristics are those exhibited by Chinese businesses everywhere. These reflect the pivotal position of the Chinese family in generating relationships of trust. Overseas Chinese capitalism has been one of the principal motors of success in China's market reform. It is the best guide to the indigenous capitalism that is emerging on the Chinese mainland.

The central characteristics of Chinese economic culture have been identified by Redding in his seminal book, *The Spirit of Chinese Capitalism*.[40] As summarized by Redding and Whitley, they are as follows:

1 small-scale and relatively simple organizational structuring;
2 normally focused on one product or market with growth by opportunistic diversification;
3 centralized decision-making with heavy reliance on one dominant executive;
4 a close overlap of ownership, control and family;
5 a paternalistic organizational climate;
6 linked to the environment through personalistic networks;
7 normally very sensitive to matters of cost and financial efficiency;

8 commonly linked strongly but informally with related but legally independent organizations handling key functions such as parts supply or marketing;

9 relatively weak in crating large-scale market recognition for brands;

10 high degree of strategic adaptability.[41]

There are about 40 million overseas Chinese in Hong Kong, Singapore, Taiwan, Indonesia, Malaysia and the Philippines. Their collective product amounts to around US $150–200 billion.

In these countries, as in the Chinese diaspora throughout the world, Chinese businesses are typically small, their internal and external relationships family-dependent and personal. They rely on *guanxi* – 'connections', reciprocal obligations and long-term negotiating relationships – rather than on formal contractual obligations for their supplies and supports. Even when Chinese businesses become large they remain family firms, with the most important decisions being taken by the head of the family, the father. Both in Taiwan and in mainland China large enterprises are nearly always state-owned. Where family-owned Chinese businesses are large, it is often in contexts in which they enjoy political protection, or because they have specialized in particular industries and markets such as shipping or property.

Though its reach is worldwide, Chinese capitalism is most highly developed in Hong Kong and Taiwan. Taiwan is particularly interesting in that it can plausibly claim to have carried off an indigenous modernization of its economy that has only lately begun on the Chinese mainland.

In the 1950s and 1960s Taiwan implemented a far-reaching land reform in which farmland was redistributed to create a rural economy of small farms. An equally far-reaching privatization programme was pursued from the 1950s onwards, reducing state-owned enterprises from 57 per cent of industry to less than 20 per cent. The Taiwanese economy is made up of small family businesses: there are none of the large conglomerates found in Korea and Japan. The growth rate of the Taiwanese economy over the past four decades has averaged around 9 per cent.

One result of Taiwan's economic modernization is that 'in terms of income distribution, Taiwan is the most egalitarian of all capitalist countries'.[42] These achievements give credibility to Wilson's claim that 'Taiwan has shown the way, offering China a Chinese model of modernity.'[43]

The family businesses that are the core of Chinese capitalism do not fit well with western theories of the firm. As Redding and Whitley comment, 'Anglo-Saxon conceptions of the legally bounded firm as the basic unit of economic action are inadequate to explain the actions and structures of *chaebol* and Chinese family businesses, both of which have complex extra-firm linkages influencing decision-making.'[44] Neither the structure nor the workings of Chinese businesses match the model of economic rationality that western theories assume is universally valid.

Like Japanese economic culture, though in sharply different ways, Chinese businesses challenge the standard account of the growth of capitalism advanced by Max Weber and other western sociologists. In the conventional western account, capitalism develops by displacing family and personal relationships from centrality in economic life. It makes the economy a separate, autonomous domain, ruled by an impersonal calculus of profit and loss, and held together not by relationships of trust but contractual-legal obligations. In this conventional narrative, capitalism develops by disembedding itself from its parent society.

This account squares fairly well with the development of capitalism in England and other Anglo-Saxon countries where there is a long history of individualism. Even there, it leaves out the role of state power in constructing the environment – the framework of laws and property holdings – in which disembedded markets work. In Chinese capitalism it has little purchase. The success of Chinese capitalism depends crucially on the resources of trust within families which it can draw upon.

The familism of Chinese business culture reflects that of Chinese society, in which trust is rarely extended beyond kin in weighty matters. In this core feature, Chinese economic culture differs as deeply and radically from Japanese capitalism as it does from the American free market. Relationships of trust and obligation extending beyond the family that are prominent in feudal and modern Japan and in the individualist societies of the Anglo-Saxon world have always been weak or absent in China. The vast transnational corporations that distinguish Japanese capitalism, with their strong corporate cultures and loyalties, open to government guidance but exhibiting a high degree of autonomy in their strategies, have no counterpart among Chinese businesses.[45]

Chinese capitalism differs equally from capitalism in Korea. There the economy is dominated by the conglomerates known as *chaebol*. The ten largest *chaebol* produce over half Korea's exports and the thirty largest are responsible for three-quarters of the country's output.[46] Korean *chaebol* are paternalistic institutions, with the founding families remaining in decision-making positions. But they are enterprises in which co-operation, often aiming at monopolistic or oligopolistic domination of markets, extends far beyond families.

Though this is beginning to change, *chaebol* have close links with government, which often frames overall strategy. A patrimonial style of management pervades these conglomerates, with reward and compensation being personalized. Beyond a base salary rewards depend not on the type of work done but on how well a superior judges it to have been performed. There are clan and regional rivalries among these organizations, and lifetime employment is not practised, or promised, in most Korean firms.[47]

Chinese capitalism has more in common with Italian capitalism, with its strong family-based firms, than it does with the economic culture of Korea, with the American free market, or with Japanese capitalism.

For reasons connected with the country's twentieth-century history, the capitalism of the Chinese mainland differs somewhat from that found in the Chinese diaspora. Mainland China is not a fully capitalist economy. Its remarkable growth rates are partly explained by the fact that Chinese workers have less bargaining power, and so lower wages, than workers in capitalist economies at comparable stages of development. Though precise measurement is difficult, economic inequality in Dengist China is almost certainly far greater than in the unequivocally capitalist economy of Taiwan.

Insofar as the economic culture of the Chinese mainland converges with that of the overseas Chinese it will in the future be a more traditionally Chinese capitalism than that which exists today. As Wilson has recorded, 'A visit to almost any part of China these days would show factories or other enterprises wholly or partly financed by overseas Chinese whose representatives are unconsciously reintroducing traditional cultural values that had been savaged by Mao and almost driven underground.'[48] Because overseas Chinese have had such a decisive role in financing the expanding private sector, Deng's market reform has in some measure retraditionalized parts of Chinese social life desolated by Mao's unsuccessful modernization.

If the economic culture of mainland China converges further with that of the overseas Chinese, China will become a fully capitalist economy on a home-grown model. That will require several generations of economic development, uninterrupted by political upheaval, environmental catastrophe, or war.[49]

Western business optimism about China passes tends to overload these facts, in particular the many periods of state disintegration that have recurred throughout China's history. Environmental degradation in China is regarded by those who anticipate a vast market in China as a incidental inconvenience, not a threat that might choke off further modernization altogether.

Barton Biggs, chairman of Morgan Stanley Asset Management in New York, has described environmental pollution as the price of economic development that the Chinese are prepared to pay.[50] Biggs may be right in his judgement of the readiness of many Chinese people to tolerate pollution, but it is surely significant that the present Chinese leadership does not share his insouciance about how high this price may turn out to be, or his optimism that it can be easily reduced by a technical fix. Unlike Biggs, China's leaders are aware that it may never become an economic superpower.

Even if China's environmental problems can be overcome and the programme of economic modernization begun by Deng Xiaoping is successful, China will not become a developed society until sometime in the latter half of the coming century.

Economic modernization in China, 1979 onwards

Mao's failed modernization made the task of later Chinese modernizers all the harder. In part, the market reforms of the era of Deng Xiaoping (1976–97)[51] came about as a reaction against the destruction of the Great Leap Forward and the Cultural Revolution; but they could not undo much of the harm Mao's Utopian experiment had done to China's social fabric and natural environment.

The origins of Deng's economic reforms are obscure. They began in July 1979 with the establishment of four special economic zones –

Zuhai, Shenzen, Shantou and Xiamen. These were chosen for their proximity and easy access to foreign capital. Two of them, Shantou and Xiamen, had been treaty ports during the British-dominated imperialist era. The idea of special economic zones seems to have been suggested to Deng by two party officials form Guangdong, but it may well be that this proposal was orchestrated by Deng himself.

In the post-Mao era, Chinese policy has been to modernize the economy while retaining strong overall political control. Deng deconstructed Mao's Soviet model and, in the policy of *kaifang*, or 'opening up', mobilized foreign capital and technology in the service of economic modernization. He loosened the grip of the centre on the regions while resisting any tendencies to separatism.[52] He did not try to orchestrate economic activity but merely to remove hindrances to it. The framework within which that relaxation of control occurred remained the Leninist state constructed by Mao.

In economic terms the policy has been an uneven but considerable success, with rates of economic growth in the coastal provinces running in excess of 10 per cent a year. A crucial factor in this success has undoubtedly been China's disregard to Soviet and western examples and advice. There has been no shock therapy in China. Market reform has been gradual and partial, pragmatic rather than doctrinal. If China's reformers have learned lessons from other countries, it has been from Singapore and Taiwan and, to a lesser but still significant extent, Korea and Japan. No western society has been used as a model.

China's economic reform has been an attempt to construct a working market economy, not to engineer a free market. It has built on China's strengths. Unlike Russia, China is not burdened by an inheritance of feudalism, and peasant traditions have not been wrecked by collectivization. Deng's reforms exploited these advantages.

Deng's successor, Jiang Zemin, appears determined to carry further the deconstruction of the planned economy begun by Deng. In August, 1997, the *People's Daily* announced: 'We cannot just add the market economy on to the base of the old system. We need a total modification of the old system.'[53] Like Deng, Jiang Zemin proposes to break up the institutions of the planned economy while retaining the Leninist state which created them.

What assures the political legitimacy of a regime whose official ideology, Marxism–Leninism, has long been discredited? A major dilemma for China's political elite arises from the contradiction between its vestigial Marxian ideology, which is embodied in the Communist Party, and the appeal to 'Chineseness' and Confucian values to which the regime resorts increasingly in an effort to establish its legitimacy. How can traditional Chinese values be mobilized in the service of modernization by a government that is the direct successor of a Maoist regime that tried to modernize by making war on old China?

In terms of ideology, China today has a hollow regime. While living standards go on rising this may not be a serious weakness. When economic slowdown interacts with regional inequalities and ecological crisis the regime's lack of any coherent ideology may become a source of instability.

China's modernizers today confront a country whose natural environment has suffered irreversible degradation and which has a formidable Malthusian population problem. In their attempt to modernize on the basis of the country's indigenous capitalism they must confront the fact that the most enduring result of Mao's failed modernization was to uproot much of China's traditional culture.

China's recent history of rapid growth is partly explained by its very low starting point.[54] It is not easy to assess its present GDP. The facts are hard to ascertain, and even the basis of calculation is disputed. But if the standard UN system of national accounts is used as a measure, rather than parity of purchasing power, then China's economy (not counting Hong Kong) is somewhat larger than Spain's and smaller than Italy's. By contrast, the GDP of Hong Kong is about a quarter of that of the Chinese mainland. One reason for this discrepancy is China's vast population; another is the low level of wages. China is a fast developing country, not a mature capitalist economy.

Whatever its current GDP the present regime depends for its stability on fast economic growth continuing. Even if growth does not falter its benefits will be very unevenly spread, with large parts of China stagnating in poverty. In 1992, according to the World Bank, Shanghai and Guangdong had per capita incomes of over $800; in inland Guizhou they were around $226. The southern and eastern coasts had average per capita incomes about twice as high as the much larger populations in the south and centre of China.[55]

These inequalities are likely to grow. Migrant workers may amount to 10 per cent of the Chinese population – around 120 million people.[56] China's Labour Ministry has forecasted unemployment in the year 2000 of 267 million people – a fifth of its population.[57] This forecast was made before the decision was announced in late 1997 to privatize most of China's state-owned enterprises.[58] The social and economic dislocations of market reform may be enough to put in question the integrity of the Chinese state.

State institutions in China have become weaker as a side-effect of economic liberalization. Corruption is pandemic. Every institution, including the PLA (People's Liberation Army), is – officially or unofficially – commercialized. The chain of command has not broken in China, as it has in Russia, but it has become weaker as a result of the ubiquitous belief, well-founded in practice, that nearly everything has its price.

Economic growth is too uneven to be relied upon as the sole source of allegiance to the regime. As parts of China's economy boom others are going bankrupt. In Shanghai the economy grew by 14 per cent in 1996, but its textile plants and other state-owned enterprises sank deeper into debt.[59] Worse, about three-quarters of the Chinese people's savings are tied up in loss-making state-owned enterprises through the investments of state banks. As MacFarqhar comments, 'That is a financial and political disaster in the making.'[60]

Yet, by comparison with Russia, China faces few serious challenges to the integrity of the state. Movements for independence or autonomy in Tibet and Sinkiang have been crushed ruthlessly, with a repression in Tibet as atrocious as any committed anywhere during this century. Over 90 per cent of China's citizens are Han Chinese; only around one in twenty belong to national minorities. China is close to being an ethnically homogenous country. Its history contains recurrent periods of state disintegration; but, for the present, China does not have a Hobbesian problem.

China's current regime is undoubtedly transitional, but rather than moving towards 'democratic capitalism', it is evolving from the western, Soviet institutions of the past into a modern state more suited to Chinese traditions, needs and circumstances.

Liberal democracy is not on the historical agenda for China. It is very doubtful if the one-child policy, which even at present is often circumvented, could survive a transition to liberal democracy. Yet, as China's present rulers rightly believe, an effective population policy is indispensable if scarcity of resources is not to lead to ecological catastrophe and political crisis.

Popular memories of the collapse of the state and national defence-lessness between the world wars are such that any experiment with political liberalization which appears to carry the risk of the near-anarchy of post-Soviet Russia will be regarded with suspicion or horror by the majority of Chinese. Few view the break-up of the state as other than a supreme evil. The present regime has a potent source of popular legitimacy in the fact that so far it has staved off that disaster.

An evolution from a soft, semi-totalitarian state towards authoritarianism would be a benign scenario for China. It need not mean dictatorship. The key political requirements for personal security and sustained economic growth are an uncorrupt rule of law and institutions which make government accountable. With regard to accountability a beginning has already been made with local government. In 1987 a law was enacted permitting villages to choose their governors and ruling councils. Over 4 million village officials are now elected representatives rather than party appointees.[61] Holding government to account need not mean the importation into China of western multi-party democracy, even though it will be harder for China to meet the requirement of an independent rule of law. But without it neither political stability nor steady economic development can be assured.

Because its circumstances are so different from those of any other country there is no model for China's economic or political development. Taiwan's experiment in indigenous capitalism teaches many lessons, but Singapore may approximate next closely to a model that can be emulated. That post-liberal city-state has many advantages China lacks. The differences in scale, history and ethnic composition of the two countries are self-evident. Yet Singapore's guided capitalism under a rule of law is the example from which China may have most to learn.

Replicating Singapore's achievements in China may not be fully feasible. But if the Chinese regime were to relinquish gradually the remnants of its totalitarian Leninist inheritance to become a modern, neo-authoritarian state it could have enduring political legitimacy. A China that was modelled on Singapore would not be a second-best approximation to western democracy. It would be an exemplar of indigenous modernization on a par with Japan.

Modern Asia and western backwardness?

There is no generic 'Asian' capitalism, any more than there is such a thing as 'western' capitalism. Each version of capitalism articulates the particular culture in which it remains embedded. This is true of the free market, which expresses local American values of individualism. In Asia, as in the rest of the world, each type of capitalism has advantages and costs.

Asia's diverse capitalisms will not converge: their underlying cultures will remain deeply different from one another. Still less will they assimilate to the practices of any western market economy. Nor will they converge in their political development.

The belief that prosperity drags liberal democracy in its wake is an article of faith, not a result of disciplined inquiry. Often it is little more than a neo-liberal variation of the Marxian tenet that the development of capitalism generates a growing middle class. The recent experience of many states supports a different Marxian view: that uncontrolled, slash-and-burn capitalism impoverishes and shrinks the middle classes.

Even if it were true that economic development produced everywhere a growing middle class it would not for that reason promote the spread of liberal democracy in Asia. Like everyone else, middle-class people in Asian countries have many needs in addition to those that require democratic institutions for their satisfaction. They need economic risk controlled, so that they and their families can have some control over their livelihoods; they need security from crime and corruption; they need good public services, and common institutions that give them a sense of membership and participation in society.

Regimes which meet these needs will be legitimate whether or not they are democratic, while regimes that do not will be weak and unstable however democratic they may be.

The deep differences between Asia's capitalisms and those in western countries will not diminish over time. They reflect differences not only in the family structures but also in the religious life of the cultures in which these diverse capitalisms are rooted. The greatest sociologist of capitalism, Max Weber, was right to link the development of capitalism in north-western Europe with Protestantism.

Western social thinkers and economists are mistaken in supposing that capitalism everywhere will come to resemble the highly individualist economic culture of England, Scotland and parts of Germany and The Netherlands. It has not done so in France or Italy. In our time, capitalism in post-communist countries whose religious traditions are Orthodox will be unlike that in any 'western', Protestant or Catholic, country: neither the institutions of secular civil society, nor the limited state of such western countries, has developed in any Orthodox culture. Russian capitalism, like capitalism elsewhere in the Orthodox world, will be *sui generis*.

The same goes for the capitalisms of Asia. Indian capitalism will never converge with that of countries whose principal religious inheritance is Confucian, Buddhist or Muslim. Its caste system may be the world's stablest social system, having survived challenges from Buddhism, Islam and Fabian secularism, and it will surely condition profoundly the growth of an indigenous Indian capitalism.

The new capitalisms in eastern Asia do not carry the western burden of doctrinal dispute over the merits of rival economic systems. This is partly because most of the religious traditions of east Asia make no claim to exclusivity. This freedom from sectarian claims to unique truths goes with a pragmatic approach to economic policies.[62]

In Asian cultures market institutions are viewed instrumentally, as means to wealth-creation and social cohesion, not theologically, as ends in themselves. One of the appeals of 'Asian values' is that by adopting a thoroughly instrumental view of economic life they avoid the western obsessions that make economic policy an arena of doctrinal conflict. That 'Asian' freedom from economic theology allows market institutions to be judged, and reformed, by reference to how their workings affect the values and stability of society.[63]

Insofar as Asian capitalisms are guided by governments with a view to preserving the cohesion of the societies they serve they are bound to come into conflict with the regime of global *laissez-faire*. In this conflict it is western *laissez-faire* that embodies backwardness.

This is not to say that Asian countries can insulate themselves from the economic instabilities, the ecological risks or the cultural hazards of global markets. The currency crises and vastly polluting forest fires of late 1997 showed their vulnerability. More profoundly, full-tilt economic modernization in Asian countries has involved accepting western values in one crucial, perhaps fatal context: their relations with the natural world. In Asia, as throughout the world, the modern western understanding of the earth as a consumable resource now holds sway. It may well be in Asia that ecological limits on economic growth are finally transgressed.

We have entered an era of Occidental twilight. It is not an era in which all Asian countries will prosper and all western countries decline. It is an age in which the identification of 'the West' with modernity is being severed. The very idea of 'the West' may already be archaic – the old polarities of East and West do not capture the diversity of cultures and regimes in the world today.

A monolithic 'Asia' is as much a chimera as 'western civilization'. The inexorable growth of a world market does not advance a universal civilization. It makes the interpenetration of cultures an irreversible global condition.

8 The ends of *laissez-faire*

The present situation is comparable to that at the turn of the
past century. It was a golden age of capitalism, characterized by
the principle of *laissez-faire*; so is the present. The earlier period
was in some ways more stable. It had an imperial power,
England, that was prepared to despatch gun boats to faraway
places because as the main beneficiary of the system it had a
vested interest in maintaining it. Today the United States does
not want to be the policeman of the world. The earlier period
had the Gold Standard; today the main currencies float and
crush against each other like continental plates. Yet the free
market regime that prevailed a hundred years ago was destroyed
by the First World War. Totalitarian ideologues came to the
fore, and by the end of the Second World War there was
practically no movement of capital between countries. How
much more likely is the present regime to break down unless we
learn from past experience?

GEORGE SOROS[1]

We can't turn history back. Yet I do not wish to abandon the
belief that a world which is a reasonably peaceful coat of many
colours, each portion of which develops its own distinct cultural
identity and is tolerant of others, is not a Utopian dream.

ISAIAH BERLIN[2]

A truly global economy is being created by the worldwide spread of
new technologies, not by the spread of free markets. Every economy is
being transformed as technologies are imitated, absorbed and adapted.
No country can insulate itself from this wave of creative destruction.
And the result is not a universal free market but an anarchy of sovereign states, rival capitalisms and stateless zones.

The command economies of the former socialist blocs could not
insulate themselves from the technological virtuosity of capitalism.

Marx noted that, by comparison with capitalism, 'All earlier modes of production were essentially conservative.'[3] This proved fatally true of the twentieth-century's planned economies. Except in a few areas, such as armaments and space vehicles (an offshoot of the missile programme), they could not match the inventiveness of capitalism, and lacked capitalism's ability to revolutionize itself, to change the very basis of its productivity. They were unable to liquidate old heavy industries, such as coal and steel, and slow to move into new information technologies. As a result there is now no alternative to capitalism, only its constantly mutating varieties.

Free market economies, strictly defined – and we have seen how local and peculiar they are – are no less exposed to this than any other variety of capitalism. As Joseph Schumpeter, who saw this aspect of capitalism with unsurpassed clarity, wrote: 'The opening up of new markets, foreign or domestic, and the organizational development from the craft shop and factory to such concerns as US Steel illustrate the same process of industrial mutation – if I may use that biological term – that incessantly revolutionizes the economic structure from within, incessantly destroying the old one, incessantly creating a new one. This process of Creative Destruction is the essential fact about capitalism.'[4]

The growth of a world economy does not inaugurate a universal civilization, as both Smith and Marx thought it must. Instead it allows the growth of indigenous kinds of capitalism, diverging from the ideal free market and from each other. It creates regimes that achieve modernity by renewing their own cultural traditions, not by imitating western countries. There are many modernities, and as many ways of failing to be modern.

A plural global economy severs one of the strongest strands in modern western thought. Karl Marx and John Stuart Mill believed that modern societies throughout the world would become replicas of western societies. The West would necessarily be a *model*, its imitators secular, Enlightenment cultures. Economic life would detach itself from kinship and personal relationships. Capitalism everywhere would promote individualism and rational calculation. If socialism were established, it would develop the rational economy that capitalism had pioneered. Modernity and the evolution of a single-world civilization were one and the same.

History has falsified this Enlightenment faith. Modern societies come in many varieties. Like nineteenth-century Japan, China and Russia, Singapore, Taiwan and Malaysia are developing as modern countries today by borrowing selectively from western societies while rejecting western models. The indigenous varieties of capitalism emerging in China and the rest of Asia cannot be contained within a framework that has been designed to reproduce the American free market. The governments of these countries will not accept policies whose effect is to uproot their economies from their parent cultures and render them uncontrollable.

The growth of a world economy could be a great advance for humankind. It could be the beginning of a many-centred world, in which different cultures and regimes could interact and cooperate without domination or war. But that is not the world that is arising around us in the vain attempt to build a universal free market.

In a world in which market forces are subject to no overall constraint or regulation, peace is continually at risk. Slash-and-burn capitalism degrades the environment and kindles conflict over natural resources. The practical consequence of policies promoting minimal government intervention in the economy is that, in expanding regions of the world, sovereign states are locked in competition not only for markets but for survival. The global market as it is presently organized does not allow the world's peoples to coexist harmoniously. It impels them to become rivals for resources while instituting no methods for conserving.

Can global *laissez-faire* be reformed?

At present global markets work to fracture societies and weaken states. Countries with highly competent governments or strong, resilient cultures have a margin of freedom within which they can act to maintain social cohesion. Where these resources are lacking, states have collapsed or ceased to be effective, and societies have been desolated by market forces over which they have no control.

History confirms that free markets are not self-regulating. They are inherently volatile institutions, prone to speculative booms and busts. Throughout the period in which Keynes's thought was a dominant influence it was recognized that free markets are highly imperfect institutions. To work well they need not only regulation but active management. During the post-war era world markets were kept stable by national governments and by a regime of international cooperation.

Only lately has a pre-Keynesian idea been revived to become an orthodoxy: the belief that, provided there are clear and well-enforced rules of the game, free markets can embody the rational expectations that participants form about the future.

In fact, since markets are themselves shaped by human expectations, their behaviour cannot be rationally predicted. The forces that drive markets are not mechanical processes of cause and effect. They are what George Soros has termed 'reflexive interactions'.[5] Because markets are constituted by highly combustible interactions among beliefs they cannot be self-regulating.

In standard economic theory the economy can be understood in the same way we understand the workings of a machine; but human societies are forever fluctuating and changeable. Social institutions are composed from human beliefs: a piece of paper counts as money only if we believe it to be money, otherwise it is only a curiosity. Theories which try to model markets on machines miss the most important fact about them: they are figments of human imagination and expectations.

Particularly in financial markets, our expectations about the future rebound upon each other. Financial markets do not tend to equilibrium. Overshoot is their normal condition. This volatility at the core of deregulated financial institutions makes a world economy that is organized as a system of free markets essentially unstable.

Those who believe that free markets enable us to form rational expectations about the future see the long American economic boom from the early 1980s to the present as evidence that the business cycle is one of history's barbarous relics. They are confident that economies which have submitted themselves to the requirements of the Washington consensus need not fear the sudden crashes and long depressions that have shaken them in the past.

The conceit that the business cycle is now obsolete has been given credence by Alan Greenspan, Chairman of the Federal Reserve Bank. Until 1989 Greenspan believed that free markets were rooted in human nature, and only tyranny prevented the rest of humankind embracing them. Commendably, it was Greenspan who, in a lecture to the Woodrow Wilson Center in June 1997, confessed that after 1989 he discovered that 'much of what we took for granted in our free-market system was not nature at all, but culture. The dismantling of the central planning function does not, as some had supposed, automatically establish (market capitalism).'[6]

Greenspan has recognized the importance of cultural norms in supporting free markets. But what cataclysm in the market will it take to convince Greenspan that a 'New Era' of stable growth is merely another myth?

Global *laissez-faire* may break down in an unmanageable crisis of the world's stock markets and financial institutions. The enormous, practically unknowable virtual economy of financial derivatives enhances the risks of a systemic crash.

How would America's fractured society cope with a collapse in the stock market such as occurred in Japan in the early 1990s? A crash of that magnitude today could trigger large-scale economic and social upheaval in the US. Whatever else such an event might portend we may be sure that no more would be heard of a global free market. The international regime of free markets could not survive an economic upheaval at its epicentre.

In reality, the idea that a free market economy is a self-stabilizing system is archaic – a curious relic of Enlightenment rationalism. It will be tossed aside when the market reminds today's investors that those who think themselves exempt from history are condemned to repeat it.

Yet a cataclysm in the market is not the most likely scenario for ending the current era of *laissez-faire*. It is more likely to unravel as America's hegemony in the world economy is challenged by the newly emerging powers.

Like the pre-1914 international liberal economic order, a global free market functions only so long as its institutions are underwritten by an effective global power. The United States today lacks the will, perhaps the capacity, to assume the burdens of an imperial power comparable to that of Britain during the *belle époque*.

More than most other democracies, late twentieth-century America is a post-military society. Yet it is the only remaining power with a reach that is global. Its continuing heavy investment in state-of-the-art technologies gives it an unchallengeable military superiority over any other state.

Despite this, the United States can sustain no military engagement that seems likely to be protracted or which carries a significant risk of high casualties. Where their technological lead confers a strategic advantage, as it did in the Gulf War, the United States can prosecute a major war. Where, as in Somalia, what is needed is a willingness to perform some of the functions of government, and to bear their costs, including continuing casualties, over the long haul, American hegemony has proved to be a chimera.

With the steady banalization of new technologies the sources of power in the late modern period are flowing away from western countries. As countries that were pre-industrial develop their own varieties of capitalism they are becoming less willing to submit themselves to the Washington consensus.

If China is successful in modernizing its economy it will play hardball with transnational organizations that attempt to enforce an American free trade agenda on it. So will Russia. The forces of the expanding world economy will break through the institutions of the global free market.

Global *laissez-faire* is a moment in the history of the emerging world economy, not its endpoint. Either the present regime will evolve into something its architects could scarcely have envisaged and certainly do not intend, or its institutions will become ineffectual and marginal.

If they do not begin to reflect the diversity of a more plural world, the transnational institutions that embody global *laissez-faire* will lose their remaining authority. Soon they may be as powerless and irrelevant as the League of Nations between the two world wars.

So, too, if the rules of the global free market are not reformed to match the needs of the emerging economic powers they will be flouted. This is happening already, with China infringing copyright and ignoring many intellectual property rights. A world economy in which the property rights recognized by transnational organisations are unenforceable is not a free market. It is an anarchy.

America's resources as the only remaining global power will not enable it to achieve its objective of projecting free markets worldwide. But they are enough to allow it to veto any reform of global *laissez-faire*.

A regime of global governance is needed in which world markets are managed so as to promote the cohesion of societies and the integrity of states. Only a framework of global regulation – of currencies, capital movements, trade and environmental conservation – can enable the creativity of the world economy to be harnessed in the service of human needs.

The specific policies that should be implemented by such institutions are less important, for the purposes of the present inquiry, than the recognition of the need for a new global regime. A global tax on currency speculation, as proposed by the economist James Tobin,[7] may be an example of the kind of regulation that could render world markets more stable and productive.

Whether or not such policies are workable is uncertain. What is beyond serious doubt is that organizing the world economy as a single global free market promotes instability. It forces workers to bear the costs of new technologies and unrestricted free trade. It contains no means whereby activities that endanger the global ecological balance can be curbed. If – as seems clear – global warming is a real threat, the global free market contains no institutions to deal with it. Organizing the world economy as a universal free market is, in effect, staking the planet's future on the supposition that these vast dangers will be resolved as an unintended consequence of the unfettered pursuit of profits. It is hard to think of a more reckless wager.

Yet the replacement of global *laissez-faire* by a managed regime for the world economy is, at present, nearly as Utopian a project as a universal free market. Such a regime could be established only by the world's great economic powers acting in concert, and conflicts of interests make cooperation for any purpose more ambitious than crisis-management almost impossibly difficult. The necessary consensus on means and ends in policies on population control and environmental conservation does not exist.

A vital condition of reform of the international economy is that it be supported by the world's single most important power. Without active and continuing American endorsement there can be no workable institutions of global governance. But so long as the United States remains committed to a global free market it will veto any such reform. So long as American policy is based on the *laissez-faire* ideology that informs the Washington consensus there is no prospect of reforming the world economy.

The end of the Washington consensus?

The ideal of minimum government which animates the Washington consensus is, at best, anachronistic. It belongs to an age in which totalitarian states were the chief threat to freedom and prosperity. Today human and social well-being is being threatened chiefly by collapsed or enfeebled states.

Reform begins with a rehabilitation of the modern state. In the coming century the condition of a country such as Somalia will be a more pervasive threat to human well-being than the activities of rogue states. Like Somalia, much of the world lacks effective government. In Liberia, Albania, Tajikstan, Pakistan, Colombia, Siberia, Chechnya, the threat to peace and economic progress does not come from tyrannous or expansionist states. It comes from the absence of effective government of any kind.

In many parts of the world, the modern state has not taken root, or else it has collapsed. In such countries the most essential precondition of peace and economic progress, of humane standards for labour and of the conservation of the environment, is lacking.

Throughout most of the contemporary world the modern state is not an institution that can be taken for granted. For most of mankind Hobbesian insecurity – the danger of violent death – is an everyday reality. Yet until that Hobbesian problem has been solved none of the rudiments of human well-being can be assured.

Without a modern state which controls the instruments of war there cannot be peace. Post-Clausewitzian wars are a more formidable obstacle to civilized existence than wars among sovereign states, because they contain no institution that can bring conflict to an end. With the withering away of Clausewitzian war, peace has ceased to be enforceable.

Effective state institutions are needed to monitor the impact of humans on the natural environment, and to limit the exploitation of natural resources by unaccountable interests. In Russia, the degradation of the environment once inflicted by a totalitarian state is being carried on by bandit capitalism. Until Russia's Hobbesian problem has been resolved Russia's natural environment will continue to be destroyed.

The Washington consensus assumes that the Hobbesian problem of maintaining order has been solved. It thereby not only passes over the condition of the majority of humankind, which lives under enfeebled or collapsed states; it neglects the many ways in which unregulated world markets threaten cohesion in society and stability in government.

A few states – Singapore, Malaysia, Japan, Holland, Britain, Sweden, Norway – may have the capacity to preserve social cohesion while responding to global competition. Most are too weak, corrupt or incompetent. Most actually existing states cannot hope to reconcile the imperatives of global markets with the needs of social cohesion and environmental conservation.

Is reform of the global market to promote the development of effective states feasible? There are signs that the need to rehabilitate the state is beginning to be accepted even in some of the transnational organizations that are the architects of the global free market. The fountainhead of the Washington consensus, the World Bank, has abandoned its endorsement of minimal government. It has acknowledged that there cannot be sustainable economic development in the absence of an effective modern state.

The World Bank's 1997 Development Report, *The State in a Changing World*, begins by declaring: 'Certainly, state-dominated development has failed. But so has stateless development . . . History has repeatedly shown that good government is not a luxury but a vital necessity. Without an effective state, sustainable development, both economic and social, is impossible.'[8] The report goes on to commend 'Thomas Hobbes's insight, in his 1651 treatise *Leviathan*, that life without an effective state to preserve order is "solitary, poor, nasty, brutish, and short".'[9]

The World Bank's repudiation of the dogma of minimal government is welcome; but it falls far short of the reorientation of thought that is needed. States which do not solve the Hobbesian problem lack legitimacy everywhere. But security from civil disorder and criminal violence is not all that people demand from their governments. They demand security from destitution, unemployment and exclusion. Unless the protective functions of states extend to the control of such risks governments will not be perceived as legitimate by their citizens.

The World Bank reiterates the conventional wisdom of the past decade when it describes 'the full complement of core public goods and services' as consisting in 'a foundation of lawfulness, a stable macroeconomy, the rudiments of public health, universal primary education, adequate transport infrastructure, and a minimal safety net'.[10]

In this account the proper functions of the state are derived from the economic theory of public goods. No doubt there are some functions of the state that can be understood in such terms. Some preconditions of a modern market economy are universal. All modern economies must contain uncorrupt law enforcement, well-defined property rights and policies for conserving the environment if they are to serve human needs.

What is lacking in the World Bank's account is recognition of the state's economic role in preserving and fostering cohesion in society. The policies dictated by this responsibility cannot be deduced from the supposed universal truths of economic theory. They will vary, according to the cultural traditions of different peoples and the kinds of capitalism they practise.

The World Bank remains faithful to the Washington consensus in treating differences between cultures, regimes and kinds of capitalism as of marginal importance in determining the economic role of the state. In fact these differences are decisive. It has not accepted – or, perhaps, fully perceived – the diversity of contemporary capitalism.

Consider two examples. Japanese capitalism depends for its political legitimacy on the renewal of the social contract which underwrites its full employment culture. Yet Japan's employment practices are under siege from transnational organizations as policies of concealed protectionism. Germany's economic dilemma has some similar features. High levels of social protection are an integral part of Germany's post-war consensual capitalism. The German state cannot relinquish its role as final guarantor of full employment, nor can it hope to achieve that objective primarily by enforcing American-style labour flexibility. Yet international economic orthodoxy continues to demand that Germany adopts the hire-and-fire practices of the Anglo-Saxon free market.

Neither the World Bank nor the other transnational organizations that are involved in the attempt to construct a worldwide free market have yet absorbed these lessons. Global regulation will be sustainable only insofar as it accepts a diversity of regimes, cultures and economies as a permanent condition.

The regulation that is needed in a truly global economy must promote a *modus vivendi* among species of capitalism that will always remain different. Consider trade. Rules for the regulation of trade which treat the practices of American capitalism as a universal standard do not respect that diversity. Regulations that prohibit governments acting to protect the cohesion of their societies and the particular type of capitalism they have evolved do not provide a framework for free trade. They privilege one species of capitalism in its competition with the rest. A framework is needed in which governments can protect what is distinctive and valuable in their economic cultures.

This does not imply any of the policies associated with protectionism. Like social democracy, protectionism belongs to a world that cannot be revived. Sovereign states will continue to shelter industries they regard as strategically vital; but the classical policies of trade protection, as applied across entire economies, are unworkable or counter-productive. When companies can split up their operations and locate them practically anywhere in the world, services can be contracted out to remote countries through the use of information technologies, financial assets are traded in cyberspace, and protectionist policies are a dead end.

But regulations that stigmatize as protectionism any policies that seek to preserve distinctive cultures or livelihoods do not promote harmony among the world's economies. They make long-term cooperation among them impossible. If such regulations are not reformed the world's new economic powers will ignore them.

In seeking to force every economy into a strait-jacket sewn from the singular practices of American capitalism transnational organizations compel countries to adopt economic policies that do not fit their histories and needs. But transnational authorities are not free agents. They operate in the shadow of the sovereign states whose purposes and philosophy they serve. Today all transnational agencies implement variations on the neo-Wilsonian philosophy that is presently the dominant strand in American foreign policy. This approach to international relations stands and falls on the assumption that, sooner or later, the countries of the world will all accept 'democratic capitalism'.

The United States is engaged in a revolutionary make-over of the world economy. Its policies on trade and competition condemn to extinction every other economic civilization. If Japanese corner stores, or European guaranteed markets for bananas, are judged to be restraints on competition as that is understood in the terms of the American free market, they must be prohibited, whatever their benefits in social cohesion.

US policy-makers and opinion-formers have not considered how the American condition is perceived in the rest of the world. They have not asked themselves why the American condition is regarded with suspicion or dread throughout Europe and Asia, and its universal claims rejected with incredulity or contempt.

The determination to subjugate and annex all other economies to the American free market cannot succeed. It exacerbates conflicts of interest between the world's economic powers. It triggers attempts to break away from American-led transnational organizations, such as the proposal (discussed in late 1997 in several Asian countries) that the IMF be supplemented or replaced by a separate Asian fund. The most lasting result of American policy may be that some countries and regions decouple themselves from the transnational institutions that embody the global free market.

By seeking to impose a single economic civilization on all of humankind America's support for the Washington consensus risks turning manageable differences among states into intractable conflicts.

The Washington consensus will not last forever. It will undoubtedly be shaken by economic shocks and geopolitical shifts. It is an episode in the search by the United States for a post-Cold War identity, no more stable or enduring than any other aspect of American opinion or policy. As the example of the World Bank's changing view suggests, it is already being questioned.

But the core project of implanting free markets throughout the world looks set to persist for the foreseeable future. Is it the case that the world must suffer a major crisis – economic, environmental or military – before the United States sheds its *laissez-faire* philosophy and uses its unmatched power to help establish working conditions of global governance?

After *laissez-faire*

The immediate post-Cold War period was captivated by hallucinatory vistas of a New World Order. That era is now over. The international landscape of the coming century can be only dimly described although the chief sources of conflict can already be seen. They are the classical divisions of ethnicity and territory, magnified by growing scarcities in vital natural resources and a terrifying inheritance of weapons of mass destruction.

The risk of a rerun of the 'Great Game' in Central and Eastern Asia, in which the world's powers compete for control of oil, is a portent of what may be in store for us. If China's consumption of energy reaches the level of Latin American countries by the end of the century, its total oil consumption could exceed that of all OECD European countries combined. Even if China reached the levels of consumption of energy of South Korea, its total would be around double that of the United States today. In 1995, China asserted its sovereignty over oil-rich waters near the Philippines. China, Taiwan, Japan, Malaysia, Brunei, Indonesia, Vietnam and Brunei all have conflicting territorial claims in the East and South China Sea. Nearly all have a crucial bearing on oil or other scarce natural resources. It is not surprising that East Asia is already the site of a regional arms race.[11]

The threat to peace has not disappeared with the end of the Cold War. The nature of war has merely mutated. One consequence of a anarchic global economy has proved to be a world awash with weapons. The former Soviet military-industrial complex has turned itself into a weapons bazaar. Even the danger of nuclear weapons being detonated has not diminished. It may well have increased, as the unregulated proliferation of nuclear power has made it more feasible for such devices to be acquired and deployed by small states and political organizations.[12]

The risk of nuclear terrorism is enhanced by the greatly extended international reach of organized crime. These unanticipated consequences of an open world economy are compounded by the enfeeblement of the state that has been actively promoted by the Washington consensus.

The world-historical movement we call globalization has momentum that is inexorable. We are not the masters of the technologies that drive the global economy: they condition us in many ways we have not begun to understand. Institutions that could monitor or counteract their dangerous side-effects are lacking. It is more than doubtful now whether any late modern society can restrain technological development even if its consequences are injurious to vital human needs. Such societies are too uncertain of their values, and too wedded to an understanding of the earth as a resource to be consumed in the service of unlimited human wants, to attempt such an heroic task.

Luddites and fundamentalists who seek to turn back the tide of invention and scientific knowledge exhibit one of the chief traits of the modern world they claim to reject – the conviction that humankind's ills can be cured by an act of will.

The flood of invention which drives the world economy cannot be controlled so that we are touched only by its benefits. The evils of new technologies are often inseparable from the good they make possible. But we can hope to tilt the balance, so that the effects of technology are less injurious to human well-being.

Science and technology form a common human inheritance. To imagine that they might be used to make (in the words of Isaiah Berlin) 'a reasonably peaceful coat of many colours', a plural world in which diverse cultures can live together, is not to envision an ideal that can never be realized. It is to voice a hope that Enlightenment thinkers have in common with all those religions and philosophies, ancient and modern, that recognize the ideal of toleration. The prospect of a single, self-regulating global free market has made this vision of a peaceful *modus vivendi* itself Utopian.

As a result, we stand on the brink not of the era of plenty that free-marketeers project, but a tragic epoch, in which anarchic market forces and shrinking natural resources drag sovereign states into ever more dangerous rivalries.

The lesson is clear. As it is presently organized, global capitalism is supremely ill-suited to cope with the risks of geo-political conflict that are endemic in a world of worsening scarcities. Yet a regulatory framework for coexistence and cooperation among the world's diverse economies figures on no historical or political agenda.

Global market competition and technological innovation have interacted to give us an anarchic world economy. Such an economy is bound to be a site for major geo-political conflicts. Thomas Hobbes and Thomas Malthus are better guides to the world that global *laissez-faire* has created than Adam Smith or Friedrich von Hayek; a world of war and scarcity at least as much as the benevolent harmonies of competition.

The likelihood must be that the *laissez-faire* regime will not be reformed. Instead it will fracture and fragment, as mounting scarcities of resources and conflicts of interest among the world's great powers make international cooperation ever more difficult. A deepening international anarchy is the human prospect.

Will the resources of critical rationality which we have inherited from the Enlightenment enable us to cope with the disorders that its most recent project has created or compounded? Or is the global anarchy in which we find ourselves an historical fate against which we are bound to struggle, but which we are powerless to overcome? It will surely be one of history's darkest ironies if the Enlightenment project of a world civilization ends in a chaos of sovereign states and stateless peoples struggling for the necessities of survival.

The spread of new technologies throughout the world is not working to advance human freedom. Instead it has resulted in the emancipation of market forces from social and political control. By allowing that freedom to world markets we ensure that the age of globalization will be remembered as another turn in the history of servitude.

Postscript

As it is presently constituted, global capitalism is inherently unstable. A worldwide free market is no more self-regulating than the national free markets of the past. Barely a decade old, it already contains dangerous imbalances. Unless it is reformed radically, the world economy risks falling apart in a replay, at once tragic and farcical, of the trade wars, competitive devaluations, economic collapses and political upheavals of the 1930s.

Mainstream parties in all countries hold that there is no alternative to worldwide free markets. This book challenges that economic philosophy. When *False Dawn* was published in Britain in the spring of 1998 it was attacked from all parts of the political spectrum. Its claim that global capitalism is deeply unstable in its present form was represented as wildly pessimistic, not to say apocalyptic. Less than a year later that claim has been largely vindicated.

False Dawn's reception confirmed one of its central theses: contemporary opinion – in politics, the media and business – has become so detached from enduring human realities that it can no longer distinguish utopia from reality. As a result, it is unprepared for the return of history – with its familiar intractable conflicts, tragic choices and ruined illusions – which we are currently witnessing.

In the short time since the book's first publication, events have corroborated its analysis. Even official opinion is beginning to suspect that economic problems in Asia are not local difficulties in faraway countries. Soon it will it will be forced to confront the fact that what it has seen as a crisis of Asian capitalism is in fact a fast developing crisis of global capitalism. There can no longer be much doubt that we are approaching a major upheaval in the international economic system. It is a pretty safe bet that, a few years hence, it will be difficult to find a single person who admits ever having supported the global regime which established opinion still insists is immutable.

False Dawn argues that a global free market is not an iron law of historical development but a political project. The deep flaws of this project have already caused much unnecessary suffering. Yet a global economy modelled on Anglo-American free markets is the avowed goal the International Monetary Fund and similar transnational organizations. Global markets are engines of creative destruction. Like the markets of the past, they do not advance in smooth, steady waves. They make progress through cycles of boom and bust, speculative manias and financial crises. Like capitalism in the past, global capitalism achieves its prodigious productivity today by destroying old industries, occupations and ways of life – but on a scale that is worldwide.

Joseph Schumpeter understood capitalism better than any other twentieth century economist. He saw that it did not work to preserve the cohesion of society. Left to itself it could well destroy liberal civilization. That is why he accepted that capitalism must be tamed. Government intervention was needed to reconcile the dynamism of capitalism with social stability. The same is true of global markets today.

Today's believers in worldwide *laissez-faire* echo Schumpeter without comprehending him. They believe that by promoting prosperity free markets advance liberal values. They have not noticed that a global free market engenders new varieties of nationalism and fundamentalism even as it creates new elites. By eating away the foundations of bourgeois societies and imposing massive instability on developing countries, global capitalism is endangering liberal civilization. It is also making it harder for different civilizations to live in peaceful coexistence.

Global *laissez-faire* has become a threat to peace between states. The present international economic system contains no effective institutions for conserving the wealth of the natural environment. The risk is that sovereign states will be drawn into a struggle for control of the earth's dwindling natural resources. In the coming century ideological rivalries between states may well be succeeded by Malthusian wars of scarcity.

The Asian crisis is a sign that global free markets have become ungovernable. A bursting bubble of historic proportions in the United States; deflation entrenched in Japan and emerging in China; depression in Indonesia and several smaller Asian countries; financial and economic crisis and a likely change of regime in Russia – these are not developments that augur stability. They show the instability of the world economy as a whole.

In this new postscript I will show how recent developments illustrate and corroborate the argument of *False Dawn*. I will then offer some scenarios for the future and consider what might be done.

Does the current crisis in Asia spell the end for Asian models of capitalism, as the conventional wisdom in western countries has been quick to conclude? Can Japan preserve its distinctive economic culture? Can the European Union, newly equipped with a single currency, insulate itself against the shocks of global markets? Can German capitalism renew itself? What will become of the US commitment to free markets when America's bubble economy has burst?

These are some of the questions suggested by events that have occurred since this book was first published that I aim to address. Before I do so it may be useful to rehearse the book's central argument. It has eight main strands.

The argument of *False Dawn*

The free market is not – as today's economic philosophy supposes – a natural state of affairs which comes about when political interference with market exchange has been removed. In any long and broad historical perspective the free market is a rare, short-lived aberration. Regulated markets are the norm, arising spontaneously in the life of every society. The free market is a construction of state power. The idea that free markets and minimum government go together, which was part of the stock in trade of the New Right, is an inversion of the truth. Since the natural tendency of society is to curb markets, free markets can only be created by the power of a centralized state. Free markets are creatures of strong government and cannot exist without them. This is the *first* argument of *False Dawn*.

It is well illustrated by the short history of nineteenth century *laissez-faire*. The free market was engineered in mid-Victorian England in exceptionally propitious circumstances. Unlike other European countries, England had long traditions of individualism. For centuries yeoman farmers were the basis of its economy. But only by Parliament using its power to amend or destroy old property rights and create new ones – through Enclosure Acts in which much of the country's common land was privatized – did an agrarian capitalism of large landed estates come into being.

Laissez-faire came about in England through a conjunction of favourable historical circumstances with the unchecked power of a Parliament in which most English people were unrepresented. By the middle of the nineteenth century, through the Enclosures, the Poor Laws and the repeal of the Corn Law, land, labour and bread were commodities like any other: the free market had become the central institution in the economy.

But the free market lasted in England for barely a generation. (Some historians have even made the hyperbolic claim that there never was an era of *laissez-faire*.) From the 1870s onwards, it was gradually legislated out of existence. By the First World War, markets had been largely re-regulated in the interests of public health and economic efficiency, and government was active in supplying a range of vital services, notably schools. Britain continued to have a highly individualistic variety of capitalism, and free trade survived until the catastrophe of the Great Depression; but political control over the economy had been re-asserted. The free market was regarded as an doctrinaire excess or else a mere anachronism – until it was revived by the New Right in the 1980s.

The New Right was able to alter political and economic life irreversibly in the countries in which it gained power – but it failed to achieve the hegemony to which it aspired. In Britain, the United States, Australia and New Zealand, together with some other countries such as Mexico, Chile and the Czech Republic, governments heavily influenced by free market ideas were able to dismantle much of their corporatist or collectivist inheritances. But in every case the initial coalitions that made free market policies politically possible were undermined by the medium-term effects of these same policies.

Selling off social housing – one of the key Thatcherite policies – was a success so long as house prices were rising. When they fell abruptly and millions were trapped in negative equity it became a political liability. Privatizing public assets and freeing up markets were politically advantageous only so long as a booming economy masked their deeper impact, which was to compound economic insecurity. When economic downturn made that effect palpable New Right governments began to live on borrowed time.

In most countries, the political beneficiary of neo-liberal economic reform has turned out to be the soft Left. As in the late-nineteenth century, so in the late-twentieth century, the socially destructive effects of free markets have made them politically unsustainable.

That leads on to the *second* strand in *False Dawn*: democracy and the free market are competitors rather than partners. 'Democratic capitalism' – the vacuous rallying-cry of neoconservatives everywhere – designates (or conceals) a deeply problematic relationship. The normal concomitant of free markets is not stable democratic government. It is the volatile politics of economic insecurity.

Now and in the past, in virtually every society, the market has been curbed so that it does not thwart too severely vital human needs for stability and security. In late modern contexts, free markets have normally been tempered by democratic governments. The withering away of the free market in its purest mid-Victorian form coincided with the widening of the franchise. As English *laissez-faire* retreated with advancing democracy, so in most countries the excesses of the 1980s have been moderated – under the pressures of democratic competition – by successor governments. Yet at the global level the free market remains unchecked.

One historic project of reconciling the market economy with democratic government has gone into what looks like a final retreat. European social democracy continues to exist as a number of actually existing regimes. But social democratic governments lack the leverage over economic life which they were able to exercise during their period of post-war success. Global bond markets will not allow social democracies to borrow heavily. Keynesian policies are not effective when in open economies from which capital can exit at will. Worldwide mobility of production allows enterprises to locate where regulatory and tax burdens are least onerous.

Social democratic governments no longer have the resources to pursue their goals by social democratic means. As a result, in most continental European countries, mass unemployment is a problem without any evident solution. In a few cases, special circumstances – such as windfall gains from oil in Norway – have given social democratic regimes another lease on life. But in general terms the contradiction between social democracy and global free markets seems irreconcilable.

There are today few effective institutions of global economic governance, and none that is even remotely democratic. Achieving a humane and balanced relationship between government and the market economy remains a distant aspiration.

Thirdly, socialism as an economic system has broken down irretrievably. In both human and economic terms, the legacy of socialist central planning has been ruinous. The Soviet Union was not a regime that achieved rapid progress at regrettably high human cost. It was a totalitarian state that killed or ruined the lives of millions of people and devastated the natural environment. Except in the enormous military sector and in some areas of public health, the Soviet Union had few genuine economic or social achievements. In Maoist China the loss of life through state-induced famines and terrors and the destruction of the natural environment may have been greater even than in the USSR.

Whatever else the coming century may bring, the collapse of socialism looks irreversible. For the future we can foresee, there will not be two economic systems in the world, but only varieties of capitalism.

Fourth, though the implosion of Marxian socialism has been welcomed in western countries, especially the United States, as a triumph for free market capitalism, it has not been followed in most formerly communist countries by the adoption of *any* western economic model.

In both Russia and China the disappearance of communism has revived indigenous types of capitalism, in both cases deformed by their communist inheritance. The Russian economy is dominated by a species of criminal syndicalism. The proximate origins of this peculiar economic system are in the Soviet illegal economy, but it has some points of resemblance with the mixed capitalism of large, state-controlled enterprises and wild entrepreneurship that flourished in the last decades of Tsarism. Capitalism in China has much in common with that practised all over the world by the Chinese diaspora, notably in the crucial role in business played by kinship relations, but it too is pervaded by corruption and by the commercialization of institutions – including the military – that have been inherited from the communist era.

Conventional opinion perceives the collapse of communism as a victory for 'the West'. In fact, Marxian socialism was a prototypically western ideology. Over the long haul of history, the disintegration of Marxian socialism in Russia and China represents a defeat for all western models of modernization. The breakdown of central planning in the Soviet Union and its dismantlement in China marked the end of an experiment in forced-march modernization in which the model of modernity was the nineteenth century capitalist factory.

In its *fifth* strand, *False Dawn* argues that, though they support different economic systems, Marxism-Leninism and free-market economic rationalism have much in common.

Both Marxism-Leninism and free-market economic rationalism adopt a Promethean attitude to nature and exhibit scant sympathy for the casualties of economic progress. Both are variants of the Enlightenment project of supplanting the historic diversity of human cultures with a single, universal civilization. A global free market is that Enlightenment project in its latest – perhaps last – form.

Much current debate confuses globalization, an historical process that has been underway for centuries, with the ephemeral political project of a worldwide free market. Properly understood, globalization refers to the increasing interconnection of economic and cultural life in distant parts of the world. It is a trend that can be dated back to the projection of European power into other parts of the world in imperialist policies from the sixteenth century onwards.

Today, the main motor of this process is the rapid diffusion of new, distance-abolishing information technologies. Conventional thinkers imagine that globalization is tending to create a universal civilisation by way of the worldwide spread of western – and, more particularly, Anglo-Saxon – practices and values.

In fact, the development of the world economy has been mostly in the other direction. Globalization today differs from the open international economy that was set up under European imperial auspices in the four or five decades before the First World War. In the global market no western power has the supremacy possessed by Britain and other European powers at that time. Indeed, over the longer run, the banalization of new technologies throughout the world works to erode western power and values. The spread of nuclear weapons technologies to anti-western regimes is only a symptom of a larger trend.

Globalized markets do not project the Anglo-American free market throughout the world. They throw all types of capitalism – not least the free-market varieties – into flux. Anarchic global markets destroy old capitalisms and spawn new ones, while subjecting all to unceasing instability.

The Enlightenment idea of a universal civilization is nowhere stronger than in the United States, where it is identified with the universal acceptance of western – that is to say, American – values and institutions.[1] The idea that the United States is a universal model has long been a feature of American civilization. During the eighties, the Right was able to co-opt this idea of a national mission in the service of free market ideology. Today the worldwide reach of American corporate power and the ideal of a universal civilization have become indistinguishable in American public discourse.

Yet the claim of the United States to be a model for the world is accepted by no other country. The costs of American economic success include levels of social division – of crime, incarceration, racial and ethnic conflict and family and community breakdown – that no European or Asian culture will tolerate.

The notion that the United States leads an expanding bloc of western nations is almost the reverse of the truth. In present circumstances, 'the West' is a category which has ceased to have a definite meaning – except in the United States, where it denotes an atavistic resistance to the unalterable realities of multiculturalism.

The United States is increasingly at odds with other 'western' societies in many of its domestic and foreign policies. In the extremity of its divisions and the militancy of its commitment to free markets, the US is a singularity. Though they continue to share vital interests, Europe and the United States are drawing further apart in their cultures and values. In retrospect, the period of close cooperation extending from the Second World War to the immediate aftermath of the Cold War may well appear as an aberration in the relations of the United States with Europe.

The longer historical pattern in which American civilization sees itself as *sui generis* and as having little in common with the Old World is reasserting itself. In a curious irony, the appropriation of the American faith that it is a universal model by the neo-conservative ascendancy seems to be accelerating the process whereby the United states ceases to be a European, 'western' country.

The fusion of American exceptionalism with free-market ideology is the *sixth* strand in *False Dawn*. The global free market is an American project. In some contexts, American companies have benefited from it, as free markets have reached into hitherto protected economies. But this does not mean that global *laissez-faire* is a mere rationalization of American corporate interests.

A global free market has no long-term winner. It no more works in the interests of the American economy than of any other. Indeed, in a large dislocation of world markets the American economy would be more exposed than many others.

Global *laissez-faire* is not a conspiracy of corporate America. It is a tragedy – one of several that have occurred in the twentieth century – in which an hubristic ideology runs aground on enduring human needs that it has failed to comprehend.

Amongst the human needs that free markets neglect are the needs for security and social identity that used to be met by the vocational structures of bourgeois societies. A contradiction has emerged between the preconditions of an intact bourgeois civilization and the imperatives of global capitalism. This is the *seventh* strand: the chronic insecurities of late modern capitalism, especially in its most virulent free-market variants, corrode some of the central institutions and values of bourgeois life.

The most notable of these social institutions may be that of the career. In traditional bourgeois societies, most middle-class people could reasonably expect to spend their working lives in a single vocation. Few can now harbour any such hope. The deeper effect of economic insecurity is not to multiply the number of jobs each of us has in a working lifetime. It is to make the very idea of a career redundant.

In the lives of the working majority, an old-fashioned career in which professional seniority tracks the normal life cycle is barely a memory. As a result, familiar contrasts between middle-class and working-class life have diminished reality. The post-war trend to embourgeoisment is being reversed, and working people are being in some degree re-proletarianized.

Though 'de-bourgeoisification' may have advanced furthest in the US, economic insecurity is increasing in nearly all the world's economies. This is partly a side effect of global free markets, whose workings mimic Gresham's Law (which says that bad money drives out good) by making socially responsible varieties of capitalism progressively less sustainable. Worldwide mobility of capital and production triggers a 'race to the bottom', in which more humane capitalist economies are compelled to deregulate and trim back taxes and welfare provision. In this new rivalry all the varieties of capitalism that competed during the post-war period are mutating and metamorphosing.

The *eighth* strand in *False Dawn* considers what can be done. The US does not have the hegemonic power needed to make a universal free market a reality, even for a short time. But it certainly has the power to veto reform of the world economy. So long as the US remains wedded to 'the Washington consensus' on global *laissez-faire* there can be no reform of world markets. Proposals such as the 'Tobin tax' – a worldwide levy on speculative currency transactions named after the American economist who proposed it – will remain dead letters.

In the absence of reform, the world economy will fragment as its imbalances become insupportable. Trade wars will make international cooperation more difficult. The world economy will fracture into blocs, each riven by struggles for regional hegemony.

'The Great Game', in which world powers struggled a century ago for control of oil in Central Asia, may well recur in the coming century. When states are rivals for control of scarce natural resources military conflicts will be harder to avert. Weak authoritarian regimes will seek to shore themselves up by military adventures. Slobodan Milosevic, the neo-communist leader of what remains of Yugoslavia, may prove a prototype for authoritarian demagogues in many other countries.

As global *laissez-faire* breaks up, a deepening international anarchy is the likely human prospect.

Asia's depression and America's bubble economy: the beginning of the end for global *laissez-faire*?

In western countries Asia's crisis has been perceived as proof that the free market is the only kind of capitalism that can survive in a global economy. Few deny that in earlier phases of economic development

Asian capitalisms may have achieved remarkable feats; but nearly all are agreed that today they are obsolete. The western consensus is that Asia's problems are proof that there is now no alternative to Anglo-American capitalism anywhere in the world.

To be sure, only a few years ago many of these same commentators were lauding Asian capitalism as an example that western countries could do well to emulate. That episode in western opinion is now forgotten. The triumph of the free market will be equally transient and just as quickly forgotten.

We are entering one of the moments of historical discontinuity at which ruling paradigms in policy and theory are abruptly abandoned. The triumph of Keynesian ideas after the Second World War was such a moment. The Asian depression seems set to do to free market ideology what the Great Depression and World War Two did to the fiscal and economic orthodoxies of the thirties.

At no point in the history of the Asian crisis has its gravity been perceived by western observers or policy-makers. Again and again transnational organisations in thrall to the project of a single global market have been wrong-footed by events. To begin with they insisted that east Asia's problems were mainly in their financial institutions and had few serious economic repercussions. When that interpretation could no longer be sustained they contended that Asia was experiencing a recession compounded by structural problems.

That revised view also fell far short of the scale of the crisis. By the second half of 1998, western banks were forecasting that gross domestic product would drop over the year by twenty percent in Indonesia, over eleven percent in Thailand and seven and a half percent in South Korea.[2] Unemployment in Indonesia was estimated as being in excess of 20 million, with at least half of the population being expected to be in poverty by the year's end.

Declines in economic activity of these magnitudes do not normally signify the approach of recession. More commonly they indicate the onset of depression.

The scale of Asia's gathering depression is beginning to be perceived; but its causes and implications for the world economy are still not understood.

The Asian depression is the first historical demonstration that unrestricted global mobility of capital can have disastrous consequences for economic stability. Footloose capital exited overnight from Asian markets; but the effects of its departure on the real economies that were worst affected will be felt for decades or generations. The social and political scars of economic crises inflicted by speculative capital movements will be long lasting.

The Asian currency movements of the late nineties will not be recorded in history as transient financial fluctuations whose effects were soon absorbed. They will be recognized as early markers of a global crisis. It is evidence of the historical illiteracy of western opinion that it expects that economic and social convulsions in east Asia on a scale that western countries have not known since the thirties should occur without shifts of government and regime comparable to those experienced in Europe during those inter-war years. The most predictable upshot of Asia's economic crisis is a prolonged period of political instability in the region. As Asia's depression gathers pace, revivified movements of anti-western nationalism, sudden shifts in regime, the rekindling of old ethnic conflicts, large movements of population and renewed experiments in authoritarian dictatorship will transform the Asian political landscape. In these developments western ideas of free markets will play little, if any, part.

The Asian crisis does not show that Anglo-American capitalism is now – if only by default, through the disarray of all other models – the only viable economic system. That is an interpretation which seems credible only in virtue of ignorance of history and continuing western racism. What it shows is that all existing capitalisms are in flux.

Asia's economies are like all others today: they are mutating continuously, with unpredictable consequences for social cohesion and political stability. Free market economies are no more insulated from this flux than any others. Far from signifying the universal triumph of the free market, the Asian crisis is a prelude to a time of major dislocation for global capitalism.

This is a development for which current opinion is notably unprepared, especially in the United States. American perceptions of the Asian crisis embody some curious contradictions. Economic difficulties in east Asia have been welcomed in the United States as a sign that Asian capitalism is in a terminal crisis. If this were so it would be a world-historical shift of vast magnitude – and long duration. Asia's economies face massive, sometimes intractable problems; but they are not an a phase of decline that terminates with their embracing free markets. Asian capitalisms express the types of family life, the social structures and the political and religious histories of Asian countries. They are not systems that can be transformed at the will of transnational regulators but largely subterranean social and cultural institutions whose practices are saturated with local history and traditional knowledge.

Only the history-blind seers who frame the policies of the International Monetary Fund could imagine that Asian countries will shed these inheritances. If history is our guide, we can be sure that Asian capitalisms will emerge from the current crisis altered unpredictably rather than remade on any western model. But even if Asian capitalisms were to converge with those of 'the West', it would be in a traumatic process of cultural and political change spanning generations.

Until recently, American opinion was confident of business as usual throughout this protracted metamorphosis. It expected the impact of Asian economic collapse on the United States to be slight, or even positive. At the same time American policy-makers recognized – indeed insisted – that in globalized markets large changes anywhere impact upon economic life everywhere.

These ill-matched expectations articulated a highly unstable view of the world. The United States believed itself to be the engine of globalization. At the same time it imagined that it was somehow insulated from globalization's disorders. It failed to understand that when capitalism has gone global the instabilities that are inseparable from it will unavoidably also be global.

When they looked at the past, America's prophets of the 'New paradigm' recognized that capitalism is necessarily both destructive and creative. Its unmatched productivity has been achieved by wrecking existing industries and overturning established forms of social life. When they looked to the present and the future they contrived to pass over these unpleasant facts. They expected – or at least promised – the prodigious productivity of capitalism without any of the pain and chaos that has always gone with it.

This cognitive dissonance between what American opinion expected and what history records produced an unreal sense of confidence which any demonstration of American economic vulnerability could easily destroy.

America's stock market boom did not occur merely, or even mainly, as a result of economic restructuring. No doubt American advances in information technology gave the economy an enhanced competitive edge. Similarly, the brutal downsizings and recurrent corporate restructurings of the early nineties undoubtedly gave American businesses significant cost advantages. To this extent, America's boom reflected real gains in economic efficiency.

Sky-high valuations on Wall Street had another crucial support. They came to reflect American confidence that the country had won an historic geo-strategic victory. The collapse of communism, the apparent economic weakness of Europe and meltdown in Asia – these rapid shifts over less than a decade appeared to many Americans as a final vindication of 'the American Creed'.

By the late nineties public opinion in the United States was confident that American values were spreading rapidly – and irreversibly – across the world. The fanciful notion that business cycles had become obsolete had become an orthodoxy. The prospect of 'a return of history', which European and Asian observers viewed as a certainty, was not considered, or else discounted. The Long American Boom had become a speculative bubble inflated by a shallow and ephemeral mood of national hubris.

That bubble could have been punctured at any time. In part it rested on assumptions about US military hegemony that events in Asia had already confounded. A nuclear arms race on the Indian subcontinent does not in itself threaten American security directly; but nuclear rivalry between India and Pakistan undermined American-led international efforts to arrest nuclear proliferation and has thereby made for a more dangerous world.

There can be no doubt that the United States has used all its leverage to avert a nuclear arms race in southern Asia. Nor is there much doubt that it has failed. In its effort to stop the spread of nuclear weapons, the United States has been forced to confront an unpalatable fact: globalization does not strengthen American power but rather tends to limit it. The United States remains the world's premier military power, but it has little control over the spreading technologies on which military efficiency now depends.

American economic power is equally limited. Competitive devaluation of China's currency would be a disaster for east Asia and a major setback for the United States. It would deepen deflation in the region and provoke a protectionist backlash in the American Congress. The effect on Wall Street would surely be traumatic. There is an overriding

American interest in forestalling such a development. Yet there is very little the United States can do to prevent it.

China is sometimes praised by western governments as a haven of stability in the Asian crisis. Insofar as this has been true it is because China has remained to some extent outside the global free market. China's government has retained considerable control over its economy. Western governments which praise China have overlooked the fact that its relative stability is a by-product of its consistent, well-founded contempt for western opinion and advice.

China's economic policies will be determined chiefly by domestic political factors. No inducement that the American government can offer China's rulers can outweigh the threat to them which is posed by rising unemployment. China is presently in the middle of the largest and swiftest movement from countryside to town in history. Unemployment already runs in excess of a hundred million people – a figure that undoubtedly needs upward revision because of the shake-out caused by the policy of allowing many state-owned enterprises to go bankrupt. The strategy of the Chinese government is to re-employ some of these workers in export industries. There have been ominous signs that deflation has taken hold in sections of the Chinese economy. In these circumstances, forestalling a further rise in unemployment is an overriding imperative of political survival.

Western opinion is confident that China's present regime will weather the Asian depression without serious difficulty. Whether China's rulers share this certainty is doubtful. They have witnessed the decomposition of an apparently immovable totalitarian regime in Russia. They have watched a seemingly well-entrenched authoritarian regime toppled by economic crisis in a matter of months in Indonesia. They can have few illusions that the same cannot happen in China.

China's rulers have a sense of history, unlike most western governments. They must know that if they survive the depression that has engulfed their neighbours it will be one of history's most remarkable feats of statecraft. They will employ any expedient to remain in power. Competitive devaluation of the currency is one among many desperate strategies to which the government will have recourse as economic conditions worsen and social and political unrest mount. It is reasonable to anticipate further episodes like that in Tiananmen Square.

A spiral of devaluation in east Asia is only one of several events that could trigger a systemic crisis in the world economy. The collapse of the Russian rouble following the devaluation of August 1998 could have the same effect. The result of a second collapse of the Russian economy is likely to be another shift of regime than a change of government. The impact of such a change of regime on 'the West', which has viewed the move to democracy in Russia as irreversible, would be profound. Ill-prepared for a renovation of Russian despotism that is by now a likelihood, western governments are likely to view any such development as a danger to the international system. Equally, any new Russian regime will be likely to exploit the bungling attempts of western governments and transnational organizations to install capitalism in Russia to fuel anti-western sentiment. Among the incalculable consequences of a shift of regime in Russia is the certainty that international economic cooperation will be much harder even than in the past.

Economic collapse and another change of regime in Russia; further deflation and weakening of the financial system in Japan, compelling a repatriation of Japanese holdings of US government bonds; financial crisis in Brazil or Argentina; a Wall Street Crash – any or all of these events, together with others that are unforeseeable, may in present circumstances act as the trigger of a global economic dislocation. If any of them comes to pass, one of the first consequences will be a swift increase of protectionist sentiment in the United States, starting in Congress.

Ordinary Americans are not well-placed to endure protracted economic setback. The dismantling of the federal welfare state makes rising unemployment insupportable. If over a hundred million mutual fund holders lose large portions of their assets in a market cataclysm popular support for a tilt to protectionism will be irresistible.

It is a commonplace of economic history that countries without welfare states are more likely than others to have recourse to protectionism when the international economy turns down. This is an historical pattern that will certainly recur if the Asian depression deepens.

At present, personal debt and bankruptcy are running at historic levels in the United States. For many Americans, present consumption has come to depend not only on the stockmarket's remaining high but on its continuing to rise. When it turns down these people will feel – and be – considerably poorer. To the perennial psychology of mass speculation must be added the crucial ingredient of geo-political triumphalism. In this feverish atmosphere a soft landing is a near impossibility. Hubris is not corrected by twenty percent.

A stock market reversal in the United States of the scale of that which occurred in Japan at the end of the eighties – in which the market dropped by over two-thirds – would leave sections of the American middle class impoverished. The sudden disappearance of large quantities of stock market-generated wealth would reveal middle class insecurity in its starkest light. The impact of a crash on those already poor would be still harsher. It is not fantastic to envisage the re-emergence of something like the nomadic American poor whose hand-to-mouth lives were chronicled by John Steinbeck in the 1930s.

The political ramifications of a large setback in the American economy cannot be known in advance. But we know that the American commitment to free markets is not long-standing. If anything, it is an aberration in the longer history of the United States, in which protectionism has been a recurring theme.

It would be wrong to interpret the neo-conservative political consensus of the last two decades as expressing the settled convictions of the American public. The rapid rise and even swifter fall of radical right-wing Republicanism in the early nineties shows the American electorate's volatility – as well as its maturity.

Any economic setback that is sharp, deep or protracted will test to destruction the hold of free-market pieties on American political life. Their abrupt replacement by American economic nationalism would be an ironic turn of events, given the messianic devotion to universal free markets exhibited by American policy-makers in recent years.[3]

It is no part of my purpose to prescribe how the American economy should be reformed. Even if I were competent to do so it is a task that falls to Americans. The argument of *False Dawn* is that no type of capitalism is universally desirable. Each culture should be free to develop its own variety and seek to live in *modus vivendi* with those developed by others.

The United States would be wrong to try to emulate the singular practices of European or Asian capitalism – just as it is wrong to attempt to impose its own practices on them. Economic reform must be guided by each culture's indigenous values. In the case of the

United States these are presently more individualist than those of European and Asian societies. It is no part of my argument that American should seek to import economic practices that have been successful in radically different cultures.

The task in the US may not be to devise alternatives to free markets but to make them friendlier to vital human needs. (Paradoxically, an item on any agenda of reform for the US is likely to be the extension of the free market to an area in which it is currently forbidden – the enormous underground drug economy.) Any large downturn in the market is sure to provoke a bout of American economic nationalism that makes economic reform of the subtle and delicate kind that is required impossible.

In late 1997, before the first edition of *False Dawn* was published, I wrote: 'When western free marketeers crow over the economic difficulties of Asian countries they are showing themselves to be – not for the first time – myopic and hubristic. No doubt some Asian economies need far-reaching reforms. But financial crisis in Asia does not augur the universal spread of free markets. Instead it may be the prelude to a global deflationary crisis, in the course of which the United States itself recoils from the regime of free trade and deregulated markets it is currently seeking to impose in Asia and throughout the world.'[4] This is a prognosis I see no reason to alter.

Can Japan preserve its distinctive economic culture?

Japan is the only Asian economic superpower and will retain that position for the foreseeable future. As the first Asian country to industrialize and the world's largest creditor it has advantages possessed by no other Asian economy. Its high levels of education and enormous reserves of capital make it better equipped for the knowledge-based economy of the coming century than perhaps any western country. Yet it confronts a financial and economic crisis in which the very existence of a distinctive Japanese economic culture is at stake.

Without a solution to Japan's economic problem the Asian crisis can only worsen. In that event the world economy risks following Japan into deflation and depression. At present Japan confronts falling asset prices and shrinking economic activity on the scale that was faced by the US and other countries in the 1930s. Unless deflation is shaken off in Japan the prospects of the rest of Asia and the world avoiding it are slight.

Western prescriptions for Japan's economic problems are an incongruous mixture. Today, as in the past, transnational organisations insist that Japan must restructure its financial and economic institutions according to western – more precisely, American – models: the solution to Japan's economic problem is its wholesale Americanization. For them, Japan will resolve its economic difficulties only on condition that it cease to be Japanese. At times this is stated bluntly. As a writer in an American neo-conservative journal has noted approvingly: 'America has the IMF to do Commodore Perry's job.'[5]

The result of such a policy of enforced westernization would not only be to extinguish a unique and irreplaceable culture. It would be to destroy the social cohesion that has gone with extraordinary economic achievement in Japan over the past half-century – without resolving the deflationary crisis that Japan presently confronts.

Western governments demand that Japan – alone, it seems, amongst advanced industrial economies – adopt Keynesian policies. The western consensus is that Japan must cut taxes, expand public works and run large budget deficits. At the same time, western transnational organizations demand that Japan dismantle the labour market that has assured full employment over the past fifty years. If Japan accedes to these demands the result can only be to import the insoluble dilemmas of western societies without resolving any of the country's problems.

Keynesian policies of the kinds that are presently being pressed upon Japan by western countries will not be effective in staving off further deflation. In the first place such policies take no account of the cultural propensity of Japanese to increase their savings in times of uncertainty. In current circumstances, the money released by further tax cuts will not be consumed but simply added to existing savings. Widespread uncertainty about the economy has already swollen saving in Japan well beyond its normal high levels. Even if tax cuts are believed to be permanent they will merely generate a yet higher rate of saving.

If income released by tax cuts in Japan is invested productively it is likely to be abroad. Nor will deficit financing have the desired effect on the economy. When capital is globally mobile there is no assurance that higher public borrowing will have the effect of stimulating domestic economic activity. As Keynes recognized, policies of deficit financing are effective only insofar as they are applied in closed economies. When capital movements are free the leverage of such policies is slight. As a result, Japan finds itself in a liquidity trap from which Keynesian policies cannot deliver it. Western governments appear not to have noticed that the regime of free capital movements and financial deregulation they have been insistently pressing on Japan for decades nullifies the effect of the Keynesian policies they seek now to impose upon it.

For Japan to accede to western demands that its labour market be deregulated would make matters still worse. If applied consistently, deregulating Japan's labour market on any western model – particularly that of the US – would double, perhaps even triple unemployment. That, of course, is what it is meant to do. But it would have the result of increasing the sense of insecurity of the working population and thereby reinforcing the Japanese propensity to save. In this way it would defeat the purpose of tax cuts, which is to stimulate spending.

Possibly the only way the Japanese government can stimulate spending is by engineering an inflation that makes saving unprofitable. But in other countries savers have responded to inflation by saving more – even when they lose money. It is unclear why Japanese savers should be so different. In any case the inevitable result of such a policy would be a collapse in the yen. Because it would provoke a tit-for-tat response from other Asian countries, notably China, this is an outcome feared more than virtually any other by western governments.

Western policy-makers have not understood that the flexibility which they seek to impose on Japan's labour market is at odds with the Keynesian policies they are trying to force on its government. Nor do they seem to have perceived that the policies that are likely to be most effective in stimulating demand in Japan will do so at the cost of triggering competitive devaluation in Asia and thereby protectionism in the US and Europe.

The increase in unemployment that labour market deregulation is designed to produce would be even more socially disruptive in Japan than it has been in western countries. It would occur in a country that does not possess a welfare state. The experience of western countries shows that this cannot be set up overnight.

If Japan imports western levels of mass unemployment it will be compelled eventually to establish a western-style welfare state. Yet western governments are paring away the welfare state on the ground that it has created an antisocial underclass. Once again, Japan is being asked to import problems which no western society is anywhere near solving.

Whether or not Japan creates a western-style welfare state the result of rising unemployment can only be a large increase in economic inequality. By insisting that Japan abandon full employment, transnational organizations are demanding that it relinquish the more egalitarian species of capitalism that has hitherto preserved social peace in the country.

By contrast with western varieties in which shareholder's interests are overriding, Japanese capitalism derives its social and political legitimacy from the employment which it generates. Some policies implemented by the Japanese government under unremitting pressure from western-oriented transnational organizations may have made this distinctively Japanese type of capitalism unsustainable.

The 'Big Bang' of 1998, in which its financial institutions were deregulated, was a fateful step for Japan. Financial deregulation is incompatible with the preservation of Japan's employment-driven capitalism. When they evaluate the performance of Japanese companies foreign banks will apply criteria of shareholder value rather than Japanese concerns about preserving employment. In joint ventures involving Japanese and western firms, there will be a one-way pressure to apply Anglo-American standards of success and productivity. Over time, if financial deregulation proceeds according to plan, the intertwined network of banks and companies that sustains full employment in Japan will unravel.

The long-term effect of these pressures must be to import western-style unemployment into Japan. Such a development would mean the end of the unwritten social contract that has contained social and industrial conflict since the fifties. Unless that contract is renewed in a new and sustainable form, the unique cohesion of Japanese society will begin to fracture. Japan could follow other Asian countries into political instability. At that point, remote as it seems at present, a sudden, radical shift of national direction cannot be ruled out.

Any solution of Japan's economic problem must be a reform of its indigenous economic culture rather than an attempt to dismantle it. The besetting flaw of western prescriptions for the Japanese economy is that they assume that Japan is, or will sooner or later become, a western country. Nothing in Japanese history supports that expectation. Japan's history shows several instances of abrupt shifts in national policy; but none of them has involved the renunciation of its indigenous culture. Japan's modernization during the Meiji period was successful largely because it was home-grown. Similarly, economic modernization will be successful in Japan today only insofar as it is *not* a policy of enforced westernization.

No reform of the economy that risks sacrificing social cohesion will be accepted as legitimate by Japan's voters. Can Japan's labour market be made more flexible without greatly increasing job insecurity? Should Japan seek to emulate other advanced industrial societies in seeking to restart economic growth? Or should economic growth itself be redefined to mean growth in the quality of goods, services and lifestyle? These are some of the questions that will be asked and answered in Japan over the coming years. But they contain no solutions for the current crisis.

The prospect of deepening deflation in Japan triggering a global depression is no longer remote or hypothetical. It is real and near at hand. The danger of the present situation arises from the fact that western governments are urging Japan to adopt policies that will not deliver it from deflation but will tear up the social contract that has preserved social cohesion and political stability since the Second World War.

Western pressure to deregulate markets has left few options open to Japan's government, and none that is without grave risks for the world economy.

Is there a future for European social market economies?

A systemic crisis in global financial institutions could derail the start of the Euro. But if it survives that crisis a single currency will give the European Union a presence in world markets it has never had before. So far discussion has focused on internal obstacles to its success rather than on its implications for the global economy.[6] Yet the latter are potentially profound.

A single currency does not enable the European Union to insulate itself from world markets; but it does create an economic power capable of negotiating on terms of equality with the United States. If all of the EU's present members enter it, the Euro zone will be the largest economy in the world and the Euro will challenge the US dollar as the world's dominant currency. If the Euro establishes itself as a credible currency, a collapse of the dollar becomes more likely. If it goes ahead the Euro will bring forward the time at which the US will no longer be able to flourish as the world's largest debtor. Over time, possibly quite quickly, a shift in the balance of economic power in the world will inexorably follow.

It is true that the internal conditions for the new currency's success are not yet in place. Under a single interest rate regime, some countries and regions will languish while others thrive. The conditions do not exist in the EU that have enabled the US to adapt to these divergences. At present Europe lacks continent-wide labour mobility and it has no fiscal mechanisms to prevent large pools of unemployment welling up in Europe's depressed regions.

Once the Euro is in operation, European institutions will be compelled to remedy these failings. They will be forced to develop policies that allow the economy to respond more flexibly to the imperatives and constraints of a single monetary regime. But they will have to recognise that Europe is not and never will be the United States. American labour mobility is impossible, and for that matter undesirable, in a long-settled continent of diverse historic communities. Nor, I venture to suggest, will there ever be a European state having the powers of the US federal government. European institutions will go on evolving, but they will remain hybrids. Europe will continue to be governed by a shifting balance of power between national governments and transnational institutions.

European capitalisms will continue to differ profoundly from American free markets. No European country – not even the United Kingdom – is ready to tolerate the levels of social dereliction produced by the free market in the United States. Boundaries between the state and civil society will remain – as they have been in the past – permeable and negotiable. Historic memories and attachments to places will block mass mobility on the American model. For all these reasons, the free market will not displace social markets in the countries of continental Europe.

Yet European social markets cannot survive in their present forms. To begin with unemployment is running at levels that are not sustainable indefinitely (over 11 percent across the EU as a whole). When the population as a whole is ageing the fiscal implications of unemployment on this scale are sobering. The fiscal problems of mass unemployment are not, however, its worst dangers.

Mass unemployment has aggravated social exclusion and political alienation throughout Europe. Most of the countries of continental Europe contain influential parties of the radical Right. In France and Austria, partly on the basis of support they receive from socially excluded groups, far-Right parties dictate the terms of political trade to moderate parties. In these European countries the centre ground of politics is no longer defined by liberal values but by anti-liberal parties.

In the early years of the single currency the danger confronting European institutions is that they will become identified in the minds of citizens with mass unemployment. Voters who perceive European institutions in this way are easily exploited by Rightist parties. The radical Right is not likely to enter national government in any EU country over the next few years. But it can condition deeply the environment in which policies are formed by centrist administrations.

In the larger Europe of which the EU is a part, far-Right parties could wield far more power. Where states are weak they are easily Balkanized. States containing significant minorities could well be casualties of ethnic nationalism. Events in parts of post-communist Europe are a telling reminder that Europe has not exhausted its capacity for disorder.[7]

In a global free market social groups that have been excluded from economic participation return to haunt political life as supporters of extremist movements. As Zygmunt Bauman has well described this development: 'An integral part of the globalizing processes is progressive spatial segregation, separation and exclusion. Neo-tribal and fundamentalist tendencies, which reflect and articulate the experience of people on the receiving end of globalization, are as much legitimate offspring of globalization as the widely acclaimed 'hybridization' of top culture – the culture at the globalized top.'[8]

Social democrats believe that Europe's social markets can be renewed within the framework of global *laissez-faire*.[9] But worldwide mobility of capital renders ineffective the Keynesian policies on which social democratic regimes have in the past relied to achieve full employment.[10] Global free trade makes the regulatory and tax costs of socially responsible capitalism harder to support. So long as these conditions prevail Europe's social markets will be under unremitting pressure from global market forces. Social exclusion and political alienation will be constant dangers.

This is not to say that the Rhine model of capitalism is destined to disappear. On the contrary, German capitalism has emerged from the trauma of unification as the dominant economic force in Europe. The question for the Rhine model is whether it can continue to subordinate the interests of shareholders to those of stakeholders. So long as the rules of global *laissez-faire* are not challenged, the answer must be that it cannot.

Global markets will bear down inexorably on the share prices of companies that attempt to do so. Even in a Europe unified by a single currency, the German social market cannot remain what it is today. Neither in Germany nor in any other country of continental Europe will social markets converge with Anglo-Saxon free markets. Nevertheless, a generation from now Europe's social markets are likely to be unrecognizable.

The single currency cannot insulate Europe from intensifying competitive pressures that arise from centuries-long processes of globalization. Long after global *laissez-faire* has passed into history Europe will still need to find its place in a world that has been altered irreversibly by industrialization.

Nor can the single currency shelter Europe from the fallout from economic collapse in neighbouring countries. If Russia descends into chaos after the rouble collapse the direct economic impact on the countries of the EU may not be unmanageable. The social and political impact may be considerable. How will countries such as Poland cope with the risk of large population movements across their eastern borders? How would such a large-scale refugee crisis affect the EU's strategy of enlargement to the east?

The single currency will be of little help to Europe in dealing with such problems. But it gives the European Union a powerful advantage in responding to the larger crisis of global *laissez-faire*. If the world market begins to fall apart under pressures that it can no longer contain, Europe will be the largest economic bloc. Its size and wealth will enable it to press for reforms limiting the mobility of capital. If it survives the turmoil of the coming years, the pivotal position of the Euro will strengthen Europe's voice in urging regulation of speculative trade in currencies. Even in a global depression like that in the thirties Europe could be less severely affected than either the United States or the countries of Asia.

The free market has never had in Europe the commanding position it has sometimes exercised in English-speaking countries. It is not inconceivable that the European Union could take the lead in building a new framework for the world economy in the wake of the collapse of global *laissez-faire*.

Can anything be done?

As yet there is still no consensus that the world economy is in crisis. Opinion in transnational organizations and mainstream political parties insists that the Asian depression can be contained. The necessity for radical reform of the world economy has not been understood. This continuing default of understanding warrants pessimism about the future.

The Asian crisis has not been understood because according to the prevailing view of the world it could not occur. In this world-view free flows of capital promote maximal economic efficiency. They do so even when – as in Indonesia – their effect is to ruin an entire economy. Within the view of the world that is dominant in our time economic efficiency has been disconnected from human well-being.

A basic shift in economic philosophy is needed. The freedoms of the market are not ends in themselves. They are expedients, devices contrived by human beings for human purposes.[11] Markets are made to serve man, not man the market. In the global free market the instruments of economic life have become dangerously emancipated from social control and political governance.

Within transnational organizations there are signs that free-market fundamentalism is being questioned. The dogma that capital must have unfettered mobility and similar tenets of the 'Washington consensus' are sometimes criticized. Nonetheless, the Anglo-Saxon free market remains the model for economic reform everywhere. The idea that the world economy must be organized as a single, universal market has not yet been challenged.

The ultimate explanation of the power of the free market cannot be found in any economic theory. It is in the recurring utopianism of western civilisation. A worldwide free market embodies the western Enlightenment ideal of a universal civilization. That is what explains its popularity – especially in the United States. It is also what makes it peculiarly dangerous at the present time.

Globalization – the spread of new, distance-abolishing technologies throughout the world – does not make western values universal. It makes a plural world irreversible. Growing interconnection between the world's economies does not signify the growth of a single economic civilization. It means that a *modus vivendi* will have to be found between economic cultures that will always remain different.

The task of transnational organizations should be to fashion a framework of regulation within which diverse market economies can flourish. At present they do the opposite. They seek to force a revolutionary make-over on the world's divergent economic cultures.

History does not support the hope that global *laissez-faire* can easily be reformed. It took the disaster of the Great Depression and the experience of the Second World War to shake the hold of an earlier version of free market orthodoxies on western governments. We cannot expect feasible alternatives to global *laissez-faire* to emerge until there has been an economic crisis more far-reaching than that we have experienced thus far. In all probability the Asian depression will spread throughout much of the world before the economic philosophy that supports the global free market is finally abandoned.

Without a fundamental shift in the policies of the United States all proposals for reform of global markets will be stillborn. At present the US combines an absolutist insistence on its own national sovereignty with a universalist claim to worldwide jurisdiction. Such an approach is supremely ill-suited to the plural world which globalization has created.

The practical upshot of American policy can only be that other powers will act unilaterally when the instability of global markets becomes intolerable. At that point, the jerry-built edifice of global *laissez-faire* will begin to crumble.

A global free market is a project that was destined to fail. In this, as in much else, it resembles that other twentieth century experiment in utopian social engineering, Marxian socalism. Each was convinced that human progress must have a single civilization as its goal. Each denied that a modern economy can come in many varieties. Each was ready to exact a large price in suffering from humanity in order to impose its single vision on the world. Each has run aground on vital human needs.

If we take history as our guide, we must expect that the global free market will shortly belong to an irrecoverable past. Like other twentieth-century utopias, global *laissez-faire* – together with its casualties – will be swallowed into the memory hole of history.

Notes

1 From the Great Transformation to the global free market

1 George Soros, *Soros on Soros*, New York: John Wiley, 1995, p. 194.
2 Karl Polanyi, *The Great Transformation: The Political and Economic Origins of our Time*, Boston: Beacon Press, 1944, p. 140.
3 Ibid.
4 I have discussed the Enlightenment project in my book, *Enlightenment's Wake: Politics and Culture at the Close of the Modern Age*, London and New York: Routledge, 1995.
5 Barrington Moore, *Social Origins of Dictatorship and Democracy: Lord and Peasant in the Making of the Modern World*, Harmondsworth: Penguin Books, 1991, pp. 21–2, p. 25.
6 E. J. Hobsbawm, *Industry and Empire*, Harmondsworth: Penguin, 1990, pp. 88–9.
7 D. Ricardo, *Principles of Political Economy and Taxation*, London: Everyman, p. 1.
8 A. J. Taylor, *Laissez-faire and State Intervention in Nineteenth Century Britain*, London: Macmillan, Economic History Society Monograph, 1972, p. 43.
9 Ibid., p. 57.
10 Ibid., p. 57.

11 Alan Macfarlane, *The Origins of English Individualism*, Oxford: Basil Blackwell, 1978, p. 199.

12 Ibid., p. 202.

13 For a balanced assessment of the evidence on the economic gains and social costs of the mid-Victorian economy, see R. A. Church, *The Great Victorian Boom 1850–1873*, London: Macmillan, Studies in Economic and Social History, 1975.

14 The description of the 1870 Education Act comes from Arthur J. Taylor, *Laissez-faire and State Intervention in Nineteenth Century Britain*, London: Macmillan, Economic History Society Monograph, 1972, p. 57.

15 Corelli Barnett, *The Collapse of British Power*, Stroud, Glos: Alan Sutton Publishing, 1984, p. 493.

16 Karl Polanyi, op. cit., p. 69.

2 Engineering free markets

1 Karl Polanyi, *The Great Transformation: The Political and Economic Origins of our Time*, Boston: Beacon Press, 1944, p. 140.

2 See Roderic Ai Camp, *Politics in Mexico*, Oxford and New York: Oxford University Press, 1996, pp. 219–20.

3 A. V. Dicey, *Lectures on the Relationship between Law and Public Opinion in England during the Nineteenth Century*, London, 1905, p. 306.

4 See Simon Jenkins, *Accountable to None: The Tory Nationalization of Britain*, London: Hamish Hamilton, 1995.

5 On *Stepping Stones*, see Hugo Young's magnificent study of Margaret Thatcher, *One of Us*, London: Pan Books, 1993, pp. 115–18.

6 National Survey by the Health Visitors Association, reported in the *Independent*, 25 November 1996, 'Dickensian diseases return to haunt today's Britain'.

7 *Transition and Transformation: Employee Satisfaction in the 1990s*, London: ISR International Survey Research, 1996.

8 A survey of some of this evidence may be found in Ruth Lister, 'The Family and Women', in D. Kavanagh and A. Seldon, *The Major Effect*, London: Macmillan, 1994.

9 For evidence about Swindon which tends to confirm the connections between labour market mobility and family breakdown, see Matthew D'Ancona, *The Ties That Bind*, London: Social Market Foundation, 1996.

10 Survey conducted by Paul Gregg and Jonathan Wadsworth at the London School of Economics, reported in the *Observer*, 10 January 1997, p. 10.

11 Source: House of Common Library, compiled by Peter Hain MP. Reported in the *Independent*, 23 December 1996.

12 *Financial Times*, Editorial, 27 August 1996.
13 See A. Sked and C. Cook, *Post-War Britain: A Political History*, Harmondsworth: Penguin, 1990, p. 354.
14 T. Morris, 'Crime and Penal Policy', in Kavanagh and Seldon, eds, *The Major Effect*, op. cit., p. 313.
15 Sked and Cook, op cit., p. 354.
16 T. Morris, in Kavanagh and Seldon, eds, *The Major Effect*, op. cit., pp. 314–15, 316.
17 *Joseph Rowntree Foundation Inquiry into Income and Wealth*, vol. 1, York: February 1995, Joseph Rowntree Foundation, p. 15.
18 Joseph Rowntree Report, ibid., vol. 2, p. 23.
19 See Hugo Young, op. cit., pp. 435–58.
20 On the passing of social democracy, see my monograph, *After Social Democracy*, London: Demos, 1995, reprinted in my book, *Endgames: Questions in Late Modern Political Thought*, Cambridge: Polity Press, 1996, Chapter 2.
21 F. A. Hayek, *The Constitution of Liberty*, Chicago: Henry Regnery, 1960.
22 Francis Fukuyama, *Trust: The Social Virtues and the Creation of Prosperity*, New York and London: The Free Press, p. 351.
23 For an early effort to track the self-destruction of conservatism in Thatcherite Britain, see my monograph *The Undoing of Conservatism*, published by the Social Market Foundation in June 1994, republished as Chapter 7 of my book *Enlightenment's Wake: Politics and Culture at the Close of the Modern Age*, London: Routledge 1995, and republished again with a new Postscript in John Gray and David Willets, *Is Conservatism Dead?*, London: Profile Books, 1997.
24 See Will Hutton's excellent polemic, *The State We're In*, London: Jonathan Cape, 1995, for a powerful critique of short-termism.
25 Jane Kelsey, *Economic Fundamentalism*, London and East Haven, CT: Pluto Press, 1995, p. 5. I am much indebted to Kelsey's indispensable study of New Zealand experiment.
26 Ibid., p. 271.
27 Ibid., p. 297.
28 Ibid., p. 275.
29 For an example of this rhetoric, see Charles Murray, *Losing Ground: American Social Policy, 1950–1980*, New York: Basic Books, 1984.
30 On this, see *The Economist*, 5 November 1994, p. 19.
31 Kelsey, op. cit., p. 348.
32 'Mexico replays loan early', *Financial Times*, 16 January 1997, p. 6.
33 Ai Camp, op. cit., p. 215; N. Lustig, *Mexico: The Remaking of an Economy*, Washington: Brookings Institution, 1992, Chapter Two.
34 Jorge G. Castaneda, *The Mexican Shock: Its Meaning for the U.S.*, New York: The New Press, 1995, p. 34.
35 Ibid., p. 33.

36 Andres Oppenheimer, *Bordering On Chaos: Guerillas, Stockbrokers, Politicians and Mexico's Road to Prosperity*, New York and London: Little Brown, 1996, pp. 293–4.

37 Carlos Salinas, 'A New Hope for the Hemisphere', *New Perspective Quarterly*, Winter 1991, p. 128.

38 Castaneda, op cit., p. 184.

39 Fernando Perez Correa, 'Modernizacion y mercado del trabajo', *Este Pais*, February 1995, p. 27. The survey is cited in Ai Camp, op. cit., p. 220.

40 One such survey appeared in *Forbes* magazine, Winter 1994.

41 Castaneda, op. cit., pp. 35–6, 38.

42 Ai Camp, op. cit., pp. 212–13.

43 Castaneda, op. cit., p. 215.

44 Andres Oppenheimer, op. cit., p. 293.

45 Source: *Financial times*, 28 October 1996.

46 On this, see Andres Oppenheim, op. cit., pp. 307 *et seq.*

47 See *The Times*, p. 15, 'Mexican drug lords aided by brother of former President', 18 February 1997.

48 For the arrest of Mexico's senior anti-narcotics officer, see *Financial Times*, 'Top Mexican official held over drugs link', 20 February 1997, p. 4. For allegations against the governor of Sonora, see the *Guardian*, 'Governor aids Mexican drug trade', 24 February 1997, p. 10. For the claim that 'the power of the drug cartels in Mexico is far greater than Mexican authorities would care to admit', see Leslie Crawford, 'Drugs scandal hits US-Mexico trust', *Financial Times*. February 28 1997.

49 Octavio Paz, 'The Border of Time', *New Perpectives Quarterly*, Winter 1991, p. 36.

3 What globalization is not

1 Joseph Schumpeter, 'The Instability of Capitalism', *Economic Journal*, vol. 38, September 1928, p. 368.

2 David Held, David Goldblatt, Anthony McGrew, Jonathan Perraton, 'The Globalization of Economic Activity', *New Political Economy*, vol. 2, no. 2, July 1997, pp. 257–77, p. 258. See also, by the same authors, *Global Flows, Global Transformations: Concepts, Theories and Evidence*, Cambridge: Polity Press, 1997. I am much indebted to David Held for making the pathbreaking paper to which I have referred above available to me prior to publication.

3 Anthony Giddens, *The Consequences of Modernity*, Cambridge: Polity Press, 1990, p. 64.

4 John Micklethwaite and Adrian Wooldridge, *The Witch Doctors*, London: Heinemann, 1996, p. 294.

5 Tom Nierop, *Systems and Regions in Global Politics*, London: John Wiley, 1994, Ch. 3.

6 Micklethwaite and Wooldridge, op. cit., p. 245.

7 See Paul Krugman, 'Growing World Trade: Causes and Consequences', *Brookings Paper on Economic Activity*, No. 1 (1995).

8 For evidence on this point, see J. Frankel, *The Internationalization of Equity Markets*, Chicago: University of Chicago Press, 1994; H. Akdogan, *The Integration of International Capital Markets*, London: Edward Elgar, 1995.

9 On the trend to global pricing of equities, see Lowell Bryan and Diana Farrell, *Market Unbound: Unleashing Global Capitalism*, New York: John Wiley, 1996, Chapter Two.

10 GATT, *International Trade 1993–4*, vol 1, Geneva: GATT, 1994; UN Development Programme, *Human Development Report 1994*, Oxford: Oxford University Press, 1994; UNCTAD, *World Investment Report 1994*, Geneva: UNCTAD, 1994.

11 *Wall Street Journal*, 24 October 1995; Bank of International Settlements, Annual Report, 1995.

12 Michel Albert, *Capitalism against Capitalism*, London: Whurr Publishers, 1993, p. 188.

13 UNCTAD, *World Investment Report*, 1994.

14 Micklethwaite and Wooldridge, op. cit., p. 246.

15 W. Ruigrok and R. van Tulder, *The Logic of International Restructuring*, London: Routledge, 1995.

16 Paul Hirst and Grahame Thompson, 'Globalization', *Soundings*, Issue 4, Autumn 1996, p. 56.

17 See Micklethwaite and Wooldridge, op. cit., pp. 243–4.

18 Kenichi Ohmae, *The End of the Nation-State: The Rise of Regional Economies*, London: HarperCollins, 1995, p. 7.

19 Paul Hirst and Graham Thompson, *Globalization in Question*, Cambridge: Polity Press, 1996, p. 6. Similar sceptical arguments about globalization may be found in P. Bairoch, 'Globalization, Myths and Realities', in R. Boyer and D. Drache, *States Against Markets – The Limits of Globalization*, London: Routledge, 1996. See also P. Bairoch and R. Kozul-Wright, 'Globalization Myths: Some Historical Reflections on Integration, Industrialisation and Growth in the World Economy', UNCTAS Discussion Paper No. 113.

20 Hirst and Thompson, *Globalization in Question*, op. cit., p. 31.

21 Held et al., *New Political Economy*, p. 6.

22 Hirst and Thompson, op. cit., p. 10.

23 Hirst and Thompson, op. cit., p. 163 *et seq*.

24 Held et al., *New Political Economy*.

25 Kenichi Ohmae, *The End of the Nation-State, The Rise of Regional Economies*, London: HarperCollins, 1995, pp. 15, 19–20.

26 Nicholas Negroponte, *Being Digital*, London: Hodder & Stoughton, 1995.

27 Bryan and Farrell, op. cit., p. 1.

28 Robert B. Reich, *The Work of Nations: Preparing Ourselves for 21st Century Capitalism*, New York: Alfred A. Knopf, 1991.

29 John Naisbitt, *Global Paradox*, London: Nicholas Brealey Publishing, 1995, p. 40.

30 Ruigrok and Van Tulder, op. cit.

31 Hirst and Thompson, op. cit., p. 12.

32 I am indebted to some aspects of the analysis of Scott Lash and John Urry, in their book *The End of Organised Capitalism*, Cambridge: Polity Press, 1987.

33 See Susan Strange, *Casino Capitalism*, Oxford: Basil Blackwell, 1986.

34 See Martin van Craveld, *On Future War*, London: Brassey, (UK), 1991, for a brilliant exposition of the decline of Clausewitzian war.

35 An interesting study of business organization as epistemic, knowledge-creating devices, is Ikujiro Nonaka and Hirotaka Takeuchi, *The Knowledge-Creating Company: How Japanese Companies Create the Dynamics of Innovation*, New York and Oxford: Oxford University Press, 1995.

36 On the contemporary interaction between resource-scarcity and military conflict, see T. Homer-Dixon, 'On the Threshold: Environmental Changes as Causes of Acute Conflict', *International Security*, Harvard and MIT: Boston, Fall 1991.

4 How global free markets favour the worst kinds of capitalism: a new Gresham's Law?

1 W. Stanley Jevons, *Money and the Mechanism of Exchange*, London: Kegan Paul, Trench Trubner, 1910, p. 81.

2 For powerful critiques of global free trade to which I am indebted, see Herman E. Daly, 'From Adjustment to Sustainable Development: The Obstacle of Free Trade', in *The Case Against Free Trade: GATT, NAFTA, and the Globalization of Corporate Power*, San Francisco: Earth Island Press, 1993, pp. 121–32. See also Jerry Mander and Edward Goldsmith, *The Case Against the Global Economy and For a Turn Toward the Local*, San Francisco: Sierra Books, 1996.

3 David Ricardo, *On the Principles of Political Economy and Taxation*, Harmondsworth: Penguin, 1971, p. 155.

4 As Michael Porter notes, in his classic, *The Competitive Advantage of Nations*, London: Macmillan, 1990, p. 12, 'The standard theory (of comparative advantage) assumes that there are no economies of scale, that technologies everywhere are identical, that products are undifferentiated,

and that the pool of national factors is fixed. The theory also assumes that factors, such as skilled labour and capital, do not move among nations. All these assumptions bear little relation, in most industries, to actual competition.' A seminal recent statement of comparative advantage theory is that of R. Dornbusch, S. Fisher and Paul Samuelson, 'Comparative Advantage, Trade and Payments in a Ricardian Model with a Continuum of Goods', *American Economic Review*, vol. 67, December 1977, pp. 823–39.

5   This is the strategy of argument of two notable contemporary writers who defend unrestricted global free trade; Douglas A. Irwin, *Against the Tide: An Intellectual History of Free Trade*, Princeton, NJ: Princeton University Press, 1996; and Paul Krugman, *Pop Internationalism*, Cambridge, Mass: MIT Press, 1996. For a classic modern version of the theory of comparative advantage, see Betil Ohlin, *Interregional and International Trade*, Cambridge, Mass: Harvard University Press, 1933.

6   For this comparison, see Peter Marsh, 'A shift to flexibility', *Financial Times*, 21 February 1997.

7   'Come to low-wage Wales', *Independent*, 13 January 1997.

8   For this comparison, see Peter Marsh, 'A shift to flexibility', *Financial Times*, 21 February 1997.

9   R. Freeman, 'Are your wages set in Peking?', *Journal of Economic Perspectives*, 9, Summer 1995.

10 *World Labour Report*, Geneva: International Labour Organisation, 1992.

11 Michael Lind, *The Next American Nation: The New Nationalism and the Fourth American Revolution*, New York: The Free Press, 1995, p. 203.

12 I owe these examples to 'Who competes? Changing landscapes of corporate control', *The Ecologist*, vol. 26, No. 4, July/August 1996, p. 135.

13 On this, see Jeremy Rifkin, *The End of Work: The Decline of the Global Labor Force and the Dawn of the Post-Market Era*, New York: G.P. Putnam, 1995.

14 David Ricardo, *Principles of Political Economy and Taxation*, London: J. M. Dent, 1991, pp. 266–7. For a more recent argument that supports Ricardo's, see Paul Samuelson, 'Mathematical vindication of Ricardo on machinery', *Journal of Political Economy*, vol. 96, 1988, pp. 274–82, and Samuelson's 'Ricardo was right!', in *Scandinavian Journal of Economics*, vol. 91, 1989, pp. 47–62.

15 See Patrick Minford, 'Free trade and long wages – still in the general interest', *Journal des Economistes et des Etudes Humaines*, vol. 7, Number 1, March 1996, pp. 123–9.

16 William Pfaff, 'Job security is disappearing around the world', *International Herald Tribune*, 8 July 1996, p. 8.

17 See Adrian Wood, *North–South Trade, Employment and Inequality–Changing Fortunes in a Skill-Driven World*, Oxford: Clarendon Press, 1994, and 'How trade hurts unskilled workers' in *Journal of Economic*

Perspectives, vol. 9, No. 3, pp. 57–80. See also P. Minford et al., 'The Elixir of Growth', in Snower and de La Dehesa, eds., *Unemployment Policy*, London: Centre for Economic Policy Research, 1996. A counter-argument has been advanced stressing the importance of controls on immigration as means whereby nation-states can protect their workers against globalized competition, especially in the non-traded services sector. On this view, globalization of labour was more advanced in the late nineteenth century than it is today. See Vincent Cable, *Daedalus*, vol. 124, no. 2, June 1995.

18 'Living with tax rivalry', *Financial Times*, 14 January 1997.

19 For a criticism of Rawls's theory, see my book, *Liberalisms*, London: Routledge, 1989, Chapter 6.

20 I have argued this more systematically in my monograph, *After Social Democracy*, London: Demos, 1996, reprinted as Chapter Two of my book, *Endgames: Questions in Late Modern Political Thought*, Cambridge: Polity Press, 1997.

21 A powerful critique of 'rational expectations' equilibrium theories of economic life is developed in G. Shackle's *Epistemics and Economics*, Cambridge: Cambridge University Press, 1976.

22 George Soros, 'Can Europe work? A plan to rescue the union', *Foreign Affairs*, September/October 1996, vol. 75, Number 5, p. 9.

23 Paul Hirst and Grahame Thompson, 'Globalization', *Soundings*, Issue 4, Autumn 1996, p. 58.

24 William Greider, *One World, Ready or Not: The Manic Logic of Global Capitalism*, New York: Simon & Schuster, 1996, p. 281.

25 The view that it was the willingness of the state to act as employer of last resort, not its active labour policy, which enabled Social Democratic Sweden to avoid mass unemployment, is argued for persuasively in R. B. Freeman, B. Swedenborg and R. Topel, *Reforming the Welfare State: Economic Troubles in Sweden's Welfare State*, Stockholm: Centre for Business and Policy Studies, Occasional Paper Number 69, 1995.

26 Michel Albert, *Capitalism Against Capitalism*, London: Whurr Publishers, 1993.

27 Ibid., p. 191.

28 Reported in David Goodhart, *The Reshaping of the German Social Market*, London: Institute of Public Policy Research, p. 22. See also Olivier Cadot and Pierre Blime, *Can Industrial Europe be Saved?*, London: Centre for European Reform, 1996, for a careful assessment of Europe's industrial record and prospects.

29 I have considered the Ordo-liberal philosophy more systematically and extensively in my monograph, *The Postcommunist Societies in Transition: a Social Market Perspective*, London: Social market Foundation, 1994, reprinted as Chapter 5 of my book, *Enlightenment's Wake*, London: Routledge, 1995.

30 It has been claimed that Erhard was advised to launch Germany's economic liberalization by two Allied economic advisers, Karl Bode and E. F. Schumacher (later author of the book *Small is Beautiful*). See Neal Ascherson, 'When Soros debunks capitalism', *Independent on Sunday*, 2 February 1997, p. 22.

31 David Goodhart, op. cit., p. 80.

32 Interview in *The European*, 16 January 1997, p. 28.

33 For 'flexible specialization' in Germany, see David Goodhart, op. cit., pp. 59–62.

34 On the Osram's–IG Metall union deal, see Peter Marsh, 'A shift to flexibility', *Financial Times*, 21 February 1997, p. 14.

35 Hirst and Thompson, *Soundings*, op. cit.

5 The United States and the Utopia of global capitalism

1 Edmund Stillman and William Pfaff. *The Politics of Hysteria: The Sources of Twentieth Century Conflict*, London: Victor Gollancz, 1964, pp. 222–3.

2 Henry Kissinger, *Diplomacy*, New York: Simon & Schuster, 1994, p. 811.

3 For an authoritative account of the American conservative ascendancy, see Godfrey Hodgson, *The World Turned Right Side Up: A History of the Conservative Ascendancy in America*, Boston and New York: Houghton Mifflin, 1996.

4 David Stockman, *The Triumph of Politics: The Crisis in American Government and How it Affects the World*, New York, 1986, p. 422.

5 Hodgson, op. cit., p. 303.

6 I have examined American liberal legalism in its left-wing as well as its right-wing varieties in *Enlightenment's Wake*, Ch. 1: *Politics and Culture at the Close of the Modern Age*, London, Routledge, 1995, and *Endgames: Questions in Late Modern Political Thought*, Cambridge: Polity Press, 1997, Ch. 2.

7 J. K. Galbraith, *The Culture of Contentment*, Harmondsworth: Penguin, 1993, p. 10.

8 *Statistical Abstract of the United States: 1991*, Washington DC, Tables 129, 133, pp. 87–8.

9 D. Puga, *The Rise and Fall of Regional Inequalities*, London: Centre for Economic Performance, November, 1996.

10 *The State of Working America*, Washington: Economic Policy Institute, December 1996.

11 Richard Layard, 'Clues to Prosperity', *Financial Times*, 17 February 1997.

12 Edward Luttwak, 'Turbo-charged capitalism and its consequences', *London Review of Books*, 2 November 1995, p. 7.

13 Bureau of Labor Statistics, 29 January 1996, and L. Mishel and J. Bernstein, *The State of Working America*, Washington: Economic Policy Institute, 1994.

14 Edward Luttwak, *The Endangered American Dream*, New York and London: Simon & Schuster, 1993, p. 163.

15 Kevin Phillips, *The Politics of Rich and Poor: Wealth and the Electorate in the Reagan Aftermath*, New York: Harper Perennial, 1991, p. 82.

16 Hodgson, op. cit., p. 302.

17 See Robert H. Frank and Philip J. Cook, *The Winner-Take-All Society*, London and New York: The Free Press, 1995.

18 Graef Crystal, *In Search of Excess: The Overcompensation of American Executives*, New York: W. W. Norton, 1991, pp. 207–9.

19 Michael Lind, *The Next American Nation: the New Nationalism and the Fourth American Revolution*, New York and London: The Free Press, 1995, p. 189.

20 Richard Layard and John Parker, *The Coming Russian Boom*, New York: The Free Press, 1996, p. 301: 'inequality (in post-communist Russia) still falls short of that in the United States; it is close to the level in Britain.'

21 Felix Rohatyn, Requiem for a Democrat, Speech delivered at Wake Forest University, Winston-Salem, NC, 17 March 1995. I owe this reference to Simon Head, 'The new, ruthless economy', *New York Review of Books*, 29 February 1996, p. 47.

22 'Many seek security in private communities,' *New York Times*, 3 September, 1995.

23 *The Times*, 11 December 1995, p. 38.

24 Louise I. Shelley, 'American crime: an international anomaly?', *Comparative Social Research*, 1985, pp. 81–9.

25 'Crime and punishment', *Financial Times*, 8–9 March 1997, p. 7.

26 Richard Layard, 'Clues to prosperity', *Financial Times*, 17 February 1997.

27 *The Times*, 11 December 1995, p. 38.

28 *New Republic*, 25 May 1992, p. 7.

29 I argued that America was undergoing Brazilianization in 1990. See my article, 'The Brazilianization of the United States', *Fortune*, vol. 122, no. 5, 1990.

30 Michael Lind, *The Next American Nation*, op. cit., p. 216. For the revival of conservative racism in the United States, see Michael Lind, *Up from Conservatism: Why the Right is Wrong for America*, New York: The Free Press, 1996, Chapter 8.

31 For a powerful argument for the reform of American drug policy, see George Soros, 'A new leaf for the law', *Guardian*, 22 February 1997.

32 *The Economist*, 22 October 1994, Survey, p. 4.

33 S. M. Lipset, *American Exceptionalism: A Double-Edged Sword*, New York and London: W. W. Norton, 1996, p. 227.

34 Layard and Parker, op. cit., p. 150.
35 Source: Center for Disease Control and Prevention, 'Young America and how it dies', *International Herald Tribune*, 8–9 February 1997.
36 Christopher Davis and Murray Feisbach, *Rising Infant Mortality in the USSR in the 1970s*, Series P-25, no. 74, Washington DC: US Bureau of the Census, September 1980.
37 N. D. Kristof and S. Wudunn, *China Wakes: The Struggle for the Soul of a Rising Power*, London: Nicholas Brealey Publishing, 1995, p. 16.
38 *Statistical Abstract of the United States: 1991*, Washington, DC, Table 320, p. 188; Table 2, p. 7; Table 319, p. 188.
39 Lipset, op. cit., pp. 227–8.
40 Francis Fukuyama's original article, 'The end of history', was published in *National Interest*, Summer 1989. His book, *The End of History and the Last Man*, in which the thesis of the original article is reaffirmed without significant revision, was published in 1992 by The Free Press, New York.
41 In an article responding to Fukuyama published in October 1989, I wrote: 'we are moving back into an epoch that is classically historical, and not forward into the empty, post-historical era projected in Fukuyama's article. Ours is an era in which political ideology, liberal as much as Marxist, has a dwindling leverage on events, and more ancient, more primordial forces, nationalist and religious, fundamentalist and soon, perhaps, Malthusian, are contesting with each other . . . If the Soviet Union does indeed fall apart, that beneficent catastrophe will not inaugurate a new era of post-historical harmony, but instead a return to the classical terrain of history, a terrain of great-power rivalries, secret diplomacies, and irredentist claims and wars.' See *National Review*, 27 October 1989, pp. 33–5; reprinted as Chapter 17 of my book, *Post-liberalism: Studies in Political Thought*, London and New York: Routledge, 1993, pp. 245–50.
42 Samuel P. Huntington, *The Clash of Civilizations and the Remaking of World Order*, New York: Simon & Schuster, 1996.
43 Ibid., p. 28.
44 Robert D. Kaplan, *The Ends Of the Earth: A Journey at the Dawn of the Twenty-First Century*, New York: Random House, 1996, p. 270.
45 On Berlin's account of the Counter-Enlightenment, see my *Berlin*, London and Princeton, NJ: HarperCollins and Princeton University Press, 1995.
46 I have criticized contemporary relativism in its most plausible variety in the work of Richard Rorty in my book *Endgames*, op. cit., Chapter 4.
47 Huntington, op. cit., p. 311.
48 Samuel Huntington, 'The West v. the rest'. *Guardian*, 23 November 1996.
49 See 'God's soldiers get political', *Independent on Sunday*, 27 July 1997, p. 16.

50 Lipset, op. cit.

51 Huntington, op. cit., p. 306.

52 'Hispanic numbers explode in US', *Guardian*, 31 March 1997, p. 8.

53 On the 'Californian model', see Charles Leadbeater, *Britain – the California of Europe*, London: Demos Occasional Paper, 1997.

54 Lind, op. cit., pp. 198–9.

6 Anarcho-capitalism in post-communist Russia

1 Bertrand Russell, *The Practice and Theory of Bolshevism*, London: George Allen & Unwin, 1920, p. 118.

2 L. Shestov, *All Things Are Possible*, London: Martin Secker, 1920, p. 238.

3 For an account of the mingling of European and Russian intellectual traditions in Leninism, see Alain Besancon, *The Rise of the Gulag: Intellectual Origins of Leninism*, New York: Continuum, 1981.

4 Richard Pipes, *The Russian Revolution, 1890–1919*, London: Collins Harville, 1990, pp. 671–2.

5 Orlando Figes, *A People's Tragedy: The Russian Revolution, 1891–1924*, London: Jonathan Cape, 1996, p. 733.

6 A reliable account of Taylor's life and work was published only in 1991. See Charles D. Wrege and Ronald J. Greenwood, *Federick W. Taylor: Myth and Reality, Homewood*, Ill.: Irwin, 1991.

7 See Figes, op. cit., p. 744.

8 Ibid., p. 724.

9 Ibid., pp. 672–3.

10 Ibid., pp. 695–7.

11 M. Nekrich and A. Heller, *Utopia in Power: The History of the Soviet Union from 1917 to the Present*, New York: Summit Books, 1986, pp. 115–36.

12 Quoted in Nekrich and Heller, op. cit., p. 120. The source quoted is given as Prokopovich, *Narodnoe khoziaistvo SSR*, 1: 59.

13 J. Becker, *Hungry Ghosts: China's Secret Famine*, London: John Murray, 1996, p. 38.

14 Ibid., P. 38.

15 Robert Conquest, *Harvest of Sorrow*, Oxford: Oxford University Press, 1986.

16 Michael Ellman, 'A note on the number of 1993 famine victims', *Soviet Studies*, 1989, quoted in Becker, op. cit., p. 46.

17 I have discussed the Marxian origins of Soviet totalitarianism in 'Totalitarianism, reform and civil society' in my book, *Post-liberalism: Studies in Political Thought*, Routledge: London and New York, 1993, Ch. 12.

18 For Zinoviev's account, see *The Reality of Communism*, London:

Gollancz, 1984; *Homo Sovieticus*, London: Gollancz, 1985; *Perestroika in Partygrad*, London: Peter Owen, 1990: *Katastroika*, London: The Claridge Press, 1990.

19 Dmitri Volkogonov, *Lenin: Life and Legacy*, London: HarperCollins, 1995, p. 334.

20 'Russian farm reform's fruit; a rural underclass', *International Herald Tribune*, 2 April 1997.

21 I have discussed late Tsarism in 'Totalitarianism, reform and civil society', in my book, *Post-liberalism*, op. cit., pp. 164–8 See also, P. Gatrell, *The Tsarist Economy 1850–1917*, London: B. T. Batsford, 1986.

22 John Gray, 'The risks of collapse into chaos', *Financial Times*, 13 September 1989, p. 25.

23 I gave an early assessment of the Soviet coup of August 1991 in my monograph, *The Strange Death of Perestroika: Causes and Consequences of the Soviet Coup*, London: Institute for European Defence and Strategic Studies, September 1991.

24 *OECD Economic Survey: The Russian Federation*, Paris: Centre for Cooperation with Economies in Transition, 1995.

25 See my monograph, *Post-Communist Societies in Transition; A Social Market Perspective*, London: Social Market Foundation, 1994, reprinted as Chapter 5 of my book, *Enlightenment's Wake: Politics and Culture at the Close of the Modern Age*, London and New York: Routledge, 1995. Powerful critiques of shock therapy can be found in Jonathan Steele, *Eternal Russia*, London: Faber, 1994; Marshall Goldman, *Lost Opportunity: Why Economic Reforms in Russia Have Not Worked*, New York: Norton, 1994; M. Ellman 'Shock Therapy in Russia: Failure or Partial Success?', *Radio Free Europe/Radio Liberty Research Report*, 3 April 1992.

   Jeffrey Sachs replied to my critique in *Understanding Shock Therapy*, London: Social Market Foundation, 1994. Samuel Brittan has provided a useful account of the differences between my own views and those of Jeffrey Sachs in 'Post-communism: the rival models', *Financial Times*, 24 February 1994; a more extended account of the debate between myself and Sachs may be found in Robert Skidelsky's *The World After Communism*, London: Macmillan, 1995 pp. 166–72. See also Robert Skidelsky, ed., *Russia's Stormy path to Reform*, London: Social Market Foundation, 1995.

26 Jonathan Steele, 'Russia: boom or bust', *Observer*, 29 December 1996, p. 16.

27 B. Russell, op. cit., p. 85.

28 Jeffrey Sachs, 'Nature, nurture and growth', *The Economist*, 14 June 1997, p. 24.

29 For a defence of Sach's views, see Jeffrey Sachs, *Understanding Shock Therapy*, op. cit.

30 Skidelsky, op. cit., p. 152.

31 On Russia's privatization programme, see J. R. Blasi, M. Kroumova and D. Ruse, *Kremlin Capitalism: Privatizing the Russian Economy*, London and Ithaca: Cornell University Press, 1997.

32 James Sherr, 'Russia's defence industry – conversion or rescue?', *Jane's Intelligence Review*, July 1992, p. 299.

33 For a moderate version of the argument that shock therapy was not consistently applied in Russia, see Richard Layard and Jon Parker, *The Coming Russian Boom*, New York: The Free Press, 1996, pp. 65 *et seq.*

34 Peter Truscott, *Russia First: Breaking with the West*, London: I. B. Tauris, 1997, p. 128.

35 Martin Wolf, 'Russia's missed chance', *Financial Times*, 18 March 1997, p. 18.

36 *Russian Economic Trends*, London: Whurr Publishers, Monthly Update, 12 June 1996, pp. 5, 16, quoted in Truscott, op. cit., pp. 130, 145.

37 Truscott, ibid., p. 130.

38 Layard and Parker, op. cit., p. 301.

39 I. Birman, 'Gloomy prospects for the Russian economy', *Europe–Asia Studies*, vol. 48, No. 5, 1996, p. 745.

40 *Russian Unemployment and Enterprise Restructuring: Reviving Dead Souls*, Geneva: ILO, 1997.

41 'Russian GDP continues to shrink', *Financial Times*, p. 2.

42 Quoted in *The Economist*, 12 July 1997, Russia Survey, p. 5.

43 'Grim jobs picture emerges in Russia', *Financial Times*, 6 February 1997, p. 2.

44 UNICEF, 'Crisis in mortality, health and nutrition: Central and Eastern Europe in transition', *Economic and Transition Studies*, No. 2 August 1994, 53.

45 Truscott, op. cit., p. 139.

46 Report of Russian Presidential Commission on Women, the Family and Demographics, as reported in the *Independent*, 15 May 1997.

47 Murray Feisbach and Alfred Friendly Jr., *Ecocide in the USSR: Health and Nature under Siege*, London: Aurum Press, 1992, pp. 4, 9.

48 I have considered the Soviet destruction of the natural environment, and its connections with Marxian humanism, in my book, *Beyond the New Right: Markets, Government and the Common Environment*, London and New York: Routledge, 1993, pp. 130–3.

49 'Russia's hidden Chernobyl', *Guardian*, 15 July 1997, p. 10.

50 Feisbach and Friendly, op. cit., p. 4.

51 Layard and Parker, op. cit., p. 300.

52 Ibid., p. 115.

53 'Russian death rate alarms doctors', *The Times*, 9 June 1997. See also, M. Ellman, 'The increase in death and disease under "katastroika"', *Cambridge Journal of Economics*, 1994, pp. 329–55; and J. C. Shapiro,

'The Russian mortality crisis and its causes', in Anders Aslund, ed., *Russian Economic Reform at Risk*, London: Pinter, 1995.

54 Report commissioned from the American-based Population Reference Service by the Russian Presidential Commission on Women Family and Demography, as reported in the *Independent*, 15 May 1997.

55 *The Economist*, 12 July 1997, Russia Survey, p. 5.

56 Truscott, op. cit., p. 131.

57 P. Morvant, 'Alarm over falling life expectancy', *Transitions*, Prague, 25, October 1995, pp. 44–5. Quoted by Truscott, op. cit., pp. 132, 145.

58 Stephen F. Cohen, 'In Fact, Russians are deep in terrible tragedy', *International Herald Tribune*, 13 December 1996, p. 8.

59 I have considered late Tsarism in somewhat greater detail in 'Totalitarianism, reform and civil society', in my book *Post-liberalism*, op. cit., pp. 164–8. On the much lower levels of repression in Tsarist Russia than in the Soviet Union, see John D. Dziak, *Chekisty: a History of the KGB*, Lexington, Mass.: Lexington Books, D. C. Heath, 1988.

60 Layard and Parker, op. cit., p. 28.

61 For an illuminating discussion of the Soviet economy which identified its unreformability, see Peter Rutland, *The Myth of the Plan: Lessons of Soviet Planning Experience*, London: Hutchinson, 1985.

62 Alain Besancon, *The Soviet Syndrome*, New York and London: Harcourt Brace Jovanovich, 1978, pp. 30–1.

63 On the criminalization of the Soviet economy and government, see Valery Chalidze, *Criminal Russia: Essays in Crime in the Soviet Union*, New York: Random House, 1977; Konstantin Simis, *USSR: The Corrupt Society: The Secret World of Soviet Capitalism*, New York: Simon & Schuster, 1982; and Arkady Vaksberg, *The Soviet Mafia*, London: Weidenfeld & Nicolson, 1991.

64 David Pryce-Jones, *The War That Never Was: The Fall of the Soviet Empire, 1985–91*, London: Phoenix, 1995, p. 382.

65 Stephen Handelman, *Comrade Criminal*, New Haven and London: Yale University Press, 1995, pp. 335–6.

66 The estimate comes from the British National Criminal Intelligence Service. It is cited in Truscott, op. cit., p. 138.

67 Handelman, op. cit., pp. 18–20.

68 Ibid., pp. 127–8.

69 Ibid., pp. 233–4.

70 Yaroslav Golovanov, 'Mech i molet' (The Sword and the Hammer), Vek, 1993. This source is cited by Yevgenia Arbats, *KGB: State within a State*, London and New York: I. B. Tauris, 1995, p. 388, fn. 56.

71 Arbats, op. cit., pp. 335–6.

72 Truscott, op. cit., p. 114.

73 James Sherr, 'Russia: geopolitics and crime', *The World Today*, February 1995, p. 36.

74 Jim Rogers, 'No new money for an old empire', *Financial Times*, 5 October 1990, p.2.

75 For an excellent discussion of the political role of the European idea in post-communist countries, see Tony Judt, *A Grand Illusion? An Essay on Europe*, London and New York: Penguin Books, 1997.

76 Boris Yeltsin, *Programme of Action for 1996–2000*, 27 May 1996, p. 109, quoted in Truscott, op. cit., p. 8, fn. 9.

77 Prince Nikolai Trubestskoi, George Florovsky and Pyotr Savitsky, *Iskhod kvostoku (Exodus to the East)*, Sofia, 1921.

78 Layard and Parker, op. cit., p. 34.

79 Nekrich and Heller, op. cit., p. 178. I have discussed the Eurasian movement briefly in 'Totalitarianism, reform and civil society', in *Post-liberalism*, op. cit., pp. 177–8.

80 For a useful account of Leontiev's thought, see N. Berdyaev, *Leontiev*, London: Geoffrey Bles, The Centenary Press, 1940.

81 Truscott, op. cit., pp. 2, 5–6.

82 Layard and Parker, op. cit., pp. 281–2.

83 Economist Intelligence Unit, *EIU Country Profile 1995–6: The Russian Federation*, 1997, p. 12.

84 'Attitude is what gives Russians the edge', *Times Educational Supplement*, 1 January 1992.

85 For an account of the strength of the Russian family in Soviet times, see Klaus Mehnert, *Soviet Man and His World*, New York: 1961, chapter on 'Family and Home',

86 Layard and Parker, op. cit., p. 106.

7 Occidental twilight and the rise of Asia's capitalisms

1 Lee Kuan Yew, Interview, *New Perspectives Quarterly*, vol. 13 no. 1, Winter 1996, p. 4.

2 Takeshi Umehara, 'Ancient Japan shows post-modernism the way', *New Progressive Quarterly*, 9, Spring 1992, p. 10.

3 Qiao Shi, Interview, *New Perspectives Quarterly*, vol. 14, no. 3, Summer 1997, pp. 9–10.

4 Jasper Ridley, *Lord Palmerston*, London: Constable, 1970, p. 387.

5 For an authoritative account of Singapore's modernization, see M. Hill and Lian Kwen Fee, *The Politics of Nation Building and Citizenship in Singapore*, London and New York: Routledge, 1995. For a highly critical account of economic development in Singapore and the other little dragons, see W. Bello and Stephanie Rosenfeld, *Dragons In Distress: Asia's Miracle Economies in Crisis*. London: Penguin, 1992.

6 For a delightful account of this unique period, see Noel Perrin, *Giving Up the Gun: Japan's Reversion to the Sword, 1543–1879*, Boston: Nonpareil Books, 1979.

7 See Arthur Walworth, *Black Ships Off Japan*, New York: Alfred Knopf, 1946.

8 Perrin, op. cit., p. 91.

9 For an ambitious argument that Japan limits or falsifies much in western social science, see David Williams, *Japan and the Enemies of Open Political Science*, London and New York: Routledge, 1996.

10 Ann Waswo, *Modern Japanese Society 1868–1994*, Oxford: Oxford University Press, 1996, p. 102.

11 Paul Kennedy, *The Rise and Fall of the Great Powers*, London: Fontana, 1988, p. 266.

12 Murray Sayle, 'Japan victorious', *New York Review of Books*, 28 March 1985, p. 35.

13 Peter F. Drucker, *Post-Capitalist Society*, Oxford: Butterworth-Heinemann, 1993, p. 117.

14 Some writers argue that the Japanese economic system cannot be classified as a variant of capitalism. For one such argument, see E. Sakakibara, *Beyond Capitalism: The Japanese Model of Market Economics*, Economic Strategy Institute, Lanham: University Press of America, 1993.

15 R. E. Caves and M. Uekusa, *Industrial Organisation in Japan*, Washington, DC: Brookings Institution, 1976, p. 59.

16 Graham Searjeant, 'Economically, jails cost more than corner shops', *The Times*, 11 December 1995.

17 The figures are taken from the OECD Report for January 1997, as reported in Martin Wolf, 'Too great a sacrifice', *Financial Times*, 14 January 1997.

18 Paul Kennedy, op. cit., p. 266.

19 S. Tsuru, *Japan's Capitalism*, Cambridge: Cambridge University Press, 1993.

20 I have examined Mill's conception of a stationary-state economy more fully in my book, *Beyond the New Right: Markets, Government and the Common Environment*, London and New York: Routledge, 1993, pp. 140–54.

21 Mao Zedong, quoted in Jasper Becker, *Hungry Ghosts: China's Secret Famine*, London: John Murray, 1996, p. 37.

22 Jonathan D. Spence, *The Search for Modern China*, New York: Norton, 1990, pp. 249–50.

23 Simon Leys, *The Burning Forest: Essays on Chinese Culture and Politics*, New York: Henry Holt, 1983, p. 114.

24 Ibid., pp. 133–4. (Italics in original.)

25 Klaus Mehnert, *Peking and Moscow*, London: Weidenfeld & Nicolson, London, 1963, pp. 104–5.

26 Ibid., p. 138.

27 Ibid., p. 87. The research to which Mehnert refers is by John Lossing

Buck, *Chinese Farm Economy*, Nanking, 1937 (footnoted in Mehnert, p. 493). Buck's wife, Pearl S. Buck, won the Nobel Prize for Literature her novel, *The Good Earth*.

28 Jasper Becker, *Hungry Ghosts: China's Secret Famine*, London: John Murray, 1996, p. 37.

29 Ibid., pp. 28–9.

30 Ibid., p. 48.

31 Spence, op. cit., p. 583.

32 Ibid., p. 48.

33 Leys, op. cit., p. 167.

34 Becker, op. cit., p. 77.

35 Vaclav Smil, *The Bad Earth: Environmental Degradation in China*, London: Zed Press, 1983. See also Smil's *China's Environmental Crisis: An Inquiry into the Limits of National Development*, Armonk, New England and London: M.E. Sharpe, 1992.

36 Vaclav Smil, 'A land stretching to support its people', *International Herald Tribune*, 30 May 1994, p. 8.

37 Smil, *China's Environmental Crisis*, op. cit., pp. 129–37.

38 Smil, 'A land stretching to support its people', op. cit.

39 Roderick MacFarquhar, 'Demolition man', *New York Review of Books*, 27 March 1997, p. 14.

40 S. G. Redding, *The Spirit of Chinese Capitalism*, Berlin: de Gruyter, 1990.

41 S. Gordon Redding and Richard D. Whitley, 'Beyond bureaucracy: analysis of resource coordination and control', S. R. Clegg and S. G. Redding, eds., *Capitalism in Contrasting Cultures*, Berlin: de Gruyter, 1990, p. 86.

42 Yu-Shan Wu, 'Marketization of politics, the Taiwan experience', *Asian Survey*, 4 April 1989, p. 387. Wu's statement is quoted by Dick Wilson, *China: The Big Tiger*, London: Little, Brown, 1996, p. 365.

43 Ibid., p. 379.

44 Redding and Whitley, op. cit., p. 79.

45 For an attempt at a comparison of Chinese and Japanese enterprises as ideal types, see Simon Tam, 'Centrifugal versus centripetal growth processes: contrasting ideal types for conceptualizing the developmental patterns of Chinese and Japanese firms', in Clegg and Redding, op. cit., pp. 153–84.

46 H. Koo, 'The interplay of state, social class, and world system in east Asian development: the cases of South Korea and Taiwan', in F. C. Deyo, ed., *The Political Economy of the New Asian Industrialism*, Ithaca, New York: Cornell University Press, 1987, pp. 41–61.

47 N. Woolsey Biggart, 'Institutionalized patrimonialism in Korean business', in M. Orru, N. Woolsey Biggart and G. G. Hamilton, *The Economic Organization of East Asian Capitalism*, Thousand Oaks, London and Delhi: Sage, 1995, pp. 215–36.

48 Wilson, op. cit., p. 394.

49 The risk of war in East Asia is real. On this, see Kent E. Calder, *Asia's Deadly Triangle: How Arms, Energy and Growth Threaten to Destabilize Asia–Pacific*, London: Nicholas Brealey, 1997.

50 For Biggs's views, see Andrew Serwer, 'The end of the world is nigh – or is it?' *Fortune*, 2 May 1994. Biggs expressed his views in the context of a debate about Robert Kaplan's book, *The Ends of the Earth: A Journey at the Dawn of the 21st Century*, New York: Random House, 1996. Kaplan cites Biggs on pp. 297, 300.

51 For the best study of Deng, see Richard Evans, *Deng Xiaoping and the Making of Modern China*, London: Penguin Books, 1997. For a useful assessment of Deng's impact, see D. S. Goodman and Gerald Segal, *China Without Deng*, Sydney and New York: Editions Tom Thompson, 1997. See also, D. Shambaugh, ed., *Deng Xiaoping: Portrait of a Chinese Statesman*, Oxford: Oxford University Press, 1995; and Deng Maomao, *Deng Xiaoping: My Father*, New York: Basic Books, 1995.

52 For an overview of central-local relations in the Maoist and post-Maoist eras, see M. Boisoit and J. Child, 'Efficiency, ideology and tradition in the choice of transactions and governance structures: the case of China as a modernizing society', in Clegg and Redding, pp. 281–314.

53 '"Thoughts of Jiang" spell end to state planning', *The Times*, 8 August 1997, p. 12.

54 On this, see Ian Little, *Picking Winners: The East Asian Experience*, London: Social Market Foundation, 1996, Ch. 5.

55 Martin Woolf, 'A country divided by growth', *Financial Times*, 20 February 1996.

56 MacFarquhar, op. cit., p. 16.

57 William Pfaff, 'In China, the Interregnum won't necessarily be peaceful', *International Herald Tribune*, 25 February 1997.

58 See Teresa Poole, 'China ready for world's ultimate privatisation', *Independent*, 12 September 1997, p. 11.

59 'Socialism "leaves its post" in Shanghai', *Guardian*, 11 March 1997, p. 11.

60 MacFarquhar, op. cit., p. 16.

61 Jim Rohwer, *Asia Rising*, London: Nicholas Brealey, 1996, p. 162.

62 For a defence of Asian values from an Islamic standpoint, see Anwar Ibrahim, 'A global convivencia vs. the clash of civilizations', *New Perspectives Quarterly*, vol. 14, no. 3, Summer 1997, pp. 31–43.

63 For an Asian statement of the view that economies serve their parent cultures, see Mahathir Mohamad and Shintaro Isihara, *The Voice of Asia*, Tokyo: Kodansha International, 1995.

8 The ends of *laissez-faire*

1 George Soros, 'The capitalist threat', *The Atlantic Monthly*, September 1996.

2 Nathan Gardels, 'Two Concepts of Nationalism: an interview with Isaiah Berlin', *New York Review of Books*, 21 November 1991, p. 21.

3 Karl Marx, *Capital*, vol 1, Moscow, 1961, p. 486, cited by G. A. Cohen, *Karl Marx's Theory of History: A Defence*, Oxford: Clarendon Press, 1978, p. 169.

4 Joseph Schumpeter, *Capitalism, Socialism and Democracy*, London: Unwin University Books, 1996, p. 83.

5 Soros's account of reflexive processes in markets can be found in his book, *The Alchemy of Finance: Reading the Mind of the Market*, New York: Simon & Schuster, 1987, Part One, and in his book, *Underwriting Democracy*, New York: The Free Press, 1991, Part Three. A somewhat parallel account is given by one of the great neglected economic thinkers of this century, G. L. S. Shackle, in his book *Epistemics and Economics: A Critique of Economic Doctrines*, Cambridge: Cambridge University Press, 1972.

6 The quotation from Greenspan occurs in William Pfaff, 'Genuflecting at the altar of market economics', *International Herald Tribune*, 14 July 1997, p. 8.

7 James Tobin, 'A proposal for international monetary reform', *Eastern Economic Journal*, July–October 1978, pp. 153–9.

8 *The State in a Changing World: World Development Report 1997*, World Bank, Oxford: Oxford University Press, 1997, p. ii. For a sharp critique of the World Bank's development policies, see Catherine Caufield, *Masters of Illusion: The World Bank and the Poverty of Nations*, London: Macmillan, 1996.

9 *World Bank*, op. cit. p. 19.

10 Ibid., p. 59.

11 See Kent E. Calder, *Asia's Deadly Triangle: How Arms, Energy and Growth Threaten to Destabilize Asia–Pacific*, London: Nicholas Brealey, 1997, pp. 50, 122, 120.

12 On the new nuclear danger, see Fred Charles Ikle, 'The second coming of the nuclear age', *Foreign Affairs*, vol. 75, no. 1, January/February 1996, pp. 119–28.

Postscript

1 Not all Enlightenment thinkers understood a universal civilization on terms that were Europocentric. For a discussion of this point in relation to the paradigm Enlightenment thinker, see my book, *Voltaire and Enlightenment*, London: Orion, 1998.

2 Figures cited by Larry Elliot from Dresdner Kleinwort Benson estimates in 'Fairytale turns to horror story', *Guardian*, Monday 20 July 1998, p. 19.

3 For an illuminating analysis of the politics of insecurity in the United States, see Richard C. Longworth, *Global Squeeze: The Coming Crisis for First-World Nations*, Chicago: Contemporary Books, 1998, Chapter 4.

4 'Forget Tigers, keep an eye on China', *Guardian*, 17 December 1997, p. 17.

5 Sebastian Mallaby, 'In Asia's Mirror: From Commodore Perry to the IMF', *The National Interest*, Number 52, Summer 1998, p. 21.

6 For an illuminating discussion, see C. Fred Bergsten, *Weak Dollar, Strong Euro? The International Impact of EMU*, Centre for European Reform: London, 1998.

7 On this see M. Hunter, 'Nationalism Unleashed: Le Pen Moves East', Transitions, Vol 5, No. 7, July 1998, pp. 18–28.

8 Zygmunt Bauman, *Globalization: The Human Consequences*, Cambridge: Polity Press, 1998, p. 3.

9 For a good statement of this social-democratic view, see Frank Vandenbroucke, *Globalisation, Inequality and Social Democracy*, London: The Institute for Public Policy Research, 1998.

10 For a more extended consideration of social democracy, see my monograph, *After Social Democracy*, London: Demos, 1996, reprinted in my book, *Endgames: questions in late modern political thought*, Cambridge: Polity Press, 1997, Ch. 2.

11 For a useful philosophical exploration of the market and human well-being, see John O'Neill, *The Market: Ethics, Knowledge and Politics*, London and New York: Routledge, 1998.

12 For an incisive critique of free-market philosophies of economic progress, see Richard Bronk, *Progress and the Invisible Hand*, London: Little, Brown and Co., 1998.

Index

ABB, 63
Africa: investment capital, 58; wage levels, 83
Albert, Michel, 62, 93
Arbats, Yevgenia, 157
Argentina, financial crisis, 224
Aristotle, 102
Arzu, Alvaro, 51
Atatürk, Kemal, 168
Australia: capitalism, 73; free market, 14; multicultural society, 129, 130

Barings Bank, 62
Barnett, Corelli, 15
Bauman, Zygmunt, 232
BBC, 36
Becker, Jasper, 138, 178
Bentham, Jeremy, 119, 124
Berlin, Isaiah, 194, 207
Besancon, Alain, 154
Beveridge, William, 6, 10, 19, 28
Biggs, Barton, 186
Blair, Tony, 34
Borodin, M., 179

Bosanquet, Bernard, 15
Bosnia, US intervention, 128
Braun, Otto, 179
Brazil, financial crisis, 224
Brezhnev, Leonid, 142, 154
Britain (England): capitalism, 73; crime rate, 30–1; development of free market, 7–14; divorce rate, 29; effects of Thatcherite policies, 25–34, 35–8, 53–4; Factory Acts, 11, 17; free market policies, 53–4, 108; Great Depression, 15; inequality, 32; labour market, 11, 29; law enforcement, 31; lawyers, 118–19; multinational state, 129; Poor Law Reform, 9–10, 29; Repeal of Corn Laws, 9; prison population, 30, 116–17; Thatcherite rule, 5, 23; underclass, 30, 42; Victorian foreign policy, 166–7; welfare state, 10, 14, 19; see also England
British Aerospace, 63
British Petroleum, 27
British Telecom, 27

Bryan, Lowell, 68
Buchanan, Pat, 130
Buck, J.L., 178
Burke, Edmund, 119
Bush, George, 109, 129

Callaghan, James, 24
Camp, Ai, 49
Canada: free market, 14; prison
    population, 116
Cardenas, Cuauhtemoc, 48
Castaneda, Jorge, 48
Castro, Fidel, 136
Ceausescu, Nicolae, 160
Centre for Strategic and International
    Studies, 148
Chechnya, war, 157, 158
Chile, public services, 41
China: business culture, 184; capitalism,
    4, 58–9, 74, 79, 182–6; communism, 3;
    copyright infringement, 199; Cultural
    Revolution, 139, 180, 186; diaspora,
    59, 183, 185–6; economic
    modernization, 186–90; economy, 56,
    66; energy consumption, 206;
    environment, 80, 149, 175, 181–2;
    famine, 175, 179; Great Leap
    Forward, 134, 175, 179–80, 186;
    labour costs, 84; market reform, 121,
    177, 187; Opium Wars, 168;
    population, 181–2; traditional culture,
    176–7
Chubais, Anatoly, 145
Civil Service, 27
Clausewitz, Karl von, 75, 201
Clinton, Bill, 44–5, 91, 109–10, 167
CNN, 60
Cohen, Stephen, 151
Colosio, Luis Donaldo, 51
Condorcet, Marie Jean de Caritat,
    Marquis de, 124
Conquest, Robert, 139
Conservative Party, 25–7, 32–3

de Gaulle, Charles, 158
Deng Xiaoping, 177, 178, 179, 182,
    185–7
de Tocqueville, Alexis, 114, 126, 130

Dewey, John, 178
Dicey, A.V., 26
Diderot, Denis, 124
Drucker, Peter, 171

East India Company, 62
Ellman, Michael, 139
England, *see* Britain
Erhard, Ludwig, 94
Euro, 230–1
European Union, 25, 33, 35–6, 57, 98,
    160

Farrakhan, Louis, 128
Farrell, Diana, 68
Fay, Michael, 167
Ferguson, Adam, 124, 169
Feshbach, Murray, 149
Fidelity, 22
Figes, Orlando, 135, 136
Foucault, Michel, 38
France, Enlightenment values, 101
Franklin, Benjamin, 124
Freiburg School, 94
Freud, Sigmund, 109
Friedman, Milton, 28
Friendly, Alfred, 149
Fukuyama, Francis, 37, 116, 120–1

Gaidar, Yegor, 134, 143–6, 151, 156
Galbraith, J.K., 111
GATT, 43, 46
General Motors, 96
Genghis Khan, 149
Germany: capitalism, 59, 93, 203;
    economy, 73, 92–9; labour costs, 84,
    85; lawyers, 119; reunification, 95;
    state intervention, 7
Gingrich, Newt, 107
Goldman Sachs, 22
Goodhart, David, 94
Gorbachev, Mikhail: coup against, 143;
    perestroika, 47, 52, 139, 142;
    presidential election, 161; reform
    programme, 47, 141–2, 154, 178
Green, T.H., 15
Greenpeace, 75
Greenspan, Alan, 197–8

Greider, William, 91
Gresham, Sir Thomas, 78
Guatemalan National Revolutionary
　Unity army (URNG), 51
Guillen, Rafael Sebastian, 50

Handelman, Stephen, 155, 156
Hayek, Friedrich von, 8, 28, 207
Healey, Denis, 27
Hegel, Georg Wilhelm Friedrich, 102
Held, David, 65
Heller, Mikhail, 161
Herder, J.G., 124
Hirst, Paul, 63, 64, 66–7, 69, 90
Hobbes, Thomas, 201, 202, 207
Hobhouse, L.T., 15
Hobsbawm, Eric, 9
Hobson, J.A., 15
Hodgson, Godfrey, 115
Hoechst, 96
Homer, 124
Hong Kong, Chinese capitalism, 183
Hoskyns, John, 28
Hudson Bay Company, 62
Hume, David, 124
Huntington, Samuel, 120, 121–9

IG Metall, 97
Ilyushin, Victor, 147
India: capitalism, 192; caste system,
　192; market reforms, 56
Indonesia, unemployment, 219
International Labour Organisation
　(ILO), 85, 148
International Monetary Fund (IMF):
　British economy, 16, 24; influence, 23,
　144, 146, 205; Mexican economy, 45,
　46; objectives, 1; policies, 221
Irish Republican Army (IRA), 75
Italy, economy, 73
Ivan IV (the Terrible), Tsar, 153

Jacques, Martin, 25
Japan: Allied Occupation, 169;
　capitalism, 4, 58–9, 169–75, 203;
　corporate culture, 60; crime rate, 118;
　economy, 73, 227; Edo period, 168,
　174; education, 164; employment
　policy, 83, 173–4; lawyers, 118; Meiji
　period, 168–9, 171–2; prison
　population, 116; state intervention, 7
Jefferson, Thomas, 2, 100, 119, 124
Jevons, W.S., 78
Jiang Zemin, 187

Kafka, Franz, 38
Kant, Immanuel, 124, 135
Kaplan, Robert, 123
Kelsey, Jane, 41, 43
Kennedy, Paul, 171
Keynes, John Maynard: influence, 6, 24,
　28, 79, 98, 196; New Liberal thought,
　15; New Zealand influence, 40, 54; on
　employment, 24, 28, 78, 90; on
　interest rates, 174; policies, 213,
　227–8; Second World War, 219
Khasbulatov, Ruslan, 161
Khrushchev, Nikita, 179
Kissinger, Henry, 103

Labour Party, 24
Layard, Richard, 148, 152, 161, 162,
　164
League of Nations, 199
Lee Kuan Yew, 166
Lenin, V.I., 135–6, 137–8, 140, 165
Leontiev, Konstantin, 161
Leys, Simon, 176
Lincoln, Abraham, 152
Lind, Michael, 86, 115, 117
Lippmann, Walter, 104
Lipset, S.M., 126
Liu Shaoqui, 179
Lloyd George, David, 15
Locke, John, 106
Lucky Goldstar, 84
Luttwak, Edward, 113, 114

Macfarlane, Alan, 13, 14
MacFarquhar, Roderick, 182, 189
Madison, James, 119
Madonna, 38
Madrid, Miguel de la, 46
Major, John, 25, 30, 31, 33
Malaysia: government, 4; multicultural
　society, 129

Malthus, Thomas, 175, 181, 182, 188, 207, 211
Mao Zedong, 139, 175–7, 179–82
Mapplethorpe, Robert, 126
Marcos, Subcommander, 50, 51
Marcuse, Herbert, 38
Marx, Karl: account of capitalism, 71, 169; Enlightenment thought, 2, 124; influence, 135, 136, 137, 169; influence in China, 175, 178; on agriculture, 138; on modernity and tradition, 37, 195; on nature, 149; theory of history, 144
Massieu, José Francisco Ruiz, 51, 52
Massieu, Mario Ruiz, 52
Mehnert, Klaus, 176, 178
Mencken, H.L., 104
Mexico: austerity programme, 50; Chiapas rebellion, 46, 50; devaluation, 22, 44, 46, 50; drug trade, 52; elections (1997), 48, 51; free market, 23, 47–8, 53–4; inequality, 48–9; labour market, 11; middle class, 48–9; modernization, 46–7; neo-liberal reform, 52–3; structural adjustment, 11, 90; US relations, 45–7, 52–3, 56
Micklethwaite, John, 59
Microsoft, 72
Mill, John Stuart, 2, 124, 169, 175, 178, 195
Milosevic, Slobodan, 218
Mitsubishi, 172
Mitsui, 168, 172
Mitterrand, François, 90
Moore, Barrington, 8
MTV, 60

Nader, Ralph, 130
Naisbitt, John, 68
National Health Service, 28
NATO, 125, 160
Negroponte, Nicholas, 68
Nekrich, Alexander, 161
New Zealand: capitalism, 73; free market, 14, 23, 53–4, 108; inequality, 32, 42; labour market, 11, 40; law enforcement, 31; multicultural society, 129, 130; neo-liberal experiment, 39–44; underclass, 41–2
Nigeria, structural adjustment, 90
North American Free Trade Association (NAFTA), 45, 49, 70
North Korea, economy, 55

Ohmae, Kenichi, 64, 68, 69
Organisation for Economic Cooperation and Development (OECD), 2, 172, 173, 206
Ortiz, Guillermo, 45
Osram's, 84, 97

Pacifico, Don, 166–7
Paine, Tom, 2
Palestine Liberation Organisation (PLO), 75
Palmerston, Henry John Temple, 3rd Viscount, 166–7
Parker, Jon, 148, 152, 161, 162, 164
Paz, Octavio, 53
Perot, Ross, 130
Perry, Commodore Matthew, 168, 227
Peter I (the Great), Tsar, 134, 145, 153, 161
Peters, Winston, 44
Pfaff, William, 87, 100
Phillips, Kevin, 114–15
Pipes, Richard, 135, 137
Plaza Accords, 73
Plekhanov, Georgi, 138
Poland, European role, 160
Polanyi, Karl, 1, 12–14, 18, 22
Pol Pot, 122
Posadas, Cardinal, 51

Qiao Shi, 166

Rawls, John, 89
Reagan, Ronald, 31, 107–8, 115–16
Redding, S. Gordon, 182, 184
Reich, Robert, 68
Rhine model (of capitalism), 233
Ricardo, David, 10, 81–2, 85, 86, 102
Rios Montt, Efrain, 51
Rogers, Jim, 157
Rohatyn, Felix, 116

Romania, national policy, 160
Ronson, 84–5
Roosevelt, Franklin D., 4, 6, 19, 109
Rowntree Report on Income and Wealth, 32
Ruigrok, Winfried, 63
Russell, Bertrand, 133, 144
Russia: anarcho-capitalism, 151–9; capitalism, 4, 134–5; crime rate, 118; defence industry, 156–7; education, 163–4; environmental pollution, 80, 149–50; Eurasian, 159–63; families, 112, 164; health, 149–51; land privatization, 140; market reform, 140–1, 147; middle classes, 164; organized crime, 154–6; prison population, 117; resources of capitalism, 163–5; shock therapy, 141–7; social costs of shock therapy, 147–51; state intervention, 7; Time of Troubles, 157, 158; Tsarist, 152–3, 165; unemployment, 148; War Communism, 133–41; *see also* Soviet Union

Sachs, Jeffrey, 144–5
Salinas de Gortari, Carlo, 46–8, 51, 52
Salinas, Raul, 52
Salomon Brothers, 22, 45
Santayana, George, 104
Sayle, Murray, 171
Schumpeter, Joseph, 55, 195, 210
Scudder, 22
Serbia, anti-western forces, 150
Shell corporation, 75
Sherr, James, 145, 157
Shestov, Lev, 133
Siemens, 85, 94, 96
Singapore: capitalism, 190; education, 164; government, 4; income and wages, 65, 83, 84; multicultural society, 129; US relations, 167
Skidelsky, Robert, 145
Smil, Vaclav, 181
Smith, Adam: account of capitalism, 169; Enlightenment thought, 124; influence on Marxism and Soviet communism, 102; influence on

Russian capitalism, 143, 151; on competition, 207; on economic man, 13; on universal civilization, 195
Solzhenitsyn, Alexander, 161
Soros, George, 1, 90, 194, 197
South Korea: capitalism, 185; GDP, 219; incomes and wages, 65, 84
Soviet Union: collapse, 47, 56, 79, 121; Enlightenment Utopia, 3; influence on China, 175; New Economic Policy, 139; organized crime, 153–5; *perestroika*, 47, 52, 139, 142; War Communism, 133–41; *see also* Russia
Spain: family role, 73; multinational state, 129
Stalin, Joseph, 133, 136, 146
Steele, Jonathan, 144
Steinbeck, John, 225
Stillman, Edmund, 100
Stockman, David, 107
Stolypin, P.A., 139
Sumitomo, 172
Sweden: economy, 73, 91; employment policy, 91–2

Taiwan: economic modernization, 183–4, 190; income and wages, 65, 84
Tawney, R.H., 179
Taylor, F.W., 136
Thailand, GDP, 219
Thatcher, Margaret: deregulation, 40; development of Thatcherism, 24–5; effects of policies, 25–34, 35–8; fall, 25; free market objectives, 5, 23; world influence, 16
Thompson, Grahame, 63, 64, 66–7, 69, 90
Thyssen's, 96
Tiananmen Square, 223
Tobin, James, 200
Trotsky, Leon, 136
Truscott, Peter, 147, 150, 161–2
Turkey: modernization, 168; political movements, 101

Umehara, Takeshi, 166
United Kingdom, *see* Britain
United Nations, 101

United States of America: capitalism, 59, 73, 79; crime rate, 118; employment, 112–13; Enlightenment values, 2–3, 101–3; expansionist policies, 91; family breakdown, 112; free market, 2–3, 79–80; Hispanic Americans, 129–30; inequality, 48, 114–16; Japan relations, 168; labour costs, 85; labour market, 11, 74, 112; law enforcement, 31; lawyers, 118; Mexico relations, 45–7, 52–3, 56; middle classes, 111–12; multiculturalism, 128–9; neo-conservative ascendancy, 103–10; new American economic insecurity, 110–14; New Deal, 4, 6, 19, 130; prison population, 30, 74, 116–19; religion, 125–7; Singapore relations, 167; state intervention, 7; underclass, 30, 42; Washington consensus, 200–5; Welfare Reform Act, 109

van Tulder, Rob, 63
Voegelin, 104
Volkogonov, Dmitri, 140

Volkswagen, 96
Voltaire, 124
von Pierer, Heinrich, 94, 96

Wales, labour costs, 84–5
Waswo, Ann, 170
Weber, Max, 37, 71, 169, 184, 191
Whitley, Richard D., 182, 184
Wilson, Dick, 184, 185
Wilson, Woodrow, 125, 204
Wolf, Martin, 173
Wooldridge, Adrian, 59
World Bank, 90, 156, 188, 202–3
World Trade Organisation (WTO), 1, 18, 43, 52

Yeltsin, Boris, 134, 142, 147, 158–9, 161

Zamyatin, Yevgeny, 136
Zapata, Emiliano, 50
Zapatistas, 50–1
Zedillo, Ernesto, 22, 49, 51
Zhirinovsky, Vladimir, 146
Zinoviev, Alexander, 139